MW00612648

COMMITTEE ON FOREIGN AFFAIRS

SUBCOMMITTEE ON EUROPE AND THE MIDDLE EAST

LEE H HAMILTON, Indiana, *Chairman*

ELIOT L ENGEL, New York
CHARLES E SCHUMER, New York
ROBERT A BORSKI, Pennsylvania
ROBERT E ANDREWS, New Jersey
SHERROD BROWN, Ohio
ALCEE L HASTINGS, Florida
PETER DEUTSCH, Florida
TOM LANTOS, California

BENJAMIN A GILMAN, New York
WILLIAM F GOODLING, Pennsylvania
JAN MEYERS, Kansas
ELTON GALLEGLY, California
DAVID A LEVY, New York
JAMES A LEACH, Iowa

KATHERINE A WILKENS, *Staff Director*
DEBORAH E BODLANDER, *Republican Professional Staff Member*
MARTIN SLETZINGER, *Professional Staff Member*

SUBCOMMITTEE ON INTERNATIONAL SECURITY, INTERNATIONAL ORGANIZATION AND HUMAN RIGHTS

TOM LANTOS, California, *Chairman*

HOWARD L BERMAN, California
GARY L ACKERMAN, New York
MATTHEW G MARTINEZ, California
FRANK McCLOSKEY, Indiana
THOMAS C SAWYER, Ohio

DOUG BEREUTER, Nebraska
OLYMPIA J SNOWE, Maine
CHRISTOPHER H SMITH, New Jersey
DAN BURTON, Indiana

ROBERT KING, *Staff Director*
MICHAEL ENNIS, *Republican Professional Staff Member*
KENNETH R TIMMERMAN, *Professional Staff Member*
BETH L POISSON, *Professional Staff Member*
MARYANNE MURRAY, *Professional Staff Member*

CONTENTS

WITNESSES

MATERIAL SUBMITTED FOR THE RECORD

APPENDIX

IRAQ'S NUCLEAR WEAPONS CAPABILITY AND IAEA INSPECTIONS IN IRAQ

TUESDAY, JUNE 29, 1993

HOUSE OF REPRESENTATIVES,
COMMITTEE ON FOREIGN AFFAIRS,
SUBCOMMITTEES ON EUROPE AND THE MIDDLE EAST AND ON INTERNATIONAL SECURITY, INTERNATIONAL ORGANIZATIONS AND HUMAN RIGHTS,
Washington, DC

The subcommittee met, pursuant to call, at 10:00 a m. in room 2172, Rayburn House Office Building, Hon Lee H Hamilton (chairman) presiding

Chairman HAMILTON. The Subcommittees on Europe and the Middle East, on International Security, International Organizations and Human Rights and on Economic Policy, Trade and the Environment meet today in open session to discuss the Iraqi nuclear program and the role of the United Nations and the Atomic Energy Agency.

Today we will hear first from Assistant Secretary of State Robert L. Gallucci.

Second, we will hear from a panel of private witnesses, including Jules Kroll, President of Kroll Associates; Gary Milhollin, Director of the Wisconsin Project on Nuclear Arms Control, Jay Davis, the Lawrence Livermore National Laboratory; and Lawrence Scheinman, Professor of Government, International Law and Politics, Cornell University

We have several topics of interest to the subcommittees, including The post-Gulf War experience of IAEA in inspection, disposal, and monitoring of Iraq's nuclear weapons program; assessments of the current status of Iraq's nuclear weapons activities; and the assessment of our witnesses of the lessons learned by the international community of the Iraqi experience and their recommendations of how to prevent a similar incident from recurring in the future

We welcome our witnesses before the subcommittees and are pleased to have them with us today We have a lot of ground to cover I want to advise the witnesses that we anticipate, once the House goes into session, a series of notes We don't know how many at this point But we may have to make some adjustments in the schedule as we move along.

Mr Gallucci, we are very pleased to have you Your statement, of course, will be entered into the record in full And before you proceed, I will ask my colleagues first if they have any comments to make.

Mr Gejdenson
Mr Lantos.

A CRITICAL JUNCTURE FOR U.S. POLICY IN THE GULF

Mr. LANTOS. Thank you, Mr Chairman And I want to commend you for holding this hearing. This hearing comes at a critical junction for U S policy in the Gulf, and for the new collective security system that is emerging from the end of the cold war

Through his despicable attempt to murder former President Bush, Saddam Hussein has shown once again, if anyone needed reminding, that he is not fit to play a role on the world's stage And yet, in recent months Saddam has attempted, with some success, to divide public opinion and drive a wedge between the United States and its allies In the Muslim world, we hear many voices rising, even from Egypt, that the United States is "over-reacting" or being "too harsh" toward Saddam, while ignoring the fate of the Bosnian Muslims who are being massacred daily by Serbian thugs In Western Europe, U S allies such as France have become increasingly reticent at the U N to support U S. military action against Saddam, lured once again by the scent of financial profits.

Following Operation Desert Storm, which I strongly supported, Iraq has become subjected to the most rigorous international sanctions ever imposed on any nation since World War II Its weapons plants have been subject to repeated inspections by United Nations teams Its assets abroad have been frozen. And yet, Iraq continues to flaunt its military power, massacring its own citizens in the North, and Iraqi Shiites in the South

The question arises. What will happen if Saddam Hussein succeeds in driving a wedge between the United States and its allies and the U N sanctions are lifted?

SUMMARY OF SUBCOMMITTEE REPORT

I called for a staff study, which has been distributed, and I will summarize just a few of the staff report's findings [1]

Despite ongoing inspections by the International Atomic Energy Agency and the U.N. Special Commission, Iraq has managed to reconstruct 80 percent of the military manufacturing capability it possessed before Desert Storm. Neither the U N , nor the International Atomic Energy Agency, has been able to do anything about this.

Despite the U.N embargo, Iraq has succeeded in reinvigorating its clandestine procurement network, relying on known front companies in Jordan, France, and Germany to purchase critical items and spare parts for its weapons industries

Despite the U.N. trade embargo, Iraq continues to ship oil to Jordan, and to Iran, using this money to feed its procurement network and to rebuild its weapons plants

Today, Iraq is manufacturing T–72 tanks, artillery munitions, and even short-range ballistic missiles, and is operating more than 40 major weapons plants

[1] The full text of the report appears in the appendix on p 77

Iraq has repaired and returned to service most of the 2,500 main battle tanks and 250 fixed-wing aircraft that survived Desert Storm

Of the more than 850 machine-tools that have now been identified and catalogued at Iraqi nuclear weapons plants by the IAEA, only a handful have actually been destroyed or subjected to future monitoring. Furthermore, the 850 machine-tools and dozen or so large computers constitute but a small fraction of the more than $14 billion worth of high-tech manufacturing gear imported by Iraq during the late 1980's. This leaves an immense production capability intact, which is already being used to manufacture conventional weapons and which could be applied in short order to a resumption of the nuclear weapons program once U N sanctions are lifted

The Chairman of the U.N. Special Commission, Ambassador Ekeus, is fully aware of Saddam's intentions. As he recently summed it up before the Washington Institute, Iraq's weapons programs are likely to "grow up like mushrooms after the rain" once the United Nations sanctions are lifted.

I think it is critical, Mr Chairman, that we paint a coherent picture of Iraq's attempt to rebuild its complex military capabilities, its support for terrorism in this country and elsewhere, and that we recognize that Saddam's Iraq continues to represent a major threat to the peace of this world

Chairman HAMILTON I thank the gentleman

Any other opening statements from my colleagues?

If not, Mr Gallucci, you may proceed, sir

STATEMENT OF HON. ROBERT L. GALLUCCI, ASSISTANT SECRETARY FOR POLITICO-MILITARY AFFAIRS, DEPARTMENT OF STATE

Mr GALLUCCI Thank you, Mr Chairman.

Mr. Chairman, Members of the committee, I am pleased to have the opportunity to discuss our assessment of the nuclear situation in Iraq and the U.N.'s capabilities to deter or detect any efforts by Iraq to regenerate its nuclear weapons program

In these remarks, I would like to briefly describe the work of the International Atomic Energy Agency in Iraq, some lessons learned, and the continuing need to give our fullest support to the IAEA as part of our overall nonproliferation efforts

Under the auspices of the U.N Security Counsel Resolution 687 and with the assistance of the U N Special Commission, UNSCOM, the IAEA his conducted 20 nuclear inspections of Iraq since the end of the Gulf War in April 1991

These inspections have forced Iraq to disclose, destroy, or render harmless all of the major nuclear weapons facilities and equipment that we are aware of, including several enrichment sites, research facilities, and weapons design facilities Along with the damage inflicted by the war and subsequent military actions, we believe these inspections have effectively put the Iraqi nuclear weapons program out of business, at least for the near term.

A LONG-TERM NUCLEAR THREAT

Over the long-term, however, Iraq still presents a nuclear threat We believe that Saddam Hussein is committed to rebuilding a nuclear weapon capability using indigenous and imported resources.

Iraq retains the most critical resource for any nuclear weapons program, namely skilled personnel and expertise

Iraq also retains a basic industrial capability to support a nuclear weapons program, including a large amount of dual-use equipment and facilities

If sanctions are lifted, Iraq would have access to additional financial resources to refuel overseas procurement activities.

Finally, Iraq has still refused to provide the U.N. with details of its clandestine procurement network, a network which could, therefore, be reactivated in the future.

To deter or detect regeneration, we need to assure that the IAEA and the Special Commission receive the political, technical, and financial support to implement their plans for long-term monitoring in Iraq These plans are contained in Security Council Resolution 715, a Resolution that Iraq has so far refused to accept

The Security Council will need to enforce the rights of the IAEA and Special Commission under Security Council Resolution 687 and 715, especially, the right to conduct challenge inspections without obstruction from the Iraqi authorities.

We must also provide technical support and information to the IAEA and Special Commission, including assistance in the use of technical monitoring devices such as water sampling, to detect covert nuclear activities

To address the risk of overseas procurement, we must continue to press Iraq to reveal its foreign suppliers and work with other suppliers to assure effective monitoring of exports to prevent diversion

Iraq, no doubt, will continue to test the U.N.'s resolve to continue inspections, especially if it perceives that support for them is waning As in the past, Iraq will use tactics such as delays or refusing access to sites, denying information, harassing inspectors, and refusing to accept Security Council Resolution 715 to reduce the effectiveness of the inspections

THE CAMERA DISPUTE

Recently, Iraq's efforts to undermine long-term monitoring has focused on two issues Iraq has refused to allow the Special Commission to install cameras at two rocket motor test stands and has refused to destroy certain chemical weapons precursors and related chemical weapon equipment

On June 18, the Security Council adopted a Presidential Statement that Iraq's refusal to cooperate with the Special Commission in these matters constitutes a "material and unacceptable breach," of U N. Security Council Resolution 687 and a violation of Resolutions 707 and 715 The Statement warned of, and I quote, "serious consequences."

On June 22, Secretary General Boutros Boutros-Ghali met with Tariq Aziz to discuss the Presidential Statement Aziz said the issue could be discussed in a technical meeting with the Special Commission on July 12

On June 24, Special Commission Chairman Rolf Ekeus told the Iraqi Foreign Minister that the meeting cannot take place until Iraq complies with the Council's demands We strongly support Chairman Ekeus in this decision

LESSONS FOR THE IAEA

I would like to relate the lessons of Iraq to the strengthening of the overall IAEA safeguards system, a system that plays a critical role in the international effort to prevent nuclear weapons proliferation.

Fundamentally, the revelations about Iraq demonstrated the need for the international community to strengthen the Agency's ability and authority to detect undeclared nuclear activities outside declared safeguarded facilities.

In response, the IAEA's Board of Governors has taken a number of important steps to improve safeguards, reflecting the view that the IAEA should give a higher priority to detecting covert nuclear activities

The Board has reaffirmed the Agency's right to perform special inspections whenever necessary to permit it to fulfill its safeguard obligations including access to undeclared sites.

The Board has determined that the Agency may rely on information supplied by member states when seeking a special inspection.

The Board has strengthened obligations to provide notice and early submission of design information on new nuclear facilities or changes to existing facilities

And the Board has established a voluntary system for reporting on nuclear exports and imports

Mr Chairman, in our view, these changes have substantially strengthened the IAEA safeguards system, which is essential to ensuring that fullscope safeguards under the Non-Proliferation Treaty are fully implemented. We have already seen evidence of this new determination in North Korea, South Africa, and Iran.

We believe that the IAEA's experience in Iraq has resulted in a substantial improvement in the IAEA safeguard system. And with the support of member states, it will continue to be an important part of the international nonproliferation regime.

Mr. Chairman, I would be pleased to try to answer any questions that the committee may have

[The prepared statement of Mr. Gallucci appears in the appendix]

Chairman HAMILTON OK. Thank you very much, Mr Gallucci, for your statement

Now, the IAEA believes that it has discovered all of Iraq's nuclear program. And it believes that it has substantially reduced or eliminated Iraq's nuclear program Do you agree with that assessment?

Mr GALLUCCI I wouldn't, Mr Chairman, put it exactly that way I would say that the IAEA, the Special Commission, and we in the U S Government, believe that the elements of the nuclear program—that we are aware of—have been essentially destroyed.

Chairman HAMILTON. How confident are you that you are aware of everything they are doing?

Mr. GALLUCCI Mr. Chairman, I think we have a fairly high degree of confidence. But it would be unreasonable, I think, to take the position that we know what we don't know.

INTELLIGENCE FAILURE BEFORE DESERT STORM

Before the end of the Gulf War, our intelligence community and the intelligence communities of others in the West, had focused on Iraq's nuclear program And it is clear, in retrospect, that they got it wrong and that there were large elements of the Iraqi nuclear program unknown to the intelligence communities.

Chairman HAMILTON. And that it was much farther advanced than U S intelligence believed? And it was much farther advanced that the IAEA believed?

Mr GALLUCCI. I think those two statements are certainly true, Mr Chairman

Chairman HAMILTON. Now, what has to happen in Iraq before you have a high degree of assurance that you know everything there is to know about their nuclear program?

Mr. GALLUCCI. Mr. Chairman, I think we have a high degree of assurance now. I am just reluctant and unwilling to say that we are absolutely certain.

The Special Commission and the IAEA can go and have gone everywhere we have reason to believe there is something related to Resolution 687 to find. And we have had that kind of assessment, that is, the Special Commission and the IAEA has

Chairman HAMILTON IAEA was able to go anywhere they wanted to go in Iraq and see anything they wanted to see in Iraq?

Mr. GALLUCCI. Yes, sir

Chairman HAMILTON. Now, there have been some criticisms, of course, of the IAEA—which some of our witnesses later today will make—that it does not share information it collects from its inspections and fails to use that information to collect further information from other sources; that some of its managers and inspectors have been timid in pursuing their mission in Iraq and have played the game largely according to the rules that the Iraqis have set, that they are too eager to claim that they have found everything that there is to find, that they haven't followed up on leads that have been gained from inspections' that a lot of their people don't have proper experience with nuclear weapon materials

What do you say to all of those criticisms? I am sure you have heard them.

CRITICISMS OF THE IAEA

Mr. GALLUCCI Mr Chairman, with respect to the professionalism of the Agency, I think the Agency has a very high degree of professionalism, and they have the right kind of people working as inspectors doing a very good job.

I want to pick up on a couple of the points you made that have been raised in criticism of the Agency The point that there may not be nuclear weapon expertise in the Agency is sort of an unfair one, even though to the extent that it is accurate.

We wouldn't necessarily want the Agency to be an expert in nuclear weapons design and development But the Agency can have attached to it, for an inspection, as it has in the case of Iraq, those experts that it needs to do an inspection job when nuclear weapons expertise is required.

With respect to what we have learned from Iraq and what the Agency has learned, what I tried to focus on in my prepared remarks is that the world learned that the IAEA's mandate, up until the time of Iraq, was to inspect facilities that were declared to it by the state in which they were conducting the inspections.

So the IAEA focused its efforts at the declared facilities at the Tuwaitha site in Iraq. When it was discovered after the war that there were a great many other facilities, the movement within the Agency and the international community that had already begun to have the Agency conduct special inspections of undeclared sites and facilities, that movement produced a change in Agency operations which we have seen take good effect in the case of North Korea within the last 6 months.

So I would say that while the Agency has always been a professional agency, its ability to do more than inspect the sites that were declared to it was limited until fairly recently

A lesson was learned, I think, by the international community, and with the support of the member states, the Agency has changed its approach and now can and does inspect undeclared facilities that are identified to it by member states that make that information available.

MONITORING WILL DETECT FUTURE NUCLEAR ACTIVITY

Chairman HAMILTON Your statement says that "in the near term." You might define near-term for me. What does that mean, first of all?

Mr. GALLUCCI. I am sorry, Mr. Chairman. The context of the sentence refers to my statement?

Chairman HAMILTON They effectively put the Iraqi nuclear weapons program out of business, at least for the near-term?

Mr GALLUCCI As long as long-term monitoring continues.

While it is to continue indefinitely under 687, any failure of the Security Council to sustain that position, we believe, would result ultimately in the regeneration of the nuclear weapons program in Iraq.

Chairman HAMILTON. And you still believe that they present a nuclear threat and that Saddam wants to rebuild his nuclear weapons capability?

So you have, on the one hand, a leader who wants to rebuild his nuclear ability and his ability to conceal the program. And, on the other side, you indicate that if the IAEA is able to proceed under U.N Resolutions and to monitor, that we think that the IAEA can determine if they launch upon a nuclear program.

Is that right?

Mr GALLUCCI Yes, Mr Chairman, I think that is correct

Chairman HAMILTON And now you say the Security Council will need to enforce the rights of the IAEA and UNSCOM.

How are we doing so far?

Mr. GALLUCCI I think we are doing reasonably well, Mr. Chairman, but not perfectly. Certainly, with respect to inspections, the IAEA and Special Commission teams have gone where they think they need to go, and under the circumstances that they thought they needed to conduct the inspections under.

At the same time, however, I noted in my remarks that the Iraqis have, so far, not formally accepted Resolution 715 They have not accepted it at all. They did accept 687 115 is, in fact, the Resolution that describes the program for long-term monitoring in Iraq. And it is, over the long-term, essential that that resolution be accepted by the Iraqis.

RELUCTANCE TO PUBLISH IRAQ'S SUPPLIER LIST

Chairman HAMILTON Before I turn to some of my colleagues, let me just ask about one aspect of this now

A very important part of keeping their nuclear capability eliminated would be to stop foreign suppliers from sending stuff into Iraq.

Do we know who these foreign suppliers are?

Mr GALLUCCI Mr Chairman, during the years before the war, there were a great many foreign suppliers to the Iraqi programs, weapons of mass destruction, not only nuclear but chemical, biological, and ballistic missile programs

Chairman HAMILTON. Do we know who they were?

Mr. GALLUCCI. We have substantial knowledge of what companies and what countries and what those countries provided

Chairman HAMILTON. Why don't we publicize it?

Mr GALLUCCI Mr Chairman, some of that information is available to us by virtue—or is available to the Special Commission and the IAEA by virtue of their inspections

Both the IAEA and the Special Commission have taken the position that information that they have about these suppliers, if published, would diminish the cooperation of the governments in the continuing efforts of the Special Commission and the IAEA to do their job.

Chairman HAMILTON Do we know the name?

Does the U.S Government know the names?

Mr. GALLUCCI. We know the names, certainly, of some companies based upon intelligence

Chairman HAMILTON. Why don't we publicize it?

Mr. GALLUCCI. I am sure there are a variety of reasons, but the one that immediately occurs to me is sources and methods, Mr Chairman

Chairman HAMILTON You mean to publicize the names of the companies would reveal sources and methods?

Mr. GALLUCCI In some cases, Mr Chairman, I think it would In other cases, I don't know that there would be any good to come from it, and there might be some diplomatic disadvantage.

Chairman HAMILTON. One good thing that might come is that they stop supplying the stuff

Mr GALLUCCI. Well, currently, Mr. Chairman, they are not And when we have information that a company in another country is cooperating in anyone's production of weapons of mass destruction, we work with that country——

Chairman HAMILTON. You are confident that suppliers are not supplying materials that could be helpful in the nuclear program?

Mr GALLUCCI With respect to Iraq, yes, sir I am confident of that

Chairman HAMILTON No materials are going into Iraq today that could be used by their nuclear program?

Mr. GALLUCCI As always, I am going to say to the best of my knowledge But I think our knowledge is very good

Chairman HAMILTON Mrs Meyers

Mrs. MEYERS. Mr Chairman, I have in front of me a document, that I presume is a public document that I believe was prepared by Mr Lantos' subcommittee And I would like to read a paragraph from that document and get you to respond to that if you would and maybe ask some other questions.

Wall Street investigator Jules Kroll, who has been tracking Iraq's procurement efforts in Jordan, alleges that the Iraqi Government transferred $5.2 billion in government funds to the Arab Bank in Amman, just as Operation Desert Storm was ending, to establish a new military infrastructure for Iraq. In addition to this, he alleges that the Central Bank of Jordan is laundering secret Iraqi funds in Switzerland through commercial banks such as the Jordan Housing Bank, the Jordan Gulf Bank, and the Arab Financial Corporation. He talks about how German companies are breaking sanctions and that they are helping Iraq to develop upgraded Scud missiles

And then he says that: Unconfirmed reports from Kuwaiti sources warned that commercial contacts have intensified in recent months between major French defense exporters and Iraqi agents in Europe in view of renewing the supply of spare parts for Iraq's fleet of Mirage F–1 fighter bombers

Now, can you comment on all of that?

That doesn't sound to me like we are seeing any build-down of defense efforts. And it certainly sounds like we are seeing a build-up of nuclear capability.

JORDAN BANKING FRONTS

Mr. GALLUCCI Mrs Meyers, first let me try to speak to each one of these and then to the general point I am afraid I am unaware of the banking activity in Jordan just prior to the war And I just cannot speak to that I have no information about that But I would take that question for the record if you would like

[State Department response follows]

We have no evidence that any transfer of funds was effected by the Iraqi Government through the Arab Bank in Amman in the period just after Desert Storm, nor any evidence of post-war involvement by the Central Bank of Jordan in laundering secret Iraqi funds through Switzerland

Because much of Iraq's legitimate trade involves Jordan, it is not uncommon for Jordanian banking institutions to show evidence of activity with Iraq It is not impossible that Iraq therefore may be able to use Jordanian banks for other activities as well When we have discussed financial issues with the Government of Jordan, they have assured us of their compliance with sanctions prohibiting unauthorized release of funds to Iraq

With respect to a German company breaking sanctions by providing equipment that would upgrade Iraqi Scud capability, I have no information about that I would personally view that as extremely unlikely——

Mrs MEYERS Have you seen this report?

Mr. GALLUCCI I don't know what you are holding, Mrs. Meyers.

Mrs. MEYERS Mr Lantos, have you distributed this report?

Mr LANTOS It is a staff report which is available And if Mr. Gallucci doesn't have it, we will be happy to provide it.

Mr GALLUCCI. Is that just available today?

Mr. LANTOS You have now been supplied a copy.

Mr. GALLUCCI I can assure you, I will read it very carefully.

SMUGGLING FROM GERMANY AND FRANCE

The German company—again, let me say I was unaware of that I find it unlikely, but we will certainly look into that

[State Department response follows]

The German Government has acknowledged that German companies account for a sizable number of items discovered in Iraq's WMD programs But the German Government has also continued its exemplary cooperation with UNSCOM, the IAEA, and other governments in identifying and punishing offenders UNSCOM and the IAEA have learned a great deal from information made available by German investigators, and have acted on this information to discover and destroy items in Iraq

Some of the shipments of German materials mentioned in the report to Iraq occurred prior to the Gulf War. We are aware of these cases, and have supported UNSCOM's and the IAEA's efforts to track down the equipment For the cases of sanctions-busting after the war, we have heard similar reports We routinely contact the source country government when we are made aware of supportable evidence of sanctions-busting We do not currently have any more significant detail on any of the suspected smuggling cases mentioned in the report

I would say the same about the French contacts. If they would involve a French company breaking sanctions that now exists, U N sanctions under Resolution 687, I would find that unlikely as well but not impossible So I will look into that as well.

[State Department response follows]

We are aware that Iraq would like spare parts for its French-made Mirage F–1 aircraft, and that Iraq has made attempts at getting parts into Iraq through the sanctions We have no confirmed deliveries of such parts, however, We will continue to watch

Let me say something more general though, because I fear there may be a misunderstanding about what was accomplished with 687. It did a number of things, but in the areas that we are addressing, as I understand it, this morning, we are focusing on the nuclear capability of Iraq and Resolution 687 in referring to weapons of mass destruction including nuclear capability and provides for, essentially, the destruction of such capability in Iraq in a certain, detailed way.

It does not, however, prevent or provide that Iraq cannot have a conventional weapon capability

Mrs MEYERS. What do you call the Scud delivery system?

Mr GALLUCCI U N Security Council Resolution 687 does not deny them a conventional weapon capability. With respect to the Scud capability, anything over 150 kilometers in range is precluded. And certainly a Scud capability is precluded

To the best of our knowledge, the Scuds that we have been able to identify and locate have all been destroyed We cannot exclude the fact that there may still be Scud or Scud variants hidden somewhere in Iraq And we, supporting the Special Commission, will continue to look for them

Yes, you are absolutely correct that capability should be destroyed. And if there were any cooperation with it, we should do what we could to cut it off, since it would be inconsistent with the Security Council Resolution.

Mrs MEYERS Do you think that we can safely assume that as long as Saddam Hussein and his party are in power that that government will do everything possible to acquire nuclear weapons?

Mr. GALLUCCI I think that is a very safe assumption.

Chairman HAMILTON. Mr. Gejdenson.

Mr GEJDENSON. What are we doing to try to preclude Iraq from getting fissionable material?

Mr GALLUCCI The most important thing, I think, is that we support the Special Commission and the IAEA in inspecting, continually, everywhere that we have any reason to suspect there may be anything having to do with either enrichment or reprocessing.

And at the same time, we focus as much of our energies as we can of assuring ourselves that nobody is exporting anything to Iraq that would provide a fissile material production capability or directly provide fissile material.

Mr. GEJDENSON. One of the things that makes us nervous is that when the Soviet Union was together, it had probably a better program than the West for preventing that kind of material from leaving its control. The West always had some breaches, but we seemed to be doing all right.

Now it seems to me we have a significant worry involving the former Soviet Union and its entities And if you look at our record with Iraq, there were a number of signals along the way

What I wonder is, following the chairman's question on the list of companies that sold to Iraq, are we a little compromised in this situation?

MIXED SIGNALS ON NONPROLIFERATION

We should have gotten a signal that there was a reason to worry about Iraq. The Israelis bombed the Osirak reactor, at least they thought there was a nuclear threat there

In 1982, when many people were concerned about Saddam's behavior and there was good indication that he was arming terrorists, we took him off the terrorists list.

In 1989, President Bush signed NSD 26 that basically was a message to help Saddam Hussein Now what I am left with is two things One, maybe we are doing as good a job as we can under the present multilateral agreements to prevent Iraq from getting new weapons capabilities

But it seems to me that, one, it is clear that you need a multilateral response in all these areas chemical, biological, and nuclear. It is also clear that our multilateral responses are wholly inadequate and that we have done things that have undermined the isolation of governments like Saddam Hussein's over the last decade

Clearly other countries now are providing missile technology to Iran, if not to Iraq as well At one point we found a White House document where, in a debate over what they were selling to Saddam Hussein, somebody used the fact that Iraq was a signatory to the Nuclear Non-Proliferation Treaty as a reason for the treatment of Iraq

How do we become more vigilant internationally when our own resolve is in question, as it was from 1982 to the invasion of Iraq?

We seem to have other political and economic motives We thought we could use Saddam Hussein. Other countries seem to think it is OK to sell missile technology to the Iranians

You have worked with international organizations and you have worked at the State Department We have got to be a little purer in this game and stop using our politicians as a frontline

How do we communicate to our allies, who do not have a seriousness about controlling nuclear proliferation, the importance of limiting weapons availability?

Mr GALLUCCI Mr. Gejdenson, I think the answer to the question—I take the question How can we do better?

NONPROLIFERATION HAS BECOME A POLICY PRIORITY

I think that, in the first instance, we have to identify the problem of nuclear weapons proliferation, as well as the other problems of proliferation—chemical, biological, and ballistic missile—as a primary national concern and an objective to do something about it And I think this administration has done that

Then we have to act consistent with that. And that means a number of things I think it means supporting international institutions that are designed to be elements in overall nonproliferation strategies. The International Atomic Energy Agency is one such agency No agency and no institution is perfect. The IAEA has come a long way And the thrust of much of my remarks this morning is that it has come a long way recently and as a result of what happened in Iraq.

And I would—as you listen to the rest of the testimony this morning, I would be concerned that one draw conclusions from parts of that testimony that may be critical of agency activity that would lead to a loss of support Because as a representative of the administration on this issue, I think supporting the IAEA is one of the critical things that needs to happen.

Mr GEJDENSON. Reports claim we now have the North Koreans making some adjustments, but I fear that they are just getting better at hiding things. I don't have an answer on how we get multilateral—I mean, can we feel confident that the Iraqis have no fissionable materials today?

Mr. GALLUCCI I am trying this morning not to make anybody feel real good about Iraq or North Korea It is just that we have to engage these countries I don't think that turning our back is the answer

Mr GEJDENSON I agree How do we get our allies, and ourselves at times, to not see any short-term political gain—as we obviously saw from 1982 to the invasion of Kuwait when, in the case of Iraq, we wanted to play off the Iranians or others in the area—to be more important than the transfer of technology that has incredible consequences today? What do we do to get them to focus on it?

Mr GALLUCCI. Without rehashing the previous 8 years or so of history, I would say that very often a nonproliferation objective is embedded in regional analysis as other objectives as well And sometimes the nonproliferation objective is best pursued within a regional context. Sometimes it isn't.

RATIONALIZE U S. EXPORT CONTROL LAWS

Mr GEJDENSON. You know, in the last 10 years we were stopping the sale of bank credit cards to England while we were selling things to Iraq that needed nuclear licenses It seems to me that if we are going to lead, we have to rationalize our export control laws to focus on the things that matter and get our friends to do the same

Chairman HAMILTON Mr Manzullo

IRAQ'S BW PROGRAMS

Mr MANZULLO. Thank you.

Mr. Gallucci, I would like to return to a question posed by Mr Hamilton. To your knowledge, have there been any sales to Iraq in violation of the 1972 Biological Weapons Convention?

Mr GALLUCCI Not to my knowledge, that I can think of No, sir

Mr MANZULLO The companies to which you referred were engaged in some type of commerce of biological weapons which you did not want to reveal——

Mr GALLUCCI I see My reference earlier to information that I am sure the U.S Government has on cooperation that companies engaged in with Iraq prior to the war, companies in other countries, clearly are over a number of the areas of weapons of mass destruction.

I myself don't know whether there was any cooperation in the area of biological weapons I know in general terms what the Special Commission found. And I know what the Iraqis declared on the eve of the first biological weapons inspection.

But I don't believe that got to the point of your question, which is, what was supplied by external suppliers? And off the top of my head, sir, I don't have any information about that

Mr. MANZULLO. Do you believe that Iraq, at present, possesses biological weapons?

Mr. GALLUCCI. I would say that it is highly unlikely, but I can't exclude the possibility The Iraqis declared themselves to have had an offensive biological weapons program, which they told the Special Commission they had abandoned. I believe they said they abandoned it in the fall of 1990. They provided some examples or specimens of biological agents they had produced to the commission But they said that the program was no longer existent.

There were a fairly large number of inspections that were aimed exclusively or partly at least at uncovering biological weapons capability in Iraq, as I am sure you know, since the capability to produce biological weapons is fundamentally a dual-use capability Many of the same pieces of equipment that one uses in a pharmaceutical or some other area of legitimate industrial activity are also useful for a biological weapons program

And that is why I am reluctant to say that such a program doesn't exist.

CW STOCKPILES

Mr MANZULLO What about chemical weapons?

Mr. GALLUCCI. The situation there is quite different There were literally thousands of fabricated chemical weapons munitions of all kinds, from missile warheads to rockets to artillery shells, and additional thousands of tons of chemical agent, both mustard and nerve agents, and tens of thousands of tons of precursor chemicals in Iraq

And at the present time, and for some time, the Special Commission has been, with the assistance of the Iraqis, drilling and draining munitions and neutralizing chemical weapons and chemical agents And that is going to continue for some time. The capability to produce chemical weapons was located at a few sites Most of that has been destroyed, all that was exclusively designed and prepared for chemical weapons production

There are still additional things that need to be destroyed that the Special Commission is working on with the Iraqis. I could not offer assurances to you—nor, I think could anybody else—that there are not stockpiles of at least mustard agent weapons somewhere in Iraq buried or hidden It is impossible to give any assurance to that

The inspection regime, however, permits, as I have indicated before, the Special Commission to go anywhere it deems necessary to do an inspection And whenever the Special Commission has received information that there is something to look at, whether it be chemical weapons themselves, agents, precursors, or equipment, they have gone there

And there has been in the chemical areas, as in other areas, a process of peeling the skin on the onion and disclosing what there is in Iraq. But I cannot preclude that there is not more that the Special Commission and we do not know about.

Mr MANZULLO Do you feel that the chemical weapons that Iraq currently possesses were manufactured by that country or shipped externally from another country

Mr. GALLUCCI. I am certain that at least a large quantity—and I am sure that all of the chemical weapons were fabricated in Iraq They have the capability to do that, and they are well able to

Chairman HAMILTON Mr Lantos.

Mr LANTOS. Thank you

Mr Gallucci, you have been a very effective and able public servant for many years, and the character and tone of my questions is not directed at you but at the palpable failure of our Government to pull together a coherent policy with respect to Iraq. So let me attempt to do that and ask you to comment on some questions.

I don't think that these items we read on the front pages—that Iraq is harassing the inspectors from the International Atomic Energy Agency, that they are threatened, that they are intimidated, that their hotel rooms are bugged—and the attempt to assassinate the former President of the United States—which has now been fully confirmed to my satisfaction—can be understood separately The attempt by Iraq to rebuild its conventional and nonconventional military capabilities is linked to its attempt to intimidate the United Nations I certainly consider it at least a possibility that the successful FBI preemption of the attack on U N. headquarters in New York was Iraqi-sponsored or financed They have a beef with the United Nations, with the United Nations Security Council, which maintains the sanctions regime I think they all hang together. And I think if we look at tiny little parts and deal with tiny little parts, we are in danger of being like a child who looks at a complex picture which is a puzzle and doesn't see what is in that picture, which can be a very clear image of something.

THE BOMBING OF IRAQI INTELLIGENCE HQ

So let me first just say for the record what a brilliant move it was by the President to bomb the facility that we did 48 hours ago It was described by some of the press as an empty building It was anything but an empty building. It was the symbol of torture for the Iraqi people.

And I would like to just quote half a paragraph from an item appearing in today's *Washington Post* by Jim Hoagland referring to that facility.

"But Baghdadis know that thousands of innocent Iraqi civilians have been tortured to death in [this intelligence] compound. In April 1980, in one of the most gruesome and significant assassinations that occurred there, Saddam's secret police drove nails into the skull of Bakr Sadr, an important Iraqi Shiite religious leader. after raping his sister before his eyes Other dissidents were poisoned with thalium. The compound was the center of Saddam's foreign espionage and terror operations "

So I think it is important to realize that our Government, within the last 2 days, took action to strike at the symptom and substance of the center of Iraqi terror and intelligence operations This is the framework in which this hearing is taking place

Now, I found your testimony, your prepared testimony, and your answers to Chairman Hamilton's questions, somewhat in conflict And I would like to ask you, if I may begin with this, to clarify this conflict

In your prepared testimony you say, "Iraq, no doubt, will continue to test the U.N 's resolve to continue vigorous inspections, especially if it perceives that support for them is waning, as in the past Iraq will use tactics such as delaying or refusing access to sites, denying information, harassing inspectors, and refusing to accept U N Security Council Resolution 715 to reduce the effectiveness of the inspections " I am still quoting "Recently Iraq's efforts to undermine long-term monitoring have focused on two issues Iraq has refused to allow the Special Commission to install cameras at two rocket motor test stands and has refused to destroy certain chemical weapons precursors and related equipment

"On June 18, the Security Council adopted the Presidential Statement that Iraq's refusal to cooperate with the Special Commission in these matters constitutes," I quote, "a material and unacceptable breach"—a material and unacceptable breach—"of U N Security Counsel Resolution 687 and a violation of Resolutions 707 and 715 The Statement warns of serious consequences."

A HISTORY OF LIES AND DECEPTION

Now, if this is your prepared testimony on behalf of the Department of State, I find it incomprehensible that in response to questions by the chairman you say that we believe that declared facilities are known to us, and of course, there may be undeclared facilities. But how can we deal with undeclared facilities? I mean, the whole history of Saddam's performance, both before and after the invasion of Kuwait, was one of deception and lies and attempts to evade the leaky system of Western controls

We now know—and I am sure you do—that a large number of firms in Germany, France, and other countries, functioned as purchasing agents for Iraq, that a large number of Jordanian companies functioned in this capacity, that there were large transfers of financial resources so that Iraq would be able to avoid the freeze on its assets.

And we all understand that there has been an enormous rebuilding of Iraq's military capability

Now it was just days before the invasion of Kuwait that the State Department gave such an optimistic picture that we can do business with these people, and we can work with these people. And I would hate to see this administration fall into the same trap We are dealing with Saddam Hussein, who, according to the statements and actions of the President of the United States, 3 days ago, attempted to assassinate the previous President of the United States.

Is it really that difficult to pull together all the information with all of the resources of the administration to demonstrate that Iraq is hell bent—hell bent on developing or redeveloping or restoring its nuclear, chemical, biological, and conventional facilities?

Mr GALLUCCI Mr Lantos, may I respond?

Mr LANTOS Please.

Mr GALLUCCI I suppose the written record will show, but I don't believe I ever said—and if I did, let's change the written record

I don't believe I said that we are inspecting and destroying facilities only that Iraq has declared. I yield to no one in my belief that Iraq lies and has repeatedly lied, gets caught at having lied, and lies again, without any show of remorse And I have personal experience with that chain of events

Mr. LANTOS Could you tell us about that, your personal events

IRAQ'S NUCLEAR PROGRAM HAS BEEN "KNOCKED FLAT"

Mr. GALLUCCI. I could, Mr Lantos, and I will But I need to—if I could first make one other comment here The point I wanted to make earlier and in the testimony that you quoted, was that we have—we the United States and other governments who have focused their energies on the Iraqi situation with respect to weapons of mass destruction, particularly the nuclear program—have provided information to the IAEA and the Special Commission on every place that we could identify, and that, therefore, the agent, the IAEA and the Special Commission, could identify They have gone to each place and any time they have found anything that deserved to be destroyed under 687, it has been destroyed We believe that program has been knocked flat.

Two other additional points that I have made I need to make again. We believe that program has been knocked flat We cannot be absolutely certain that there isn't something hidden we haven't found And nobody, I think, is going to want to make that assertion to you

And the second point is that, given the intent that we believe that regime, Saddam Hussein, has to rebuild the nuclear program and the other programs, given the resources that would fall to that government if the embargo were lifted and if they could sell oil, and given the fact that it is an industrial society and the experts, the scientists, and the engineers are still there, we believe they could, in the proper environment, rebuild And, therefore, we believe the sanctions are vital and the long-term monitoring of the regime is absolutely vital that the IAEA and the Special Commission would implement

Chairman HAMILTON Do you have another question?

Mr LANTOS Yes, I do

With what degree of assurance can you say that no other country, ranging from Jordan to individual companies in Western Europe, is functioning today as a front organization for Iraq's military procurement network?

Mr GALLUCCI. At the current time, I am unaware of any organization acting in the way that you just described I cannot exclude the possibility But I myself am unaware of companies breaking the embargo and acting in that way.

Mr. LANTOS Are you aware that as we speak German customs is investigating well over 100 German companies with respect to this issue?

Mr. GALLUCCI. I am not

Mr. LANTOS Thank you, Mr. Chairman

Chairman HAMILTON. Mr. Hastings

IRAQ IS STILL PREVENTING INSPECTION FLIGHTS OVER BAGHDAD

Mr HASTINGS. Thank you, Mr. Gallucci, for being patient I will be brief

Iraq has demanded that IAEA and UNSCOM not fly over Baghdad proper And this is a demand, of course, which has been rejected but apparently not directly challenged.

The demand that Iraq makes conflicts with United Nations Security Council Resolution 707

My question, Mr. Gallucci, is why has IAEA and UNSCOM not tried to fly over Baghdad proper to challenge Iraq on that restriction?

And, second, what is the United States doing to help the inspectors gain unrestricted access and achieve their rights under the United Nations cease-fire Resolution?

And should military action be contemplated in this case?

Mr GALLUCCI Mr Hastings, the specific case you referred to of the overflight of helicopters of Baghdad proper, which the Iraqis have refused to permit the Special Commission to do, is one of a number of cases in which we have had noncooperation from the Iraqis And they vary in importance And when they get important enough, then, in the past, actions have been taken by the international community

In each individual case, an assessment in the first instance is made by the Chairman of the Special Commission, Rolf Ekeus Then he takes it to the Security Council, and the Security Council, of course, needs to consult to see whether that incident is of sufficient moment to act. That is the sequence we have been proceeding under for the last year and a half or so.

I know that the Special Commission regards the Iraqi refusal to permit the helicopter flights as an infringement on their inspection activities, and they very much want to conduct those flights They have been taking other steps to compensate. They are not as efficient They are not as good. But I don't think they have been fundamentally hampered on their ability to move about

I think over the long-term it is like Resolution 715. Acceptance by Iraq is something that the Special Commission will want to have and will insist upon having.

As I say, in a general way, though, every time an issue like this comes up, we in the United States need to consult with our allies and see what action is appropriate Right now we have a case before us where the Iraqis are refusing on two issues: one, the stationary cameras at the test stand, and two, some movement of chemical precursors and equipment. This is a matter on which the United States will consult the Security Council and others; and appropriate action, I am sure, will be taken if this issue isn't otherwise resolved.

But we must, in every case, ensure that the case before us is one that will sustain whatever action is contemplated

Mr. HASTINGS. Saddam is saying you can't fly over Baghdad. The U N. is saying that this is an inappropriate response to unrestricted access. If then we don't fly over Baghdad what we are saying, in essence, is that all of your clandestine procurement opportunities are being fostered, or at least, if they are happening in Baghdad, we aren't immediately in a position to do anything about it

I am sorry, Mr Chairman, but I couldn't resist a followup.

Mr. GALLUCCI Let me followup. It is not that the Special Commission cannot move around with freedom in Baghdad. It does that It has any number of vehicles available to it, and it moves all about Baghdad

There is an advantage to being able to move about with helicopters and to do monitoring with helicopters. And that is something that we support the Special Commission in seeking to have They have compensated, as I said. And they do have movement and access

Chairman HAMILTON. Mr. Fingerhut.

CONCERN OVER IRAN'S NUCLEAR PROGRAM

Mr FINGERHUT. Thank you.

I know we are here to talk about Iraq, but in your written testimony and also in a number of other questions, including Mr. Lantos' and others, we expanded the scope of the discussion a little bit. And since I think we have covered Iraq pretty thoroughly, what disturbed me about the issue of the nuclear proliferation is that, even in the case of Iraq, where we have extraordinary access as a result of the Gulf War and where we have the United Nations backing up, literally day-by-day, as we do battle with Saddam Hussein over inspections and all of the technicalities of the important work in which you are engaged, even there we still have some question as to whether or not we have effectively stopped Saddam Hussein from getting back into the nuclear weapons business

How much behind the eight ball must we be in all of the neighboring countries—Iran particularly concerns me, but other countries do as well—where we don't have the kind of constant attention and access and international backup that you have in Iraq? And what would it take—I guess two questions

First, how concerned are you that, as we sit here and critically, but also in a way, sort of self-congratulatory way, applaud our work in Iraq—how close are we to losing the game in neighboring countries?

And what would it require of us if we were serious about making these same efforts in other countries?

Mr. GALLUCCI. I think that the point is that we are engaged actively in addressing the problem of nuclear weapons proliferation in neighboring countries and in countries in other regions. The point is that it will require active engagement You are absolutely correct.

There are countries with regimes that are dedicated to the acquisition of nuclear weapons, we believe. And we must be as dedicated to preventing their acquisition. The means to doing that, I think, in the first instance, is the acquisition of information about their intentions and how they are proceeding.

And so, I think, in the first question—and I think it is embedded in the question that you asked—is how good is our information and are we putting enough resources in the effort to prevent proliferation? I think the answers are moving initially in that direction, and our information in some cases is very good and in other cases not so good, depending on how difficult the problem is.

In terms of the activity that we launch after we have information, part of that is diplomatic activity to prevent exports As hard as it is to believe, most countries do not build nuclear weapons indigenously They purchase the equipment and facilities they need to produce the fissile material and to produce the triggering mechanism.

That gives us an opportunity to prevent sensitive exports to countries that wish to build nuclear weapons And we are doing that So I think that is extremely important

The final element is the international regimes. And I would put at the top of the list the international safeguards regime

THE U S. SEEKS A NUCLEAR EMBARGO ON IRAN

Mr FINGERHUT Should we be at five-alarm stage in any of the neighboring countries or, indeed, in another region? Obviously, we have talked about North Korea and Iran

Mr. GALLUCCI I don't know how many alarms are appropriate But very high on our list is our concern about Iran It is not so much of concern because of their present capability to produce nuclear weapons but rather their intentions Given the enormous financial resources available to them, and our concerns that are based upon their interest in acquiring research reactors—heavy water moderated or graphite moderated natural uranium reactors—our position is that we would like no country to engage in nuclear cooperation of any kind with Iran in light of the political orientations of its regime

Chairman HAMILTON. Mr Fingerhut, I apologize for interrupting. We have a series of votes on the floor We will have to recess at once When we get to the floor, we will see how long it is going to take us to vote. But I am told there will be one 15-minute vote which is pending now, and then several shorter votes I am not too sure how many at the moment

Mr Gallucci, what is your schedule? Do you have to leave very shortly?

Mr GALLUCCI Yes, I do, as a matter of fact, Mr. Chairman

Chairman HAMILTON. I think we will have to excuse you with appreciation for your testimony this morning and thank you for it.

I don't think it is going to be possible to keep you here because it is going to be at least a half-hour or more before we are able to get back.

So we will recess now.

Mr. Oberstar.

Mr. OBERSTAR May I pose a question for the record?

Chairman HAMILTON. Certainly

SAFEGUARDS ON NUCLEAR MATERIAL

Mr. OBERSTAR In subsequent testimony from the Nuclear Control Institute, a statement is raised that I would like you to respond to, and that is that the IAEA continues to perpetuate the myth that its safeguards on nuclear materials are effective and goes on to state that the materials are fundamentally unsafeguardable and the proof came at the time of the Gulf War when Iraq secretly removed its nuclear stockpile to the Tuwaitha facility

In your statement you say, "We must continue to press Iraq to reveal its foreign suppliers, and work with other suppliers to ensure effective monitoring of exports to prevent diversion " That seems, to me, rather naive, to believe that Iraq will voluntarily reveal information.

So I would like your comment on the Nuclear Control Institute statement. And I would like a comment on what specific things the United States is doing, not just to be polite with Iraq but to press our allies—this is no great secret, you know, who these suppliers are and how to apply pressure to them

And since we don't have time for you to respond, I will just leave it at that

Mr LANTOS [presiding] You will submit the response in writing, Mr. Gallucci? Or would you like to comment on it now?

Mr GALLUCCI I would like to briefly comment, and I will also provide in it writing

On the question of pressing the Iraqis to provide the names of their suppliers, I think we should, and do, press the Iraqis to provide what they ought to provide. That doesn't mean that we expect them to. And I don't believe that we are naive when it comes to the State of Iraq and their leadership.

With respect to the safeguarding of material and what I assume is meant in the quote by the Nuclear Control Institute, this raises the difficulty of assuring that fissile material—that is to say uranium or plutonium, subject to safeguards—can be assuredly prevented from becoming a part of a nuclear weapons program. They can be subject to safeguards, which means that material can be accounted for. It doesn't mean that there is an assurance that it will not be taken out of safeguards and used for weapons.

The basic misunderstanding is what one can expect from safeguards Safeguards cannot prevent. Inspectors are not policemen. They can provide assurances on where it is located. That is all we ask of it, and that is all we could expect of it It requires for states to do otherwise

[The response by the Department of State follows:]

The argument suggests that safeguards are fundamentally flawed because Iraq, during the course of the war, removed the fuel from its research reactors and moved that fuel to a secret location to secure the fuel against attack However, Iraq promptly informed the IAEA that the fuel was removed They told the IAEA that the new location would remain secret during the war to protect the fuel from attack

Iraq's actions do not indicate that this nuclear material is unsafeguardable, they indicate that IAEA safeguards were designed to provide assurances during times of peace The IAEA's record of verifying nuclear materials accounting demonstrates that nuclear materials are safeguardable, and that the IAEA is up to the job we give it

Before the Gulf War the international community did not accept the premise that the IAEA should search for covert nuclear activities Iraq's secret enrichment programs, uncovered after the Gulf War, demonstrated that the IAEA must be strengthened and given the tools to detect covert nuclear activities The IAEA's Board of Governors has acted and we are now giving the IAEA the necessary tools, including wider access, more kinds of information, and environmental monitoring capabilities

Mr LANTOS Mr Gallucci, on behalf of the committee, I want to thank you very much for your testimony.

The subcommittees will be in recess for approximately 30 minutes

[Whereupon a brief recess was taken]

Mr LANTOS [presiding]. The hearing of the joint subcommittees will resume

We would like to ask the four witnesses of the second panel—Mr Jules Kroll, Gary Milhollin, Jay Davis, and Lawrence Scheinman—to please take their seats

I am delighted to have all of you I want to apologize for the disjointed character of the hearing, but we are still in a heavy voting mode, so we will undoubtedly have some interruptions.

We will begin, with you Mr Kroll

Your prepared statement will be entered in its entirety in the record You may proceed in any way that you choose I would ask to you speak very close to the microphone.

STATEMENT OF JULES KROLL, PRESIDENT, KROLL ASSOCIATES

Mr KROLL Mr. Chairman, thank you for your interest in this subject and staying the course while many others have not I think my statement is rather self-explanatory, and in the interest of time, I have a few statements to make and will let the written record speak for itself

Mr LANTOS You will summarize the prepared statement?

Mr. KROLL. Yes I think the key point that I would like to present today, very simply, is that the network and the arrangement that was set up in the years prior to the invasion of August of 1990 still exists Some of the players have changed, but the strategy is essentially the same. Some of the air has gone out of the balloon, but the balloon itself exists. And some of the same persons that were active before still exist in the same roles as they previously had

That is my first point, very simply.

SMUGGLING ACROSS THE BORDERS

Secondly, that in an age where we depend so much on technology and satellite photos and cameras, et cetera, to track what's going on in the world, some very fundamental observations indicate to us that things are going on In particular, if one were to stand at the border, or the borders, of Iraq—at the Jordanian/Iraqi border, at the Syrian border, at the Iranian border—you would see on any given day hundreds and hundreds of semitrailers and other forms of large vehicles going into Iraq and leaving Iraq And the degree of inspection at the various points along those borders is extremely modest.

The fact is that, without human inspections, without technical use of equipment to monitor what is coming over those borders, no one really knows what's in those trucks Steel can easily be buried underneath lettuce, and military equipment can easily be buried underneath pharmaceuticals And it is, very simply, a question of needing a policeman on the beat in each of those locations

So I have two essential points to make: One is the kind of procurement network that existed previously still exists Many of the same businessmen who were operating in France, Germany, the UK, Switzerland, Austria and other countries, are still there. Many of those people are still individuals of immense wealth The question is still an open one as to whose wealth is that, really?

Clearly——

Mr. LANTOS. Are you suggesting that these individuals may well be using Iraqi Government funds on behalf of the Iraqi Government and are used merely as facades, as surrogates, as front organizations to pursue the procurement policy of Iraq?

Mr KROLL. I think that is a distinct possibility.

One of the lessons we learned from the prior procurement network, a part of which was exposed TDG, Matrix Churchill, et cetera, in some of the other countries, is that seemingly commercial enterprises were run as Iraqi front organizations

And I don't believe that has changed very much. You still have some individuals who were active today as they were then.

I think at this point, it might be more productive in terms of the use of time and the time of the other witnesses if you had some questions for me in your areas of interest I would like to try to respond

[The prepared statement of Mr. Kroll appears in the appendix]

Mr. LANTOS Well, we do have a number of questions to ask of you. But before I come into questions, I want to ask you to comment on the general issue of the financial network

THE ROLE OF JORDAN

In your prepared statement, and I quote, you are saying the following "The financial network, until recently under the control of Barzan Al-Tikriti, Saddam's half brother and formerly Iraq's permanent representative to the U.N in Geneva, continues to transact business out of Switzerland

"The military procurement network, under the control of Hussein Kamel, Saddam's son-in-law and former head of the Ministry of Military Industrialization, has received more publicity as a result of the Matrix Churchill investigations in the U S and abroad. Although several of these individuals and companies have been exposed, we believe that the network has been, or will be, reestablished."

What do you think is the role of Jordan in all of this at the moment?

Mr. KROLL. Well, the role has changed somewhat. I think in the spring of 1992, due to the pressures from the United States, the level of activity going from Jordan to Iraq and back was somewhat reduced

However, one must realize that a substantial portion of the commercial infrastructure of Baghdad moved lock, stock, and barrel to Amman where trading activity, commercial activities, financial arrangements, were more easily and more freely set up I don't think that that has changed very much

I think today if you want to seek to do business with Iraq on any series of subjects, you are more likely to be able to conduct that transaction in Amman So it is still a very important location. I don't mean to necessarily imply that this is something backed and sponsored by the Jordanian Government.

I found the King's comments in recent weeks to be very interesting regarding Saddam Hussein But Jordan is clearly at the center of commercial transactions vis-a-vis Baghdad

I think the second most important location is Geneva, and the third is Vienna

IRAQI ASSETS ABROAD

Mr LANTOS Now, what is the extent—even if you can just give us a ballpark figure—of preexisting Iraqi resources which were moved out of the country so as to avoid the freeze on Iraqi assets? Are we talking about billions?

Mr. KROLL Yes.

Let me try to break those into three categories of assets. There are the assets that are well known and documented that are currently frozen Those are in the billions. Many of those assets sit in banks today and are demarcated as the assets of the Iraqi Government.

I think the second level of assets, also in the billions, are monies, stock in companies, gold, that was moved out either shortly before the invasion or shortly after the invasion That would be the second category.

And then you have the third——

Mr LANTOS And you say that the second category, which are basically Iraqi Government assets, are currently at the disposal of the

Iraqi Government, contrary to United Nations Security Council Resolution, and used to obtain military and other supplies?

Mr KROLL Yes My problem with giving precise estimates is that we don't know Without a chance to look at the books and records of the financial institutions in question, which I think is critical because you can have all the inspectors and all the cameras and all the spy satellites you want, but quite often in a business matter you are going to learn more from books and records than anything else

Mr LANTOS But you believe these are in the billions?

Mr KROLL Yes, they were I think it has been diminished somewhat. They are no longer paying quite as frequently in gold That has essentially stopped in the last 6 to 9 months But it is in the billions

SLEEPING ASSETS

The third category of assets are assets that I would call sleeping assets These are assets that have appeared for years and belong to individuals in companies that are really a mix of Saddam's personal assets, the assets of the Ba'athist regime and the Iraqi Government And this category, as well, is very substantial, I would say in the billions

Estimating the precise amounts of these is difficult without access to the books and records I would urge the international community to spend more time trying to get at those books and records I think we would learn a great deal

Mr LANTOS I will ask this question of all witnesses, and since you are our first one, you are getting this question first There are certain sanctions currently in effect on Iraq. In order to achieve the goals of the international community, which aims basically at stabilizing the region and of having a modicum of peace, do you believe that sanctions currently imposed on Iraq should be, one, lifted, two, weakened, three, maintained, or, four, strengthened?

Mr. KROLL Again, given where I come from and given my perspective on this, I would argue for strengthening those embargoes, in part, because you need to analyze how effective the embargoes have been to date They have been partially effective

I think the direct sale of oil has been pretty much stymied

Mr LANTOS. Not entirely?

Mr KROLL No There is significant movement that we know of, but of a limited amount, moving over the borders by these trucks with these enormous tanks underneath We believe, but cannot yet substantiate, that there are countries friendly to Iraq that are supplying credit by selling their own oil and giving credit to vendors who wish to sell things to Iraq without literally having to sell Iraqi oil. We have a proof problem there.

But given the fact that Iraq has rebuilt so much of their infrastructure, they have clearly not done it purely out of existing inventories and parts and supplies So they have gotten it from outside.

With the passage of time and with the international community weakening by the day because of their desire for commercial gain, logic tells me that what you'll have is increased desire for increased trade.

The number of delegations going to Baghdad and going to Amman seeking to sell things is not diminishing; it is increasing And that is where the pressure will continue to come from.

I think we need to strengthen the embargo if we want to achieve the purpose of the U N. resolutions

Mr LANTOS Thank you very much, Mr. Kroll

We will need to briefly suspend the hearing because we have a vote We will resume in about 10 minutes

The meeting is in recess.

[Whereupon a short recess was taken]

Mr. LANTOS. The joint hearing of the subcommittees on Europe and the Middle East, on Economic Policy, Trade and Environment, and on International Security, International Organizations and Human Rights will now resume.

Our next witness is Mr Milhollin

Your prepared statement will be entered into the record in its entirety You may proceed in any way that you choose

STATEMENT OF GARY MILHOLLIN, PROFESSOR, UNIVERSITY OF WISCONSIN LAW SCHOOL AND DIRECTOR, THE WISCONSIN PROJECT ON NUCLEAR ARMS CONTROL

Mr. MILHOLLIN Thank you, Mr Chairman

I am pleased to have this opportunity to address these three distinguished subcommittees

I would like to begin by giving a little background on this situation I think it is useful to point out that in roughly 1 month we will pass the third anniversary of Iraq's invasion of Kuwait If Iraq had not invaded Kuwait, it is very likely that Saddam himself would be passing a milestone about now He would be assembling his first atomic bomb

Two U N inspectors, David Kay and Jay Davis, have estimated that at the time of the invasion, Iraq was 18 to 30 months away from producing its first critical mass of nuclear weapon material We have now passed the 30-month mark

THE IAEA WAS ASLEEP AT THE SWITCH

One of the most frightening things about this possibility is that the International Atomic Energy Agency did not and never would have detected it Before the invasion, the Agency rated Iraq's compliance as exemplary And in fact it was exemplary at the locations where they inspected, but they did not inspect where Iraq was making the bomb. The Agency only inspects locations that are declared by the country being inspected, and so far no country has made a bomb at a disclosed site.

Now, Iraq is a member of the Non-Proliferation Treaty and, as such, it promises not to make the bomb and it promises to declare all of its work with plutonium and enriched uranium to the IAEA Iraq secretly broke both of these promises at the time when the Agency was rating its performance as exemplary or its compliance as exemplary.

Mr LANTOS Mr Milhollin, what you are saying is so imminently sensible and reasonable that I wonder how long this charade will continue on the part of much of the international community of concluding that, since declared sites appear not to be production facilities for nuclear weapons, we can say with a high degree of assurance that nothing is happening

And as you point out, all of the activity that is interestingly taking place, obviously, is at undeclared sites And since undeclared sites are difficult to find in some instances, the degree of assurance that the international community has vis-a-vis Iraq, Iran, North Korea, whatever, is really—by force is—very limited, isn't it?

Mr MILHOLLIN. Yes, it is. And it turns out, if you simply look at the history of the development of bomb programs around the world, you see that international safeguards have been pretty much irrelevant to this activity, precisely because it has not occurred at sites that were inspected

We were lucky in Iraq If Iraq had not invaded Kuwait, this strategy would have worked. They could have joined the Non-Proliferation Treaty, enjoyed all the benefits and still have developed the bomb.

Iran is following the same strategy and so is Libya and so is North Korea In a sense, though, it is unfair to criticize the Agency for not doing a job that it was not set up to do The Agency's primary function has been to promote the spread of nuclear technology. It runs training programs, it sends out experts of its own; and, most of all, it agrees to inspect exports by more advanced nuclear countries to less advanced nuclear countries

THE IAEA'S CONFLICT OF INTEREST

If a supplier, for example, wants to sell a reactor to a country like India or Pakistan, the Agency provides a guarantee that the reactor's plutonium will not be used to make nuclear weapons. Without this guarantee, it would not be possible politically to make the sale. The result has been that because the Agency stands ready to cooperate in nuclear exports, nuclear technology has spread more rapidly around the world India and Pakistan both got reactors under Agency safeguards And since getting those reactors, both countries have made the bomb

The Agency has a built-in conflict of interest If it catches somebody making a bomb with an export, that means that the export was too dangerous to have been sold in the first place and should not have been promoted

So there is an institutional incentive at the Agency always to find that nothing is wrong

In the United States, we had this same problem with the old Atomic Energy Commission, it had the dual functions of promotion and inspection until Congress wisely split those functions in 1974.

Now the Nuclear Regulatory Commission regulates nuclear power, and the Department of Energy promotes it The regulation of nuclear power in the United States gained great credibility from this separation It seems to me that we ought to do the same thing internationally and separate the Agency's promotion function from its inspection function I think the Agency would gain great credibility from this, and it would get over this problem of a conflict of interest.

THE CHINESE REACTOR SALE TO IRAN

I'd like to mention the fact that the Chinese are now planning to sell a reactor to Iran, as everyone knows. The reactor will be at least 300 megawatts, enough to make enough plutonium for 10 bombs per year at a minimum

The Agency, the International Atomic Energy Agency, stands ready to cooperate with this deal and make it politically possible to achieve the export.

So, in Iran, we will be essentially relying on a piece of paper signed by the Iranians saying that the plutonium from this reactor will not be diverted. The United States opposed this deal because it is a giant nuclear technology transfer to Iran, moving them a long way down the road to nuclear weapons, regardless of what promises are made.

The IAEA, however, stands ready to cooperate with it The subcommittee has asked specifically about Iraq So far as we can tell, from the Special Commission, which is in charge of the chemical and missile inspections, there has been good progress in destroying chemical agents, munitions, and precursors. The commission expects to have destroyed all of them by the end of this year.

With respect to missiles, the U N inspectors report that they have narrowed the uncertainty as to how many Soviet-supplied Scuds the Iraqis may have left The uncertainty is in the number launched from 1980 to 1982. And the Iraqis have not provided the kind of documentation necessary to substantiate their claims. So there is an outstanding issue there

I think the committee has already alluded to the current deadlock over destroying equipment used to make chemical weapons and the deadlock over placing cameras at missile test sites. Those issues are still outstanding

I expect that the Special Commission will demand that they be resolved because it goes to the core of their inspection and monitoring efforts And so I think there is a real live question now about what we must do to get Iraq to back down and cooperate.

I would like to make a few other points First of all, I think the inspectors deserve a lot of credit They have carried out a difficult, dangerous job that is physically and mentally exhausting and dangerous even to their safety. They, I think, deserve the greatest possible support and cooperation from the Agency's management But I don't think they have always received it.

THE IAEA CHIEF INSPECTOR HAS "UNDERMINED" MORALE

The chief inspector, in particular, has said repeatedly to the press that, in effect, there is nothing more to find in Iraq I think the effect of these statements has been to undermine the ability of the inspectors to to keep their morale up and keep the pressure on the Iraqis

The Special Commission doesn't agree with the statements by the chief inspector. The Special Commission thinks there are still things to find And the Special Commission doesn't think the Iraqis have given up their desire or their goal to make nuclear weapons And as we have just heard this morning, neither does the U S Government.

The Special Commission, and I think also the U.S Government, hopes the following things can still be found in Iraq. These are things that we are still looking for.

First we are still looking for parts of the giant machines that Iraq used to enrich uranium. These particular parts will tell us how much uranium they managed to enrich and at what level of enrichment.

There also is a part of the centrifuge program that we think still exists that hasn't been found.

Also, the identities of the Iraqi nuclear personnel have not all been established, and we don't know what these persons are doing

We don't have all the records of explosive tests that Iraq carried out to see how far they got with nuclear weapons design.

We have never found the entire database describing all the nuclear weapon programs That is very important. We know it exists, but we haven't found it

Nor have we identified Iraq's foreign sources of technical advice so we can cut them off.

And we have not identified Iraq's network of foreign suppliers. These mercenaries stand ready to go back into action as soon as Iraq gets the money to pay them.

SPLITTING THE IAEA'S FUNCTIONS

Finally, the subcommittee has asked me to comment on how the International Atomic Energy Agency's inspections can be improved I could recommend that the Agency's functions be split up so as to get rid of the conflict of interest, as I have already said I think the Agency should continue to inspect declared locations It knows how to do that.

But I think we need a new entity that can look for undeclared locations I think the entity should report directly to the Security Council, which can back it up with force whenever it runs into noncooperation

The new entity also should be able to use and receive and protect intelligence information. The current agency does not have that capability

U S. intelligence officials say that the Agency has been a one-way street. Information goes in, but no information comes out That is because the Agency still regards its safeguarding functions as confidential.

The Agency's inspections play only a minor role in the effort to stop the bomb As I said already, in countries like Israel, India, Pakistan, and South Africa, the Agency's inspections have been virtually irrelevant We need more powerful tools I would say that they include, first, tougher diplomacy, second, trade sanctions; third, aid cutoffs; and, fourth, denials of technology through export controls

It is important to keep the Agency's inspections as strong as possible, and it is certainly possible to improve them But I think it would be a mistake to think that by tinkering with the Agency's inspection system we are going to seriously affect proliferation

Mr. LANTOS Thank you

Our next witness is Mr Jay Davis of the Lawrence Livermore National Laboratory.

Your prepared statement will be entered in the record in its entirety You may proceed in any way that you choose.

STATEMENT OF JAY C. DAVIS, DIRECTOR, CENTER FOR ACCELERATOR MASS SPECTROMETRY AND PROGRAM LEADER, GEOSCIENCE AND ENVIRONMENTAL RESEARCH, PHYSICAL SCIENCES DIRECTORATE, LAWRENCE LIVERMORE NATIONAL LABORATORY

Mr DAVIS. Thank you Today's hearing is particularly timely, as yesterday was the second anniversary for the unannounced inspection and subsequent truck chase at Fallujah——

Mr LANTOS. Could you briefly describe that episode, because not everybody may be aware of it, as I think you are, and, to some extent, I am

THE NUCLEAR CHASE AT FALLUJAH

Mr. DAVIS. On the second U N inspection, the team was in Iraq to look for the technology of electromagnetic isotope separation, the redeployment of the uranium enrichment program employed by only the United States and then abandoned by us and all other countries

The equipment is large, and the pieces weigh 60 tons. So the Iraqis assembled a truck convoy of 100 tank transports carrying this equipment that had been moving around the country and staying ahead of inspections

Assistant Secretary Gallucci and I, 3 days before the events at Fallujah, took a group of inspectors to Al Gahrib The Iraqis denied us access to that facility. We withdrew back to Baghdad When the U.N. gained us access 3 days later, the facility was inspected and found empty To our surprise, we got an intelligence update to go to Fallujah And after some planning, which I will describe further, we ran the first-ever unannounced, zero-notice inspection carried out by any agency

In the process of that inspection, we were able to panic the Iraqis They tried to flee from the compound with the equipment. We were successful in photographing that equipment, producing evidence of a covert program and Iraqi activities to not comply with the U.N. resolution. It involved shots being fired at U.N inspectors, but it was a very successful and aggressive operation.

Mr. LANTOS Well, if equipment or documentation or materials that the Iraqis don't want the world to find they move around, even equipment as vast and as complex as this, 100 trucks carrying huge pieces of equipment, and they attempt to hide this, doesn't it make elementary, common sense that materials which are much easier to hide or documentation that is much easier to hide, they clearly will also attempt to do?

Therefore, the statement that "we know what they have, what they are doing," is really a very naive statement because Iraq is a, physically, large country with enormous capabilities for hiding such materials or facilities or documentation

Would you agree with that, Mr Davis?

Mr. DAVIS I might disagree in a small sense, Mr. Chairman, in that the events at Fallujah so totally shocked the Iraqis, the threats made by both the United States and the Security Council, after we were withdrawn from the country were quite substantial, that they divulged much more than we expected and perhaps much more than they needed to We have likened the process to peeling an onion

And I think we have been able to combine the divulgations they made and the inconsistencies in those divulgations to draw a pretty complete picture. I think the bottom line is that you have stated it properly We will never know what we don't know by staying on the ground We must inhibit, irritate, and postpone. And that may be the future character of this activity.

It is useful for the committee to understand a bit of my personal background to put these comments in perspective.

I am an experimental nuclear physicist I also have other activities I have been both an emergency duty officer for the Livermore Laboratory and a senior scientific advisor for the Department of Energy's Nuclear Emergency Search Team and Accident Response Team In both of these roles, I have trained with and operated with security personnel at Livermore and trained with the FBI and U.S. military. I am both medically and psychologically screened for high-stress field work. So I look at the Iraqi inspections with an attitude somewhat different from that of a scientist on a site visit to a foreign facility

The three questions you have posed, I will answer very briefly How successful have the efforts of the international community been in identifying and rendering unusable Iraqi resources?

I think the U.N. has been very effective in finding, dismantling, and destroying Iraq's programs for weapons of mass destruction. Aided by intelligence, the process has forced Iraqi disclosure of relocated equipment, of records concealed, and of personnel involved At present in the ballistic missile area, completion of the process seems to be hindered by the lack of good intelligence leads.

Given that the work is done by unarmed inspectors operating within a country in full control of its military and security forces, I think the results have been remarkable

However, the process has now quite clearly shifted from discovery and destruction of Iraqi facilities to frustration of Iraqi attempts to restart their programs Keeping inspectors on the ground in Iraq inhibits Iraqi resumption of prohibited activities, but the process will become more dangerous as Iraqi frustration rises and world political support erodes. That change should be noted and its consequences anticipated

GIVE UNSCOM THE LEADING ROLE

The second question: How well has the IAEA accomplished its task? I think its performance could have been improved by giving the leadership to UNSCOM directly and relegating the IAEA to a technical support role in its traditional areas of nuclear fuel cycle and safeguards techniques.

Mr LANTOS. UNSCOM is the United Nations Special Commission which was set up for this purpose?

Mr. DAVIS. Yes UNSCOM has the primary responsibility for the inspections in Iraq Many of the IAEA staff, and some of the leadership, was burdened by the perceived need to protect the Agency's role, to defend its past performance in Iraq and to protect themselves from criticism and potential career damage within the Agency.

Institutionalizing the leadership for the nuclear inspections in the IAEA made it difficult to remove timid leaders and provided an opening between the commission and the IAEA that made possible both information loss and Iraqi political intrigue The IAEA has been accused of being both politicized and suffering from clientitis

From my perspective, both of these accusations are justified. The IAEA shows little appetite for intrusive inspection or aggressive behavior, both of which are essential to this inspection regime The IAEA fielded very different sorts of team leaders in Iraq. David Kay, who led the two inspections in which I participated, was aggressive and active in the field, thereby, accomplishing positive ends. Maurizio Zifferero was more the diplomat, concerned, if not burdened, by politics of the situation and the IAEA's interests Demitri Perricos was a classic IAEA inspector principally concerned with detailed verification of previously declared activities

"CLIENTITIS" AT THE IAEA

As an example of clientitis, Perricos chided me on several occasions for my estimates of Iraqi design goals and costs These had appeared in the media and had offended the Iraqi Atomic Energy Commission, leading them to protest that there was political motivation behind the numbers.

As these estimates were made possible only after defeating exhaustive Iraqi concealment and deception activities, partly in the inspection confrontation in Fallujah in which Iraqi agents had fired upon and detained members of our team, I felt his concerns for Iraqi sensibilities to be poorly considered

It is very important for the committee Members to realize that the aggressive surprise inspection of Fallujah was hardly a typical IAEA inspection activity The entire scenario was orchestrated and carried out by David Kay, four U.S and British technical experts, and two non-IAEA support staff using authority guaranteed by Rolf Ekeus, head of the U.N. Special Commissions

We quite literally wrote the script for Fallujah while walking through Baghdad back alleys after midnight, decidedly not the IAEA style Had that operation failed, as it threatened to at several moments, we might never have realized the full scope of Iraqi program This forced a great deal of Iraqi disclosure

As far as what steps can be taken to strengthen the IAEA to deal with such challenges in Iraq and elsewhere in the future, as my comments indicate, I do not believe that IAEA should have the lead role in these matters

We are at present strengthening the IAEA's analytical abilities both through access to their own facilities and by helping them field improved techniques in their own laboratories. Staff from Livermore and the other national laboratories are involved in these efforts now I think the IAEA has a very important support role in sample acquisition, maintenance of chain of custody, and technical analysis of materials returned I am not sanguine about granting the Agency routine access to intelligence information or allowing it to acquire genuine sophistication in nuclear weapons design and technology

In the chemical, biological, and ballistic missile areas, the UNSCOM has shown adequate ability to field effective teams and to accomplish its missions without having a long, previous history on the ground in Iraq

UNSCOM has been able to evaluate and replace leaders and to evolve operational doctrine without institutional inhibitions. I strongly recommend that future nuclear inspections be run under direct Special Commission control in a similar fashion.

One should allow UNSCOM, or its successor agency, to collect the inspection team leaders, evaluate the quality of intelligence, select the inspection targets, and staff the teams as appropriate, detailing IAEA staff in support roles as needed This change would relieve the IAEA of its conflicting roles—well described by other speakers—of first friendly teacher and inspector of the nuclear technology, and then suddenly the operator of adversarial and accusatory special inspections Such a change would allow more readily the fielding of teams of mixed specialists likely to be more suitable for future inspections in troublesome places

Let me close with a comment on the future I think it important to emphasize in Iraq that the IAEA and the Special Commission have been asked to do a task without precedent, operating under conditions and restraints that have been applied to no previous inspections

A NEW INTERNATIONAL INSPECTION AGENCY IS NEEDED

To criticize the IAEA for its performance on institutional grounds fails to recognize that it is trying to do a task for which it was neither created nor enfranchised Criticism on grounds of inadequate personal performance and the failure to deal with it is allowable. We need new institutions operating with different access to information, different team selection, and training approaches, and very different access to supporting military and political power if we are to be prepared for future events

Those of us who participated in the Iraqi inspections have come away feeling that their multinational character and U.N direction were essential to success. We are very proud of what was accomplished on an ad hoc basis by teams that made up doctrine and procedures as they went along. This approach will not suffice in the future where intrusive inspections may have to be carried out in states that have not recently been shocked by massive aerial bombardment and ground combat as Iraq was An ad hoc approach will similarly not suffice if we are to undertake such missions as seizing control of the nuclear weapons of a collapsing proliferant state, an event of increasing probability

If we are to succeed in these tasks in the face of deception, frustration, organized attempts to defer us, we need doctrinal development, specialized equipment, and frequent practice with our peers from other countries. None of those useful preconditions is being accomplished at present. Almost all discussion of improved non-proliferation programs has focused on technology, not on doctrine and operations.

This deficiency in present planning is an error that will have fatal consequences, both personal and political, for participants at all levels It would be very dangerous for both governments and to individuals to presume the successes in Iraq demonstrate a general case Iraq may, in fact, be the easiest case we ever face

Thank you for your consideration of my insights

[The prepared statement of Mr. Davis appears in the appendix]

Mr. LANTOS Our final witness today is Professor Lawrence Scheinman from Cornell University, who has also served as a consultant to IAEA Director, Hans Blix, and participated in IAEA-sponsored panels on improving the international safeguards system

We are pleased to have you, sir. Your prepared statement will be entered in the record in its entirety.

You may proceed any way you choose

STATEMENT OF LAWRENCE SCHEINMAN, PROFESSOR OF GOVERNMENT, INTERNATIONAL LAW AND POLITICS, CORNELL UNIVERSITY

Mr SCHEINMAN Thank you. I will follow along the text of my prepared remarks, but I will skip over quite a bit

I must say that following the two previous speakers, I find myself, as most would suspect, in a rather different position of assessment I would like to be able to respond point by point to many of the observations that were made, but I hope that my testimonial statement will accomplish part of that task

As in the case of the other members of this panel, I was asked three questions how well the United Nations has accomplished the task of eliminating weapons of mass destruction from Iraq, how well the IAEA has done; and what can be done to improve IAEA safeguards. I will try to focus most of my remarks on that last question However, I would like to say something about each of the previous two in at least an abbreviated form from my formal testimony.

I think—and this goes to a point that everybody I believe agrees with—that a fundamental point of departure in answering a question about whether we have succeeded in eliminating weapons of mass destruction from Iraq, is that it is virtually impossible to be certain about success

The only prudent approach is to be certain of uncertainty Leaving aside the obvious problems of scientists, engineers, theoretical knowledge, technical expertise, records, reports, design activities which would be very easy to hide and difficult to ferret out, there also can be no definitive assurance that nothing remains in Iraq in terms of tangible resources and capabilities to produce weapons of mass destruction, and there never can be

I think we have to have that as our fundamental point of departure This reality is one of the reasons for long-term monitoring in Iraq as described in United Nations Security Council Resolution 715 You may recall that it would provide for full and ready access to sites, materials, and persons and give the Agency the ability to restrict and/or stop movement of suspected material, equipment, and the like.

Such a verification system, even if based and implemented on a presumption that Iraq will again try to build nuclear weapons, can severely limit but not absolutely foreclose a successful clandestine effort And we have today a complicating factor, and that is the breakup of the former Soviet Union and the risk of the possibility that Iraq or others might be able to purchase, directly, weapons—usable material, or compete nuclear devices, thereby bypassing the need for mounting a program for producing fissile material which would be highly vulnerable to detection by a robust verification system

This underscores a fundamental point that the ultimate effectiveness of a verification system is not self-contained but contingent on other considerations such as a vigorously applied comprehensive export control system and resolute political support by the United Nations Security Council and the key states in the international system

As Mr Gallucci testified earlier, a great deal has been done Given the adverse conditions described by Mr. Davis, under which the IAEA and UNSCOM have had to operate, those achievements are even more impressive UNSCOM and IAEA, despite these difficulties, appear to have substantially exposed the Iraqi development

There is a sense that while not everything has been found, the vast majority of what existed has been identified

Mr. LANTOS. Could I stop you there for just a moment?

You listened, along with me and everybody else, to Mr Davis' rather dramatic description of——

Mr. SCHEINMAN. Yes, I did

Mr LANTOS [continuing]. Really a cops and robbers chase scene of the Iraqis running away with 100 trucks of heavy equipment, hiding it when unexpectedly the inspectors appeared. They panicked They shoot at them. They don't let them into the facility These people go back to Baghdad A couple of days later they come back. The place is clean. And the materials have been moved farther north

This clearly doesn't give me a great deal of confidence in our ability to state that the danger is gone.

Mr SCHEINMAN I fully agree And I didn't say that the danger is gone

Mr LANTOS I am not saying you do But here you have the international community acting through the International Atomic Energy Agency, the United Nations Special Commission, with a whole team of highly qualified people, and as it were, through creativity and good luck, they chase down the big secret And had that episode not occurred, we wouldn't know anything about it.

Isn't that true?

Mr. SCHEINMAN. That I agree with.

However, I would, in turn, ask a question Can we conceptualize a viable alternative method of getting at this kind of a problem than the one that was put forth in trying to deal with Iraq?

THE IAEA SOLUTION IS THE ONLY IMAGINABLE ONE

I have thought about this. And I find it very difficult to conceive of an effective multilaterally supported approach to the problem that is fundamentally different from what we had in the case of dealing with Iraq

The United States could choose to be an international policeman for all and to walk around the world and enter and push its way into doors and into sites as it saw fit because its intelligence service told it that that is where it ought to go But I don't think that would produce that world under the rule of law that we all understand is fundamental if we are going to have a stable international order

So we do have to find international strategies or internationally supported strategies to deal with these problems And it seems to me that whatever deficiencies may still exist—and they do still exist in the case of Iraq under these extraordinary circumstances—the task before us is to improve our capabilities, to strengthen and build our base, and to create the possibility to more effectively carryout the mission of limiting, if not ultimately preventing states that have undertaken to not acquire nuclear weapons, from doing so And I think this would apply to all other weapons of mass destruction, as well.

If I may just go on, Mr. Chairman, it seems to me that the balance sheet seems to say that we have done pretty well in Iraq, but we still have a large number of uncertainties.

The second question is really like the first, but it deals only with the International Atomic Energy Agency And I have a different answer to that question than the ones given by previous speakers on this panel.

THE IAEA HAS PERFORMED WELL

It seems to me that the IAEA has fulfilled its responsibilities, professionally and effectively, earning it the confidence of the Security Council, the Secretary General, and many governments for whom resolute implementation of the provisions for the elimination of weapons of mass destruction and the ability to produce them by Iraq are of paramount concern

I think the best judges of this are not any one of us sitting here as an outside observer, nor is it the IAEA But I believe that those who are close to the situation, outside the IAEA, may be able to offer us a better insight This is an insight that is based upon a 2-year experience and not a one-time situation And it is based upon an overall institutional assessment rather than on the assessment of the performance or behavior of specific individuals who were specified in testimony just a few moments ago

An UNSCOM spokesman, in a recent article in Arms Control Today, made the comment that, the initial understanding in implementing the verification regime was that Iraq would, in good faith, make declarations about its former activities that are now banned

Instead, it quickly became evident that Iraq was consistently concealing the extent of its programs As a result, the verification regime had to be tightened, and the UNSCOM teams—and in the nuclear sphere, the IAEA—were forced to change the basic premises of their approach to the inspection relationship Iraq, it seems, had to be presumed guilty until proven innocent.

It would appear that if the IAEA approached its tasks with some naivete and caution, as has been noted, it was not at all alone in this regard. That judgement relates to the period at the early stages of the now 19 completed inspections.

The assessment that I would like to note, again turns to the statement of the UNSCOM spokesman That comment, in the same article that I referred to a moment ago, was that, through their diligent work, the IAEA inspection teams with the assistance and cooperation of UNSCOM, uncovered three major programs for the enrichment of uranium to weapons grade materials, laboratory scale preparation of plutonium, and a full-scale program of weaponization

This is a public document in a popular journal, so you might want to go further in your assessment The Deputy Executive Director of UNSCOM, Ambassador Michael Newlin, speaking before The Washington Council on Nonproliferation, and now in a published document, commented that the Agency had to adapt to an intrusive type of inspection primarily at undeclared sites as mandated in Resolution 687 He went on to say that in his view, "the IAEA has adjusted to the new inspection requirements with remarkable success, a fact illustrated to UNSCOM by IAEA's very thorough, excellent reports Beyond inspections, the IAEA has also done well in the destruction phase of Resolution 687 "

THE IAEA HAS LEARNED IN IRAQ

And we can go further still At Mr Davis's institution, the Lawrence Livermore Laboratory last November, Ambassador Ekeus himself made the statement that "Iraq's nuclear program has been halted. The IAEA did a truly magnificent job in this respect "

And again that is in the written record This conformed with similar statements that Ambassador Ekeus reportedly made in periodic reports to the Security Council itself So I think the record, on the whole, and taking the institution as a whole, seems to indicate that the IAEA, while it may have started out slowly and with a bit, perhaps, of uncertainty and hesitation that was just described a moment ago, certainly has gone on the traditional learning track and has become a much better institution for dealing with the kinds of problems and responsibilities that have been assigned to it under Resolution 687, and that may come afterward

This brings me to the third question about improving IAEA safeguards And here is where I would like to focus my remaining remarks

What can be done to strengthen the ability of IAEA to deal with Iraq-type challenges in the future?

I fully concur with what has been said by previous speakers, that Iraq is not the last and probably not the most difficult problem we are going to have to face

Mr LANTOS The reason you are saying it is not the most difficult problem is because, as a result of Iraq's defeat in the war, it had to accept intrusive inspection, which clearly North Korea or Iran currently do not have to put up with?

Is that your point?

Mr SCHEINMAN. Those two countries do not have to put up with as intrusive inspection as Iraq has to put up with under Resolution 687; but there has been a change in the IAEA attitude, and behavior, and implementation of safeguards in the course of the last 2 years as part of that learning process, and that is what I would like to focus on That change makes it more difficult for a Korea or an Iran to get away with something. But this is not just because of the defeat of Iraq, it is because the IAEA has learned what Iraq could hide and where Iraq was or was not successful with respect to acquiring materials, equipment, et cetera, from outside In fact, my memory is that North Korea is probably better at hiding things than anybody, including Iraq, over past history

I think in approaching the question of what we do for the future, it is absolutely essential to understand that the Draconian and punitive measures applied in Iraq under the Security Council Resolutions cannot be taken as a standard for normal international verification by any institution whatsoever.

It is absolutely implausible that sovereign states would freely and voluntarily submit themselves to so onerous and intrusive a regime

If anything underscored this truth, it is the reversal of the United States' position regarding "any time, any place" inspection under the chemical weapons convention For many years we promoted that idea, but when it came down to the rock and the hard place, we backed down.

But in recent arms control agreements and in changes brought about by IAEA safeguards, there is considerable support for taking significant steps to ensure credibility and to reinforce confidence. States are willing to accept more today than they were willing to accept 20 years ago

However, any regime of the future is still going to have to strike a balance between the demands of international confidence and national sovereignty A point that I feel cannot be repeated too often is that the safeguard system applied by the IAEA in support of the NPT was commensurate with the expectations and desires of the international community at the time that system was put in place

THE NPT WAS DESIGNED TO BE NONINTRUSIVE

The NPT was devised to apply comprehensive safeguards principally to the fuel cycles of advanced industrial states, which were at the time that the NPT was being negotiated, the only states with significant nuclear activity These states, Germany, Japan, Sweden, and Italy, and so on were determined to minimize any risk that the distinction between themselves and the nuclear weapon states inherent in the NPT would extend into the peaceful realm of nuclear activity and competition

To ensure the adherence of these states to the Non-Proliferation Treaty, the United States and the Soviet Union endorsed a verification regime that kept intrusions to the minimum, consistent with credible verification that resulted in a system that focused on the flow of declared nuclear material that we have heard a lot about. It is important to understand as well that governments—and I will come back to this—speaking through their representative on the Board of Governors of the IAEA, establish the tone of the times.

And the tone of the time was verify, but don't push all that hard Just make sure that you feel reasonably confident that you know what the situation is and that you independently verify that safeguarded material can be accounted for, but don't go overboard

Now, given the structure of global competition at the time between the Russians and the Americans, it was also presumed that those two would control any real threat of proliferation among their allies or clients and as their competition reached to every region of the world that assumption applied to the world at large.

The periodic 5-year reviews of the NPT have resulted in endorsements over the years of the efficiency and credibility of the safeguard system, despite differences raised by activist nongovernmental institutions over the adequacy of the material control in large scale facilities

The end of the cold war——

Mr LANTOS You are referring to activist nongovernmental institutions?

Mr SCHEINMAN Not in a pejorative way.

Mr. LANTOS. Not in a pejorative way I appreciate that

Don't we need these activist nongovernmental gadflies to keep governments honest?

Mr SCHEINMAN Absolutely That is why I say it was not a pejorative statement

Mr LANTOS Maybe we could refer to them as treasured activist nongovernmental institutions

Mr SCHEINMAN Yes I think they have as a rule done very good public service in the questions that they have raised

A NEW PROLIFERATION ENVIRONMENT

The end of the cold war changed one of the assumptions about superpower predominance and control The discovery of a massive and largely unknown nuclear weapons development program in an NPT state, Iraq, changed another It changed the notion that it is only the advanced industrial states that are capable of mounting a sophisticated nuclear weapons program

In this new environment, the expectations are that, with the diffusion of technology, more states that are no longer under the watchful eye of the superpowers can engage in nuclear weapons development and, because of security and political concerns, no longer are being subordinated to the superpower competition Some of these states may seek to satisfy their security interests with nuclear arms, and Korea, Iran, and Iraq are certainly on that list.

All of these factors have had an impact on international institutions, not the least of which the IAEA, notably, the credibility of safeguards is now seen to be a function of their capacity to detect undeclared or clandestine nuclear activities.

Both Mr Davis and Mr Milhollin described the IAEA verification system as it was several years ago They did not describe it as it is today The concept of verifying declared nuclear material and activities no longer exists It is now a total verification of declared or undeclared activities.

CAN THE IAEA RELIABLY SEEK OUT UNDECLARED ACTIVITY?

Mr LANTOS May I just ask, Mr Davis and Mr Milhollin to comment on this point at this stage, if you care to

Mr MILHOLLIN. My comments had to do with the Agency's history and capability up until the time of the Gulf War I think the Agency still has the basic problem that I pointed out. it has a fatal conflict of interest which produces a culture in which they really don't want to find things that have gone wrong.

And I think that still exists and will exist as long as the Agency has a promotion function And so, even though the Agency, having suffered a tremendous defeat in Iraq, is now talking bravely about changing its ways, I don't believe it really can

Mr LANTOS Mr. Davis, would you care to comment?

Mr DAVIS I think my only comment is that I acknowledge the conflict of interest problem, which has been with us for a long time and is of concern. I am unsure that we understand the mechanisms by which we will pursue undeclared activities with or without the IAEA This is a difficult task, and I have seen no clear road map that suggests how we will pursue such things with any confidence of success.

Mr SCHEINMAN. As long as Mr. Davis says "with or without the IAEA," I think I concur on the difficulty of the problem.

THE IAEA HAS REFORMED ITSELF

However, the IAEA has done a number of things to try to bring itself into the modern world, if you will Mr. Milhollin referred to this as tinkering, but I think it is more than tinkering. There has been the examination of existing safeguards authority that prevailed through the statute and safeguards documents And upon that analysis was built a new approach. The main focus has been the so-called special inspections

And as the Chair is aware, the Board of Governors, a year ago, a year and a half ago, concluded that the Director General's assessment that the authority to conduct special inspections in full scope safeguard states extended to undeclared activities and that the use of outside information, including national intelligence information, was appropriate information upon which to base a request, was endorsed

Now, the authority to invoke an inspection of this nature is one thing. The willingness to do it is another And I think that we are very fortunate at this time to have a case in point. That case is North Korea It provided the testing ground, in my view, for agency determination

As the Chair is aware, there was a discrepancy with respect to the initial inventory The Agency came to the conclusion that the North Koreans had not revealed all that they should have revealed; and as a consequence of this, the Director General and subsequently the Board of Governors called for special inspections Upon refusal, the Board of Governors reported the failure to comply with safeguard obligations by North Korea to the Security Council

I submit that the IAEA acted with deliberation and decisiveness, giving a clear indication that the new political environment was, indeed, well understood and that it was prepared to exercise its authority

I think it is also interesting to note that the board came to a decision to report noncompliance while the United Nations Security Council had more difficulty in deciding whether or not and what nature of sanctions to apply. And the reason was that there is a veto power in the Security Council, and China was unwilling to go along with the more severe sanctions, and so we have a modified sanctions arrangement now in place in North Korea That does not occur at the level of the IAEA where no veto is possible.

MORE TRANSPARENCY

As you know, early submission of information, including reporting of design information and the like, was included in a Board of Governors measure reinforcing the safeguards system.

The point I want to make is that the IAEA has moved to establish increasing transparency in the nuclear arena to acquire a better early warning basis, a basis upon which it can call into question the integrity or the completeness of the record provided by states with respect to their total nuclear activities

Again, I refer to the North Korean case as a case in point I also think that there have been changes on the cultural side. There is increased awareness. There is now a system of country officers in place to consolidate all available information, all sources regarding the nuclear activity of states under safeguards and to assist with briefing and debriefing of inspectors as they go into and return from the field.

Still other measures are being considered now to improve the internal dynamics of the agency. But this brings me to my last point, Mr Chairman, and that is that we cannot stop with just improving the quality of safeguards, reorganizing activities within the context of the IAEA secretariat, or the like We need to make some additional things. I would like to mention four things that need to be done

ADDITIONAL CHANGES ARE STILL NEEDED

First I think it is unequivocally clear that the ability of the IAEA, or any other institution, to optimize safeguards capabilities and to create the greatest probability for detecting clandestine activities depends to a substantial degree on the availability to it of sensitive information which only a limited number of states are able to provide The flow of relevant information to the IAEA should be regularized and institutionalized

Contrary to the remark made by Mr. Davis, to my knowledge, there have been few, if any, questions seriously raised about the ability of the IAEA to receive and utilize national intelligence information provided to it pursuant to its responsibilities under Resolution 687 And there is every reason to think that they have been pretty good about protecting the source and the nature of the information that has been provided

I think that the United States should take a lead in moving forward on such regularization as well as ensuring any other operational or logistic support the IAEA may need to fulfill our expectations.

Second, it is a truism that international organizations lack meaningful enforcement power The exception is the United Nations Security Council which, if it invokes Chapter VII of the U.N charter, as it did in the Gulf War, can take enforcement action and pass mandatory resolutions binding upon member states

The January 1992 summit statement of Heads of State and Government of the Council declared that the proliferation of nuclear weapons constitute a threat to international peace and security, which is the key to opening the door to Chapter VII and enforcement

That same statement acknowledges the integral role of IAEA safeguards in implementing the NPT and asserted that members of the Council will take appropriate measures in the cases notified to them by the IAEA, which is what they did when the North Korean case came before them.

Given that the statement was made in the midst of a continuing crisis in Iraq and a strong sense of uniformity of purpose on the Council, I think it would be pertinent to the strengthening the international consensus against safeguards or nonproliferation violations to codify this statement in a formal United Nations Security Council Resolution.

This would provide an important element of enforcement and enforceability to IAEA safeguards, especially in view of the fact that, by statute, the IAEA has direct access to the Security Council in cases of safeguards noncompliance

I believe it is the only international organization in the U N family that has this direct access

A third measure requiring political leadership and action is to ensure that the IAEA is adequately funded to meet growing responsibilities, responsibilities flowing from North Korea, Argentina, Brazil, South Africa, and eventually, we hope, the non-Russian states of the former Soviet Union

USE THE IAEA TO VERIFY NUCLEAR WEAPONS MATERIAL

Finally, the United States should take the lead with the Russian Government to make use of the IAEA to verify dismantled nuclear warhead material I am going in a opposite direction of my colleagues Such a measure would be a strong demonstration of confidence in the system and the openness it implies could have a potentially powerful precedent setting value

The consignment of verification responsibility for dismantled warhead material would be less costly and more useful than applying safeguards on all peaceful nuclear activities in the weapons states. I think it is a step the United States should take now.

But the single most important element in strengthening the ability of the IAEA to meet the challenge of verification is the political will and the political support of its member states and of the Security Council

International organizations, as we know, are creations of sovereign states They lack sovereignty or independent political authority, and they are dependent on the political will of their sovereign members Secretariats can influence and cajole, but it is the governing bodies of the international organizations that are repositories of political authority

Sovereignty is a vigorous and contradictory force against empowering international institutions with far-reaching authority. But threats to international peace and security cannot be successfully addressed unilaterally They do require a collective action. While international verification may have to be supplemented by regionally verified arms control and security arrangements, it is something that cannot be done if there is to be any confidence in the world at large regarding the status of nuclear programs and the absence of clandestine nuclear activity

That is why it is all the more important that governments like ours that are committed to international verification, take whatever measures are possible to strengthen the hand of our chosen international instruments, in this case, the IAEA We and others have developed expectations for our international institutions

Now, we must ensure that the necessary authority, operational and financial support and political backing for vigorous implementation is made available to them

My closing comment is that the best of all possible verification arrangements is only the first step on a very tall staircase to achieving a global order free of the threat of nuclear proliferation or the proliferation of other weapons of mass destruction We are talking about a regime strategy which embraces many, many aspects, only a few of which have been touched upon today.

Thank you.

[The prepared statement of Mr Scheinman appears in the appendix.]

Mr. LANTOS. Well, I want to thank all you for excellent statements and for shedding a great deal of light on what may well be the single most important issue facing the globe, the danger of nuclear proliferation.

EXPORT CONTROLS SHOULD BE TIGHTENED

You mentioned that this is only the first step. Would you not agree that the first step, perhaps, is to dramatically tighten export controls and to bring about a degree of cooperation we certainly have not seen for years?

Isn't it infinitely easier to prevent technology and materials and high-tech equipment getting into the hands of countries like Iran, Iraq, Libya, North Korea, rather than, once there, trying to pursue this cat and mouse game of chasing trucks as they runaway with materials?

I mean, it seems to me if there is a Western failure—and I profoundly believe that there was both Western failure—when I say Western, I include Japan in that—both Western failure and irresponsibility in, say, during the decade of the 1980's.

It really was focused on not controlling Western companies from supplying rogue regimes with lethal capabilities.

Would you agree with that?

Mr SCHEINMAN. I do, Mr. Chairman I pride myself on having been one of a few outside experts invited by the German Bundestag several years ago to testify about their nonproliferation organization, law, policies, and the like Export control was one of the very fundamental points that was addressed in that Bundestag hearing

tal changes in internal German law, which has certainly come 180 degrees from where it was a few years ago.

But when I spoke of a regime, I meant precisely the idea of verification, export control, and delegitimizing nuclear weapons, establishing the concept that they are not only not usable, but that there is no legitimacy to having them as a deterrent in the final analysis.

I am referring also to the question of enforcement and to the question of working to resolve regional controversy, which is at the core in most cases, but not all, of the interest of states in acquiring nuclear weapons.

There is always the renegade problem A Kim Il-Song or a Saddam Hussein, who may see nuclear weapons not as defensive or as a means of deterring others from attacking them, but as a means of promoting an expansionist policy. That is the problem that the world has confronted since the state system emerged at the Treaty of Westphalia in the 17th century. And it is a problem that we will have to deal with until we have transcended the basic order of the world community that we have known for the past century. There is no final answer to that one either

It is a question of striving and organizing and bringing to bear as much of a concerted multilateral effort that provides a legitimate basis for dealing harshly with the recalcitrant state, and that deals with the good states in a constructive and positive way and helps to reensure security that we have to work toward

Mr. LANTOS. I mentioned earlier I will ask each of you the same question with respect to the sanctions regime And the question that I would like, first, Mr. Milhollin to respond to, do you favor lifting sanctions on Iraq, weakening sanctions, maintaining them as they are, or strengthening them?

Mr MILHOLLIN I favor strengthening them.

Before I go into that, I would like to make a request of the Chair.

Mr. LANTOS. Sure

Mr. MILHOLLIN. I have, as I am sure you know, written a couple of articles recently on this subject, one in The New Yorker magazine and another in the *New York Times* in April. The one in the *New York Times* lists those things that we have found in Iraq and the things that are still missing.

I would request that they be included in the record.

Mr. LANTOS. Without objection, they will be included in the record.

[The articles appear in the appendix]

Mr. MILHOLLIN. I think that the sanctions on Iraq should be strengthened. Certainly they should be maintained.

I believe that the inspectors have now, in effect, shifted into a monitoring mode in Iraq rather than a search mode I think that such a shift may be premature

I think there have been suggestions—the U S Government has suggested an inspection arrangement that would be far more aggressive, and that I think, will be more likely to yield results than the one that has been used The Special Commission and the IAEA have not adopted however.

As a substitute for it, the helicopter flights over Baghdad were proposed Of course, they are not happening now. So there was a time when it was agreed that we needed a more aggressive effort, we needed to engage the Iraqis more frequently, we needed to concentrate on certain areas where the government believes—our Government believes—that Iraq has the infrastructure and the people and the communications equipment, for example, to carry on the nuclear research effort.

And we thought—the U S Government—thought that it would be possible to concentrate on those areas and flush things out and get things to move so that we could see them from above. Those plans were not adopted.

And so I think we are moving into a phase in which we will simply monitor what we have found. I think it may be premature to do that So this goes a little beyond your question, but I think one safeguard could be more aggressive inspections. And I recommend that that course be adopted

Mr. LANTOS. Mr. Davis.

Mr DAVIS It is always dangerous, Mr. Chairman, to ask a scientist a political question, but I will give you an answer as the only person here who has been on the ground in Iraq and has seen the pain inflicted on the citizens of Iraq

I think I would favor altering them to make them more effective And perhaps a suggestion is to let the Iraqis sell their oil, but declare that all exports will come down the Jordan highway—or all imports come down the Jordan highway And inspect the 20,000 trucks a day that Mr Kroll says crosses that border very, very rigorously to see what is brought in.

I think in so doing, it would strengthen the support of the Arab countries in the region who are both concerned about the impact on 18 million people and have a vested interest in seeing that this regime is contained and controlled

It strikes me as much less risky and cheaper to put a powerful and effective inspection process on that border than to continue to impose an unsuccessful set of economic controls

THE FIRST U S BOMB WAS BUILT WITH THIRD WORLD TECHNOLOGY

There is one additional remark I must make. I am not very sanguine about export controls as a way of deterring nuclear weapons, and I have taken to stating that in a rather blunt way It is useful for people to remember that the first nuclear weapons were conceived, built, and used by a Third World country. The United States, at the end of the World War II, was a Third World country by our definitions: no computers, no numerically controlled machine tools, no jet aircraft; very primitive systems by the standards we now use.

A particular problem of the Iraqi business has been to shock people currently involved in the weapons program who look at Iraqi accomplishments and say they are not significant because they tend to think of it as we now do or as the Russians are doing it rather than as we did 50 years ago Much of the discussion about dual-use technologies is, I think, flavored by that

There were interesting arguments on the inspection teams between the scientists and the engineers and the politicians over when dual-use technology should be destroyed Most of the weap-

then you have said to the Iraqis, we will hold you in the Third World. That is a very powerful political statement I think part of the enigma is how do we achieve the degree of transparency that lets us override many of these dual-use problems

Mr SCHEINMAN. I concur with the idea that the sanctions should at least be maintained, possibly strengthened, but I really haven't given much thought to what kind of strengthening I would pursue

However, when we speak of strengthening or maintaining the sanctions, we have to remember that it is not us alone. There are other countries that would have to concur. This would require a collective decision, again, at the level of the Security Council.

I think we have to proceed carefully to know that we have got a concurrence of view, that a strengthening of sanctions, in one way or another, is going to achieve a desired outcome before we will be able to proceed to bring about stronger sanctions.

I would also like to comment that the remark that was just made by Mr Davis goes to the heart of the point, that preventing proliferation or bringing about a favorable result can only be done through an interdependence of measures or an interdependence of action

Not one of these safeguards or export controls or anything else is going to prevent a state from acquiring nuclear weapons. The only thing that will ever prevent that from happening is the political decision of the leadership of that country that it is not in their interest to acquire such weapons We have to bring about the conditions in which that frame of mind can prevail That is the biggest challenge of all.

Mr. LANTOS. Well, if you cannot change the mind of the political leadership on that point, then perhaps change the political leadership

I want to thank all of you for an insightful series of comments.

The hearing of the joint subcommittees is now adjourned

[Whereupon, at 1 50 p.m., the subcommittees adjourned to reconvene at the call of the Chair]

APPENDIX

TESTIMONY OF ASSISTANT SECRETARY OF STATE
ROBERT L GALLUCCI
TO THE
HOUSE FOREIGN RELATIONS COMMITTEE

June 29, 1993

Mr Chairman, I am pleased to have the opportunity to discuss our assessment of the nuclear situation in Iraq and the UN's capabilities to deter or detect any efforts by Iraq to regenerate its nuclear weapons program In these remarks, I would like to briefly describe the work the International Atomic Energy Agency (IAEA) in Iraq, some lessons learned, and the continuing need to give our fullest support to the IAEA as part of our overall non-proliferation efforts

Impact of Inspections

Under the auspices of UN Security Council Resolution 687, and with the assistance of UN Special Commission (UNSCOM), the IAEA has conducted 20 nuclear inspections of Iraq since the end of the Gulf War in April 1991. These inspections have forced Iraq to disclose, destroy, or render harmless all of the major nuclear weapons facilities and equipment that we are aware of, including several enrichment sites, research facilities, and weapons design facilities Along with the damage inflicted by the war and subsequent military actions, we believe these inspections have effectively put the Iraqi nuclear weapons program out of business -- at least for the near term

Regeneration a Problem

Over the long-term, however, Iraq still presents a nuclear threat We believe that Saddam Hussein is committed to rebuilding a nuclear weapon capability, using indigenous and imported resources.

- Iraq retains its most critical resource for any nuclear weapons program, namely skilled personnel and expertise
- Iraq also retains a basic industrial capability to support a nuclear weapons program, including a large amount of dual-use equipment and facilities
- If sanctions are lifted, Iraq would have access to additional financial resources to refuel overseas procurement activities

Finally, Iraq has still refused to provide the UN with details of its clandestine procurement network, a network which could therefore be reactivated in the future

Focus On Long-term Monitoring

To deter or detect regeneration, we need to ensure that the IAEA and UNSCOM receive the political, technical, and financial support to implement their plans for long-term monitoring in Iraq These plans are contained in Security Council Resolution 715 -- a resolution that Iraq has so far refused to accept.

- The Security Council will need to enforce the rights of the IAEA and UNSCOM under Security Council resolutions 687 and 715, especially the right to conduct challenge inspections without obstruction from the Iraqi authorities

- We must also provide technical support and information to the IAEA and UNSCOM, including assistance in the use of technical monitoring devices, such as water sampling, to detect covert nuclear activities

- To address the risk of overseas procurement, we must continue to press Iraq to reveal its foreign suppliers, and work with other suppliers to ensure effective monitoring of exports to prevent diversion

Sustainability

Iraq no doubt will continue to test the UN's resolve to continue vigorous inspections -- especially if it perceives that support for them is waning As in the past, Iraq will use tactics such as delaying or refusing access to sites, denying information, harassing inspectors, and refusing to accept UN Security Council Resolution 715 to reduce the effectiveness of the inspections

Recently, Iraq s efforts to undermine long-term monitoring has focused on two issues

- Iraq has refused to allow the Special Commission to install cameras at two rocket motor test stands and has refused to destroy certain chemical weapons precursors and related equipment

- On June 18, the Security Council adopted a Presidential Statement that Iraq's refusal to cooperate with the Special Commission in these matters constitutes a 'material and unacceptable breach' of UNSCR 687, and a violation of UNSCRs 707 and 715 The Statement warned of "serious consequences "

  On June 22 UN Secretary General President Boutros Boutros-Ghali met with Iraqi Deputy Foreign Minister Tariq Aziz to discuss the Presidential Statement Aziz said that the issues could be discussed in a technical meeting on with UNSCOM on July 12

On June 24, UNSCOM Chairman Rolf Ekeus told the Iraqi Foreign Minister that technical meetings between the Commission and Iraq cannot take place until Iraq complies with the Council's demands We strongly support Chairman Ekeus in this decision

Strengthening of IAEA Safeguards

Finally, I would like to relate the lessons of Iraq to the strengthening of the overall IAEA safeguards system -- a system that plays a critical role in the international effort to prevent nuclear weapons proliferation Fundamentally, the revelations about Iraq demonstrated the need for the international community to strengthen the Agency's ability and authority to detect undeclared nuclear activities outside declared safeguarded facilities In response, the IAEA's Board of Governors has taken a number of important steps to improve safeguards, reflecting the view that the IAEA should give a higher priority to detecting covert nuclear activities. The Board has

- Reaffirmed the Agency s right to perform special inspections whenever necessary to permit it to fulfill its safeguards obligations, including access to undeclared sites.
- Determined that the Agency may rely on information supplied by Member States when seeking a special inspection.
- Strengthened obligations to provide notice and early submission of design information on new nuclear facilities or changes to existing facilities
- Established a voluntary system for reporting on nuclear exports and imports

In our view, these changes have substantially strengthened the IAEA safeguards system, which is essential to ensuring that fullscope safeguards under the Non-Proliferation Treaty are fully implemented We have already seen evidence of this new determination in the Agency's performance in North Korea, South Africa, and Iran We believe that the IAEA's experience in Iraq has resulted in a substantial improvement in the IAEA safeguards system and, with the support of member states, it will continue to be a important part of the international non-proliferation regime

Jules Kroll
Chairman
Kroll Associates

June 29th, 1993 - Testifying before the Subcommittee on International Security, International Organizations and Human Rights

Kroll's involvement with the issue of Iraq's military procurement program began as an outgrowth of our assignment for the Government of Kuwait. In October of 1990, Kroll Associates was hired by the Government of Kuwait to locate covert assets of the current Iraqi regime and identify the individuals and/or companies controlling those assets. As the investigation progressed, it became apparent that prior to the war, Iraq had set up two worldwide networks: a military procurement network that used front companies to acquire restricted technology and a financial network used to hold and invest the hidden funds of the Iraqi regime.

The financial network, until recently under the control of Barzan Al-Tikriti (Saddam's half-brother and formerly Iraq's permanent representative to the United Nations in Geneva), continues to transact business out of Switzerland.

The military procurement network, under the control of Hussein Kamel (Saddam's son-in-law and former head of the Ministry of Military Industrialization), has received more publicity as a result of the Matrix Churchill investigations in the U.S. and abroad. Although several of the individuals and companies involved in this network have been exposed, we believe that this network either has been, or will be, re-established.

While there is no doubt that the sanctions have had a devastating effect on the people of Iraq, the evidence suggests that the current regime, with the apparent help of several countries, has not suffered and in fact, has solidified its control over the country.

It should be noted that Jordan, frequently cited for its aid to Iraq, appears to be making a serious effort to cooperate with the international community's efforts to control Iraq. I have insufficient knowledge at this point to evaluate the current level of these efforts

From an historical perspective however, any discussion of the regime's survival begins with Jordan, as its role both during and after the Gulf War cannot be overestimated

After Iraq's invasion of Kuwait, we received numerous reports of Iraqi government funds being transferred into Jordanian bank accounts to shield them from the international freezes on all Iraqi assets imposed shortly thereafter.

After the end of the Gulf War, Jordan provided a safe haven for the Iraqi government to conduct business and Amman subsequently became Iraq's business center for all trading operations These trading operations were funded by previously transferred funds held in Jordanian banks as well as periodic shipments of gold from Baghdad.

In addition to its role as depository for Iraqi assets, Jordan allowed the formation of trading companies controlled by Saddam Hussein's family members including his son, Udai, and his half-brothers. These companies are believed to handle the import of all types of materials. However, Khaled Marzoumi, Iraq's commercial attache in Amman, reportedly has primary responsibility of trade in military goods

Numerous sources have also reported on the frequent appearance of several Iraqi officials in Jordan including members of Iraq's Ministry of Industry and Military Industrialization as well as Safa Habobi, a major player in Iraq's procurement network who has been indicted in the United States for his role in the Banca Nazionale del Lavoro scandal.

Jordan, however, does not bear sole responsibility for the regime's ability to survive under international sanctions. Several other countries, including Turkey, Iran and Syria have all contributed on some level to Iraq's sanctions-busting activities.

More importantly, international pressure on countries to abide by the sanctions has not eliminated the network of individuals and companies willing to assist the current Iraqi government. In addition to those listed as "specially designated nationals" of Iraq by the Office of Foreign Assets Control, I believe that a substantial network of Iraqi bankers and businessmen continue to assist the regime while operating in coalition countries.

If the manner in which Iraq built up its military prior to the Gulf War is any indication, the mere existence of covert networks may not be as significant as the ease with which these networks conducted business. In particular, the ability of Iraq to purchase, through the use of front companies, stakes in companies in countries such as the United States, Great Britain and Switzerland provided it with ready access to military materials while decreasing the effectiveness of export laws

Events of the last few years suggest that we must address both the short-term and long-term issues affecting Iraq's ability to re-establish itself as a threat to peace in the region. Without pressure from the international community, countries will continue to assist Iraq in breaking sanctions, without increased attention to Iraq's covert networks, Iraq's agents will continue to conduct business as usual; and without monitoring of foreign investments in companies dealing in sensitive technology, Iraq will continue to have access to the materials necessary to rebuild its military capabilities.

In closing, I would like to thank the committee for the opportunity to share my thoughts on this matter It has been a honor to assist in this matter and I am available at the committee's convenience if additional questions arise.

JULES B. KROLL
CHAIRMAN

s B. Kroll is the founder of Kroll Associates and is Chairman and Chief Executive Officer. He has been ited with creating a new professional service of rnational corporate investigations and consulting which nes sophisticated fact-finding and investigative iques to the needs of the multinational business, ncial and legal communities. Kroll Associates has ces throughout the United States as well as London, s, Hong Kong and Tokyo.

Kroll is recognized as a leading authority on the ention and detection of white collar crime, defensive ics in contests for corporate control, industrial ter-espionage, and the management of complex investi-ons. He has been featured on Sixty Minutes, ABC's line, BBC, ITN and in such noted publications as Time, week, The New York Times, Fortune, Business Week, orate Finance, The Times of London, and many other ing international publications.

Wisconsin Project
on Nuclear Arms Control

Gary Milhollin
Professor, University of Wisconsin School of Law
Director

PREPARED STATEMENT OF GARY MILHOLLIN
PROFESSOR, UNIVERSITY OF WISCONSIN LAW SCHOOL
AND DIRECTOR, WISCONSIN PROJECT ON NUCLEAR ARMS CONTROL

Before the Committee on Foreign Affairs
Subcommittee on Europe and the Middle East,
Subcommittee on Economic Policy, Trade and Environment,
and
Subcommittee on International Security, International Organizations and Human Rights

June 29, 1993
10.00 a.m

Good morning. I am pleased to have this opportunity to address these three distinguished Subcommittees of the Foreign Affairs Committee

The Subcommittees have asked me to address the question of the inspections in Iraq and the effectiveness of the International Atomic Energy Agency.

In roughly one month, we will pass the third anniversary of Iraq's invasion of Kuwait. If Iraq had not invaded Kuwait, it is very likely that Saddam Hussein would be passing a different milestone about now. he would be assembling his first atomic bomb Two former U.N. inspectors, David Kay and Jay Davis, have estimated that at the time of the invasion, Iraq was 18 to 30 months away from producing its first critical mass of nuclear weapon material We have now passed the 30-month mark.

One of the most frightening things about this possibility is that the International Atomic Energy Agency did not, and never would have, detected it. The Agency's inspections were not set up to do so. Before the invasion, the Agency consistently rated Iraq's compliance with its inspections as "exemplary." In fact, Iraq's cooperation was exemplary at the locations the Agency was inspecting. The problem was that the Agency was not inspecting the locations where Iraq was making the bomb The Agency only inspects locations declared by the country being inspected, and so far, no country has made a bomb at a declared site. All A-bomb programs have been carried on at secret, undeclared sites

Iraq is a member of the Nuclear Nonproliferation Treaty, which means that Iraq promised not to make nuclear weapons and also promised to declare all of its work with plutonium and enriched uranium to the Agency. (Plutonium fueled the Nagasaki bomb, enriched uranium the Hiroshima bomb). But Iraq secretly broke both of these promises at the very time that the Agency was rating its Treaty compliance as exemplary.

To make matters worse, Iraq broke its promise by diverting equipment that the Agency's current chief inspector in Iraq had helped sell--over U S objections--to the Iraqis in the late 1970s Thus, the very equipment that the chief inspector helped supply was used to break the promise he is now supposed to be enforcing. Worse still, the Agency was later told about the violation by an Iraqi official who was himself a former Agency inspector. The former inspector had used his experience at the Agency to help outwit the current inspectors.

It is now clear what Iraq's strategy was. Iraq joined the Nonproliferation Treaty, enjoyed the diplomatic and trade benefits that come from membership, but still tried to make the bomb by outwitting the inspectors. If Saddam had not been foolish enough to invade Kuwait, the strategy would have worked. Iran is now following this same strategy, and so are Libya and North Korea. These countries cannot be expected to invade their neighbors on the eve of nuclear capability.

It is unfair, however, to criticize the Agency for not doing a job that it was not set up to do. The Agency's primary duty is to promote the spread of nuclear energy, especially to developing countries. It does a good job of that by running training programs, by sending out exports of its own, and--most of all--by agreeing to inspect exports made by the more advanced nuclear countries to the less advanced ones.

When a nuclear supplier wants to sell a reactor to a country like Pakistan or India, the Agency provides a "guarantee" that the reactor's plutonium won't be used to make atomic bombs. Without such a guarantee to make the export palatable, such transfers would be politically impossible. The result has been to encourage the proliferation of nuclear technology around the world. India and Pakistan both got reactors under Agency guarantees, and both have since made atomic bombs.

The Agency's conflict of interest is obvious. If the Agency catches somebody making bombs, it means that the nuclear exports were too dangerous to have been sold in the first place and should not have been promoted. Thus, the institutional incentive is always to find that nothing is wrong.

In the United States, the old Atomic Energy Commission had the job of both promoting and regulating nuclear energy until 1974, when Congress wisely split the functions. The Nuclear Regulatory Commission now regulates; the Department of Energy promotes. The U.S. regulatory process gained great credibility from this separation.

The situation in Iran illustrates the Agency's dilemma. The Chinese are now planning to sell Iran at least one 300MW power reactor. The reactor will make enough plutonium for at least ten atomic bombs per year The world will be relying only on a piece of paper, signed by Iran, promising that the plutonium will never be diverted.

The United States opposes the deal because it will be a
t nuclear technology transfer, moving Iran a long way down
road toward a bomb. James Woolsey, Director of Central
lligence, told Congress in February that Iran intends to make
ear weapons. The IAEA, however, stands ready to facilitate
export by promising to inspect it--providing the necessary
tical cover. I hope the Subcommittees will ask the IAEA
esses here this morning why the IAEA is willing to cooperate
this deal.

The Subcommittees have asked specifically about Iraq--about
progress in destroying Iraqi weapons of mass destruction
e the Gulf War. According to the U.N. Special Commission in
York, which is in charge of the chemical and missile
ections, there has been good progress in destroying chemical
ts, munitions and precursors. More than one thousand tons of
ical weapon precursors have been destroyed so far, but a
e amount remains. The Commission expects to have destroyed
of the identified nerve gas, mustard gas and precursors by
end of this year.

With respect to missiles, the U.N. inspectors report that
have narrowed the uncertainty as to how many Soviet-supplied
missiles remain in Iraq. The uncertainty is in the number
ched from 1980 to 1982. The Iraqis have not provided the
ments necessary to verify their claims.

Both the missile and chemical inspectors are now being
ed, however. The U.N. Security Council has just condemned
for refusing to move chemical equipment to a site for
ruction, and for refusing to allow surveillance cameras to be
alled at rocket test sites. The Special Commission believes
these refusals threaten the core of its inspection effort,
he question is what action to take if Iraq does not back
. The matter is now under consideration.

With respect to the nuclear program, there is less progress
more uncertainty. I have described the nuclear inspections
n article that I wrote for the New Yorker in February. Also,
pril the New York Times published a list of the main nuclear-
ted items that still appear to be missing in Iraq. The list
n estimate, compiled by the Wisconsin Project from Agency
rts and other sources. It gives a general picture of what
Agency is still looking for. I would like to submit both
cles for inclusion in the record.

The Subcommittees have asked me to comment on the adequacy
he Agency's inspection effort in Iraq. The Agency is in
ge of the nuclear inspections. I think that the inspectors
selves deserve our deepest gratitude and admiration. They
carried out a difficult, dangerous job that is both
ically and mentally exhausting. The inspectors are entitled

to the greatest possible support from the Agency's management, but they have not always received it.

One of the main problems has been the chief inspector's statements to the press. As early as February 1992, he said that "practically the largest part of Iraq's nuclear program has now been identified--probably what is missing is just details." And in September, he told Reuters that Iraq's nuclear program "is at zero now," and "they [the Iraqis] have stated many times to us that they have decided at the higher political level to stop these activities." He even made the improbable statement that "this we have verified."

The U.N. Special Commission flatly rejects these statements The Commission believes that Iraq has not given up on any of its mass-destruction weapon programs, including the nuclear one. Because of his press statements, the chief inspector has undermined the other inspectors' credibility. How can they plausibly search for things that their leader says don't exist?

The Special Commission still wants to find the following:

* parts of the giant machines the Iraqis used to purify uranium to nuclear weapon grade, to find out how much of this uranium the Iraqis made

* a suspected experimental array of centrifuges, also used to purify uranium to weapon grade

* a suspected underground reactor that could secretly make plutonium for bombs

* the identities of Iraqi nuclear personnel, to find out what these persons are doing

* records of explosive tests, to find out whether the Iraqi bomb design succeeded

* other records of the nuclear weapon program, to find out whether all of its components have been discovered

* Iraq's foreign sources of technical advice, to cut them off

* Iraq's network of foreign equipment suppliers, to make sure that it does not revive as soon as the embargo is lifted.

Finally, the Subcommittees ask how the Agency can be strengthened. I believe that the United Nations should follow the lead of the Congress and separate the Agency's promotion function from its inspection function This would increase its credibility by removing its conflict of interest. The inspections in Iraq, for example, would be carried out better by the Special Commission, which has no promotion function and acts directly under the United Nations Security Council.

In other countries, the Agency could continue to inspect declared locations, but inspections of undeclared locations should be done by a new entity whose sole job would be verification; no promotion function would interfere. This new entity could concentrate its resources on inspecting countries where the threat of proliferation is greatest, rather than dissipate its inspection resources as the Agency presently does. The Agency currently spends most of its scarce inspection funds looking at Germany, Japan and Canada, hardly the most acute proliferation risks today. This leaves fewer resources for countries like Iran.

This new entity should report to the U.N. Security Council, rather than to the Agency's Board of Governors. The Board typically includes countries like Algeria, China, India, Iran, Iraq, Libya, Pakistan and Syria. This amounts to letting a committee of arsonists decide where to send the fire truck.

This new entity should also be able to receive, use and protect intelligence information. The Agency has never had that ability, which is why it has never been able to do anything more than inspect declared locations. Even in the case of Iraq, where the Agency has been provided intelligence information, the Agency's secrecy rules have kept the providers from finding out what their intelligence produced U.S. intelligence officials say that the Agency has been a one-way street: information goes in, but nothing comes out.

I would like to end with an important reminder, which is that the Agency's inspections play only a minor role in the effort to stop the spread of the bomb. In countries like Israel, India, Pakistan and South Africa--countries that have successfully proliferated--the Agency's inspections have been virtually irrelevant. These countries made the bomb at places where the Agency never had any right to look To stop the bomb from spreading further, more powerful tools are needed. They include tougher diplomacy, trade sanctions, aid cut-offs, and denials of technology through export controls. It is important to make the Agency's inspections as strong as possible, and it is certainly possible to improve them, but it would be a mistake to think that by tinkering with them we are going to seriously affect proliferation

The United Nations Inspections of Iraq:
Accomplishments and Operational Lessons

House Committee on Foreign Affairs

Joint Hearing

Subcommittee on Europe and the Middle East

Subcommittee on Economic Policy, Trade and Environment

Subcommittee on International Security, International Organizations, and Human Rights

June 29, 1993

Dr Jay C. Davis
Director, Center for Accelerator Mass Spectrometry
and
Program Leader, Geoscience and Environmental Research
Physical Sciences Directorate
Lawrence Livermore National Laboratory

Chairman Hamilton, Chairman Gejdenson, Chairman Lantos and Members of the Subcommittees, I am pleased to appear before you to discuss my insights from the Iraqi inspection process Properly learning the lessons of these inspections, clearly an on-going process, is vital to the success of future efforts to control and inhibit proliferation of nuclear weapons to states or non-national organizations that might readily choose to use them. Today's hearing is particularly timely, as yesterday was the second anniversary of the unannounced inspection and subsequent truck chase at Fallujah That inspection and confrontation produced the first irrefutable evidence of Iraq's covert nuclear weapons program, its violation of its obligations under the Nonproliferation Treaty, and its efforts to evade the requirements of Resolution 687 As a principal in the events at Fallujah, I must confess that I never imagined that two years later we would still be dealing with so many uncertainties regarding both Iraq and the inspection process

I should begin with an important caveat I speak to you as an individual, not as a representative of either the Lawrence Livermore National Laboratory or the Department of Energy My impressions of the inspections and the inferences with respect to policy that I draw from them are mine alone, neither Livermore nor DOE should be burdened with them

It is perhaps useful for the Subcommittee to understand a bit of my personal background to help put my comments in perspective I am an experimental nuclear physicist, having spent over twenty years at Livermore as both a research leader and engineering project manager I have built several accelerator facilities and am familiar with nuclear weapons design, fabrication and testing and with the various technologies used to produce plutonium or to enrich uranium for weapons purposes My principal research interests are in the application of accelerator and isotopic techniques to problems as disparate as the dosimetry of carcinogens and mutagens, the mechanisms of global climate change, and the development of verification techniques for nuclear arms control I served as a technical expert detailed to the United Nations Special Commission (UNSCOM) on two of the early confrontational and productive inspections, Nuclear 2 and Nuclear 4 in the summer of 1991, to assess Iraqi efforts in these areas

In addition, I have been both an Emergency Duty Officer for the Livermore Laboratory and a Senior Scientific Advisor for DOE's Nuclear Emergency Search Team (NEST) and Accident Response Group (ARG) In both these roles, I have trained and operated with security personnel at Livermore and have trained with the FBI and US military for NEST/ARG activities I am both medically and psychologically screened for high-stress field work In consequence, I look upon the Iraqi Inspections with an attitude somewhat different from that of a scientist on a site visit to a foreign facility

You have posed three questions. I will answer them as directly as is possible for a scientist, feeling that your subsequent questions will elicit further detail as necessary

1. How successful have the efforts of the international community since the Gulf War been in identifying and rendering unusable Iraqi resources and capabilities to develop and produce weapons of mass destruction?

The United Nations has been very effective in finding, dismantling, and destroying Iraq's programs for weapons of mass destruction Aided by intelligence, the process has forced Iraqi divulgement and disclosure of relocated equipment, of records concealed, and of personnel involved At present, particularly in the ballistic missile area, completion of the process seems to be hindered by lack of good intelligence leads Given that the work is done by unarmed inspectors operating within a country in full control of its military and security forces, I think the results have been remarkable However, the process has shifted from discovery and destruction of Iraqi facilities to frustration of Iraqi attempts to restart their programs Keeping inspectors on the ground inhibits Iraqi resumption of prohibited activities, but the process will become more dangerous as Iraqi frustration rises and world political support erodes That change should be noted and its consequences anticipated

2. How well has the International Atomic Agency accomplished the tasks in Iraq that were given to it by the United Nations Security Council?

Performance could have been improved in the nuclear inspections by giving the leadership role to UNSCOM and relegating the IAEA to a technical support role in nuclear fuel cycle and safeguards techniques Many of the IAEA staff, and some of its leadership, were burdened by the perceived need to protect the Agency's role, to defend its past performance in Iraq, and to protect themselves from criticism (and possible career damage) within the Agency Institutionalizing leadership for the nuclear inspections in the Agency made it difficult to remove timid leaders and resulted in an opening between UNSCOM and the IAEA that made possible both information loss and Iraqi political intrigue The IAEA has been accused of being both politicized and of suffering from clientitis From my perspective, both these accusations are justified The IAEA shows little appetite for intrusive inspection or aggressive behavior, both of which are essential to this inspection regime

The IAEA fielded very different sorts of leaders in Iraq David Kay, who led the two inspections in which I participated, was aggressive and active in the field, thereby accomplishing positive ends Maurizio Zefferero was more the diplomat - concerned, if not burdened - by the politics of the situation and the IAEA's interests Demitri Perricos was a classic IAEA inspector, principally concerned with detailed verification of previously declared activities As an example of clientitis, Perricos chided me on several occasions for my estimates of Iraqi design goals and costs These had appeared in the media and had offended the Iraqi Atomic Energy Commission, leading them to protest that there was political motivation behind the numbers As these estimates were made possible only after defeating exhaustive Iraqi concealment and deception efforts, partly in the inspection confrontation at Fallujah in which Iraqi agents had fired upon and detained members of our team, I felt his concerns for Iraqi sensibilities to be poorly considered It is very important for Committee Members to realize that the aggressive surprise inspection at Fallujah that forced the Iraqis to disclose their covert program was hardly a typical IAEA inspection activity The entire scenario was orchestrated and carried out by David Kay, four US and British technical experts, and two non-IAEA UN support staff, using authority granted by Rolf Ekeus, head of the UN Special Commission We quite literally wrote the script for Fallujah while walking through Baghdad back alleys after midnight, decidedly not the IAEA style Had that operation failed, as it threatened to at several moments, we might never have realized the full scope of the Iraqi program

Placing leadership for the nuclear inspections in the hand of UNSCOM, as was done for the chemical, biological, and ballistic missile inspections, would have allowed evaluation of team leaders based on their performance in the field and their replacement if needed without institutional questions arising This step would have also provided the IAEA with a useful mechanism for evading the political costs associated with the conduct of intrusive inspections I strongly recommend such an arrangement in the future The Security Council's direct authority is much stronger than that of the IAEA and should be appropriately utilized

3. What steps can be taken to strengthen the IAEA to deal with such challenges in Iraq and elsewhere in the future?

As my comments above indicate, I do not believe that the IAEA should have the lead role in such matters in the future We are at present strengthening the IAEA's analytical abilities, both through access to our own facilities and by helping them field improved techniques in their own laboratories Staff from Livermore and the other national laboratories are involved in these efforts now I think that the IAEA has an important support role in sample acquisition, maintenance of chain-of-custody, and technical analysis of materials returned I am not sanguine about granting the Agency routine information to intelligence information or allowing it to acquire genuine sophistication in nuclear weapons design and technology

In the chemical, biological and ballistic missile areas, the United Nations Special Commission has shown adequate ability to field effective teams and to accomplish its mission without having a long previous history on the ground in Iraq UNSCOM has been able to evaluate and replace leaders and to evolve operational doctrine without institutional inhibitions I strongly recommend that future nuclear inspections be run under direct Special Commission control in a similar fashion Allow UNSCOM (or its successor agency) to select the inspection team leaders, evaluate the quality of intelligence, select inspection targets, and staff the teams as appropriate, detailing IAEA staff in support roles as needed This change would relieve the IAEA of its conflicting roles of first friendly teacher and inspector of nuclear technology, and then suddenly operator of adversarial and accusatory special inspections Such a change would allow more readily the fielding of teams of mixed specialists, likely to be more suitable for future inspections in troublesome places

There is perhaps one consequence of the Iraqi program that has not been ully realized and that is appropriate to point out to the Subcommittee Members concerned with economic effects Much of the Iraqi investment in the covert uranium enrichment program was dual purpose The Iraqis intended not only to create weapons but to produce an infrastructure of trained people and state-of-he-art production facilities that would make them a first-world nation in economic terms They discussed this goal in terms of human capital and return on investment in a fashion that would be perfectly understood by the Clinton Administration It is useful to remember that Jaffar Dhia Jaffar, the head of their overt program, is both Vice-Chairman of the Iraqi Atomic Energy Commission and Deputy Minister of Industry Although they failed to produce nuclear weapons, the Iraqis succeeded in creation of first-world production facilities for mechanical and electrical hardware, a fact verified and broadcast by our inspections While much of the dual use infrastructure has been destroyed, the Iraqis quite cheerfully state that they can rebuild it The size and sophistication of this act of industrialization, unprecedented among the Arab countries of the Middle-East, is a threat to their Arab neighbors and a destabilizing force, even if the Iraqis magically adopt a pacific and democratic governmental style The Iraqis openly express a desire for educational, economic and political leadership of the Arab states Many of us on the teams feel that they have the capability to emerge as the Japanese of the Middle-East, that such emergence may not be welcomed by their neighbors should be anticipated

Finally, let me close with a comment on the future I think it important to emphasize that in Iraq the IAEA and the Special Commission have been asked to do a task that is without precedent, operating under conditions and restraints that have been applied to no previous inspections To criticize the IAEA for its performance on institutional grounds fails to recognize that it is trying to do a task for which it was neither created nor enfranchised, criticism on grounds of inadequate personal performance and the failure to deal with it is allowable We need new institutions, operating with different access to information, different team selection and training approaches, and very different access to supporting military and political power if we are to be prepared for future events

Those of us who participated in the Iraqi inspections have come away feeling that their multi-national character and UN direction were essential to success We are proud of what was accomplished on an ad-hoc basis by teams that made up doctrine and procedures as they went along This approach will not suffice in the future where intrusive inspections may have to be carried out in states that have not recently been shocked by massive aerial bombardment and ground combat as Iraq was An ad-hoc approach will similarly not suffice if we are to undertake such missions as seizing control of the nuclear weapons of a collapsing proliferant state, an event of increasing probability If we are to succeed in these tasks in the face of deception, frustration, and possible violence, we need doctrinal development, specialized equipment, and frequent practice with our peers from other countries None of those useful preconditions is being accomplished at present Almost all discussion of improved nonproliferation programs has focused on technology, not on doctrine and operations This deficiency in present planning is an error that will have fatal consequences, both personal and political, for participants at all levels. It would be very dangerous, both to governments and to individuals, to presume that the successes in Iraq demonstrate a general case Iraq may in fact be the easiest case we ever face

Thank you for your consideration of my insights

Biography

Jay C Davis
Lawrence Livermore National Laboratory
University of California
P O Box 808, L-397
Livermore, CA 94551

Jay C Davis is a nuclear physicist at the Lawrence Livermore National Laboratory At Livermore since 1971, he has worked as a research scientist and as an engineering manager, having led the design and construction of several unique accelerator facilities used for basic and applied research He has also worked as a manager in magnetic fusion and laser isotope separation

In 1988, Dr Davis was appointed Director of the Center for Accelerator Mass Spectrometry, a multi-disciplinary, multi-organizational group applying accelerator analytical techniques to problems in biomedicine, geochemistry, materials science, and arms control In 1993, he also became Program Leader for Geoscience and Environmental Research at LLNL, overseeing the Laboratory's efforts in global climate change, environmental sciences, earth sciences and the emergency response to airborne release of toxic or radioactive materials

Dr Davis received his BA in Physics from the University of Texas in 1963, his MA in Physics from the University of Texas in 1964, and his Ph D in Physics from the University of Wisconsin in 1969 From 1969 to 1971, he was an AEC Postdoctoral Fellow in nuclear physics at the University of Wisconsin

Dr Davis has numerous publications on research in nuclear physics nuclear instrumentation, plasma physics, accelerator design and technology nuclear analytical techniques and analytical methods, and treaty verification technologies He holds patents on spectrometer technologies and methods for low-level dosimetry of carcinogens and mutagens, and the study of metabolic processes He has been a scientific advisor to the UN Secretariat, several US agencies, and to scientific agencies of the governments of Australian and New Zealand He participated in two UN inspections of Iraq in 1991 He is an avid backpacker, biker and cross-country skier

6/22/93

Prepared Testimony of Professor Lawrence Scheinman, Cornell University Joint Hearing before the Subcommittee on Europe and the Middle East, the Subcommittee on Economic Policy, Trade and Environment, and the Subcommittee on International Security, International Organizations and Human Rights, of the House Committee on Foreign Affairs June 29, 1993

Thank you very much for the opportunity to participate in these important hearings on UN and IAEA efforts to identify and destroy Iraqi weapons of mass destruction and establish a long-term monitoring regime I propose to focus most of my remarks on the questions of how well the IAEA has accomplished the tasks assigned to it by the United Nations Security Council under Resolution 687, and what steps can be taken to strengthen the IAEA's ability to deal with the challenge of proliferation in Iraq and elsewhere in the future However, I would like to begin with a few remarks on the general question of how successful have been the efforts of the international community in identifying and rendering unusable Iraqi resources and capabilities to produce nuclear weapons, as well as other weapons of mass destruction

A fundamental point of departure in answering this question is the understanding that it is virtually impossible to be certain about success The only prudent approach is to be certain of uncertainty Leaving aside the obvious problems of the continued presence of thousands of scientists engineers and technicians, and the consequent residual theoretical and technological knowledge and expertise, accrued technical and experimental experience and copies of records, reports, and design activities related to nuclear weapons development which are easy to hide and difficult to ferret out there can be no definitive assurance that nothing remains in Iraq in terms of <u>tangible</u> resources and capabilities to produce weapons of mass destruction, and there never really can be

This reality is one of the underlying reasons for long-term monitoring in Iraq as prescribed by UNSC/RES 715 Long-term monitoring is intended to ensure continuous verification of Iraqi compliance with extensive nonproliferation undertakings defined in the Security Council cease-fire resolution that go beyond those agreed by Iraq as a party to the NPT, and to minimize the risk that Iraq could successfully reconstruct a nuclear weapon development program RES 715 among other things authorizes the IAEA to carry out anytime/anyplace on-site inspections, to secure full and free access to all sites material and persons that the Agency judges necessary to fulfill its monitoring and verification activities and to restrict and/or stop movement of suspected material equipment and other items As the Committee is aware, Iraq has thus far refused to formally accept this Resolution, insisting that it is an unwarranted intrusion on its national sovereignty although elements such as a water-sampling program already are under way

So far-reaching a verification system especially if based and implemented on a presumption that Iraq will try again to build nuclear explosives can severely limit but not absolutely foreclose a successful clandestine effort An additional complicating factor that did not exist at the onset of the Gulf War, is the breakup of the former Soviet Union and the increased risk that would-be proliferators such as Iraq might be able to purchase directly weapons-usable material, or even acquire complete nuclear devices, thereby bypassing the need for mounting a program for producing fissile material which would be highly vulnerable to detection by a robust verification system This underscores a fundamental point the ultimate effectiveness of the verification regime is not self-contained, but contingent on other considerations such as a vigorously applied comprehensive export control system embracing all relevant suppliers, and, of course, resolute political support by the United Nations Security Council and the key states in the international system I will return to this theme in addressing the question of steps to strengthen the IAEA

This having been said, it is clear that a great deal has been accomplished in stripping Iraq of its capability to develop weapons of mass destruction Given the rather adverse conditions under which the IAEA and UNSCOM have had to operate, the achievements are all the more impressive Inspection in Iraq is not a cooperative venture Although accepting the terms and conditions of the cease fire resolution that established the rights and responsibilities of the IAEA, UNSCOM and Iraq Iraqi authorities have attempted to redefine their obligations and the rights of inspecting authorities and have interposed difficulties all along the way This includes failing to disclose information until it was clear that inspectors had irrefutable evidence of the existence of a facility, material or equipment, attempted continuous concealment of equipment and documents, denial of use of airfields to UN personnel, complicity in hostile behavior toward inspectors, and so on This is a continuing problem As noted by the UNSCOM spokesman, rather than making good faith declarations of former activities that were now banned, Iraq consistently concealed the full extent of its programs UNSCOM and the IAEA were forced to change the basic premises of their approach to the inspection relationship from good faith to using information from independent sources and backed by threats of continuing the embargo and resuming hostilities (T Trevan, Arms Control Today, April, 1993, p 11)

Despite these impediments, UNSCOM and the IAEA have substantially exposed the Iraqi programs to develop weapons of mass destruction There is a sense that while not everything has been found the vast majority of what existed has been identified that the broad infrastructure for the production of nuclear weapons has been identified and rendered harmless, destroyed or taken into custody, that all declared nuclear material and quantities of undeclared material have been accounted for and where relevant either already removed or readied for removal, that dual-use equipment has been identified although the question of its ultimate disposition in a number of instances remains unresolved Uncertainties persist about the continued presence of unacknowledged and undiscovered items or facilities such as an alleged hidden reactor, with the IAEA following up all plausible leads regarding the possible location of such a facility, a process that will continue as long as plausible information is made available or other indicators arise suggesting the existence of an undeclared facility The possibility that more undeclared nuclear material may exist in Iraq has not been excluded There is also a widely shared presumption that Iraq has not given up in its quest for weapons of mass destruction, and that given the opportunity it would reinstitute its program As well, it is recognized that given its human resource and technical experience base a rejuvenated program could move forward more rapidly than in the case of newly aspirant states Remaining gaps in information regarding the possible existence of hidden components as well as incomplete information on the Iraqi supply network both in the nuclear and missile areas are well understood by UNSCOM and IAEA and this guides their definition of future actions

In short, the efforts of the international community in identifying and disabling Iraqi resources and capabilities to develop and produce weapons of mass destruction appear to have been remarkably successful even if incomplete and limited by the reality that the only certainty is uncertainty But if policy is developed and implemented on that premise the risks associated with uncertainty will be commensurately reduced

The second question asks how well the IAEA accomplished the tasks in Iraq that were given to it by the United Nations Security Council The short answer to this question is that the IAEA has fulfilled its assigned responsibilities professionally and effectively, earning it the respect and confidence of the UN Security Council, the Secretary General, and many governments for whom resolute implementation of the provisions for the elimination of weapons of mass destruction, and the capability to produce them by Iraq, are a paramount concern

There are also those who have criticized the Agency's performance of its assigned tasks Some have done so because of what they considered to be deficiencies in how the IAEA carried out its mission A second kind of criticism reflects the intrinsic distrust of international organizations to deal with security-related matters that some people share Still other criticism is based, in my view, less on the question of how the IAEA performed in Iraq than on a concern that an organization that has a mandate both to promote and to safeguard the peaceful use of nuclear energy and that has been focussed on verifying declared nuclear materials and activities and operating more as a confidence-building mechanism than as a verification mechanism (searching for clandestine activity and invoking mandatory no-notice on-site inspections of declared or undeclared sites) might not be able to adequately accommodate to the requirements of a more demanding verification regime that will have to deal not just with declared nuclear activities, but increasingly with the threat of future Iraqs and of undeclared and clandestine nuclear operations In part this reflects a misunderstanding of the process of international safeguards in part, an intuitive preference not to rely on a technically-anchored international organization to carry out what is seen to be a political and security function This raises sizable issues about the future of the non-proliferation regime and its supporting institutions that cannot be adequately addressed in the time available today

Turning back to the first criticism concerning quality of performance there are several points to make First a number of the tasks assigned by the Security Council to the IAEA broke new ground While the Agency had a long experience in material control and accounting and in identifying and evaluating the capabilities of nuclear plant, it had not before been called upon to deal with national military activities or to take physical control of nuclear materials and assets Yet RES/687 charged the IAFA with responsibility to identify and evaluate weaponization facilities and nuclear weapons infrastructure, and to take control of and supervise the removal, destruction or rendering harmless of items specified in the resolution The earlier cited remark of the UNSCOM spokesman is particularly relevant here he noted that "The initial understanding in implementing the verification regime was that Iraq would, in good faith, make declarations about its former activities that are now banned " Instead, it quickly "became evident that Iraq was consistently concealing the full extent of its programs As a result, the verification regime had to be tightened, and the UNSCOM teams, and in the nuclear sphere, the International Atomic Energy Agency, were forced to change the basic premises of their approach to the inspection relationship, Iraq, it seems, had to be presumed guilty until proven innocent " (Trevan, loc cit) It would appear that if the IAEA approached its tasks with some naivete and caution, it was not at all alone in this regard

In the course of 18 nuclear inspections in Iraq the IAEA-led teams have, as indicated mapped out a substantially comprehensive picture of Iraq's nuclear development program, while acknowledging that they do not, and cannot, have an absolutely complete picture All known major facilities that could contribute to a weapons development program have been destroyed and all dedicated or single purpose equipment and components either destroyed or placed under seal Some quantities of dual-use equipment have been left intact This appears to follow the UNSCOM policy, as described by its spokesman of "not destroying many dual-use items that could be irreversibly converted for permitted purposes " (Trevan op cit, p 14) The full extent of the weapons development program however is not clear, knowledge of the sources of supply for equipment and components is incomplete and it is uncertain that all special nuclear material in Iraq has been located and taken into custody Recognizing that some activities, especially those involving small-scale research and progress in theoretical work and design, cannot be known except under the circumstance of extraordinary luck the IAEA emphasizes the monitoring of nuclear material pursuant to the very broad range of inspection rights referenced earlier, as approved by the Security Council in the long-term monitoring plan (RES/715)

How should one assess IAEA performance in all of these tasks? That judgment is best made by those outside the IAEA closest to the events In the course of evaluating two years experience under RES/687, the UNSCOM spokesman remarked that "Through their diligent work, the IAEA inspection teams with the assistance and cooperation of UNSCOM uncovered three major programs for the enrichment of uranium to weapons-grade material laboratory-scale preparation of plutonium and a full-scale program for nuclear weaponization " (Trevan, op cit p 13) The Deputy Executive Chairman of UNSCOM Ambassador Newlin speaking before a small professional group assembled by the Washington Council on Nonproliferation this past October, after noting the past limitations of IAFA inspections commented that " the Agency has had to adapt to the intrusive type of inspection primarily at undeclared sites as mandated by resolution 687 In my view the

IAEA has adjusted to the new inspection requirements with remarkable success, a fact illustrated to UNSCOM by IAEA's very thorough, excellent reports Beyond inspections, the IAEA has also done well in the destruction pnase of resolution 687 The Agency performed magnificently at the Al Atheer site in supervising the destruction of a very large number of buildings that were involved in the weaponization program " Finally, Ambassador Ekeus, the UNSCOM Executive Chairman, while questioning the current adequacy of the nonproliferation regime to halt the spread of nuclear weapons in a talk at the Lawrence Livermore National Laboratory last November, remarked that "Iraq's nuclear programme has been halted--the IAEA did a truly magnificent job in this respect " This conforms with similar statements he has reportedly made in periodic reports to the Security Council

If, as some others contend, the IAEA record has been less than sterling, I submit that one should look not at isolated instances but at the record as a whole, and that one should focus on the institution in its entirety rather than on any single individual Perfection is beyond human reach The consensus among those objectively viewing events seems to be that the IAEA has performed very competently in meeting its responsibilities under RES/687

This brings us to the final question raised, namely what steps can be taken to strengthen the ability of the IAEA to deal with Iraq-type challenges in the future As the Committee is well aware, this question has been the focus of attention for several years dating in some respects to pre-Iraqi times But the events in Iraq and the implications of the end of the Cold War for non-proliferation have served to concentrate the mind and energy of governments, IAEA leadership and non-governmental organizations In approaching this question one must, of course, understand that the draconian and punitive measures applied under the UNSC resolutions in Iraq cannot be taken as a standard for normal international verification It is implausible that states would freely and voluntarily submit themselves to so onerous and intrusive a regime If anything underscores this truth it is the reversal of the United States position regarding anytime/anyplace inspections under the chemical weapons convention On the other hand, as demonstrated in recent arms control and disarmament agreements, and in changes brought about in IAEA safeguards, there is considerable support for taking significant steps to ensure credibility and to reinforce confidence But any regime of the future will still have to strike a balance between the demands of international confidence and national sovereignty

A point that cannot be repeated too often is that the safeguards system applied by the IAEA in support of the Nonproliferation Treaty was commensurate with the expectations and desires of the international community The NPT system was devised to apply comprehensive safeguards principally to the nuclear fuel cycles of the advanced industrial states which at the time were the only states with any significant nuclear activity at all These states Germany Japan Italy, Sweden and so on were determined to minimize any risk that the distinction between themselves and the nuclear weapon states inherent in the NPT would extend into the realm of peaceful nuclear activity and competition This deep-seated concern, parenthetically, was the reason why President Johnson offered to submit all US peaceful nuclear activities to the IAEA safeguards regime to be applied to the non-nuclear weapon states under the Treaty

To ensure the adherence of these states to a non-proliferation treaty the United States and the Soviet Union endorsed a verification regime that kept intrusion to the minimum consistent with credible verification This resulted in a system that focussed on the flow of nuclear material and resulted in certain constraints on how the IAEA exercised the rather liberal rights originally granted it in its statute Governments, speaking through their representatives on the Board of Governors, established the tone of the times Participating non-nuclear weapon states were obligated to declare all of their nuclear material to the IAEA which would then verify that the material could be accounted for

Given the structure of global competition between the two superpowers it was always presumed that they would control any threat of proliferation among their allies or clients, and as their competition reached into every region of the world, that assumption applied to the world at large The periodic five year reviews of the NPT have resulted in consensus endorsements of the sufficiency and credibility of the safeguards system despite some differences [raised by activist non-governmental institutions] over the adequacy of the material control and accounting system upon which the regime was based to detect diversions of quantities of nuclear material suitable to produce a single nuclear explosive device in certain large-scale facilities

The end of the Cold War changed one of the assumptions upon which the nonproliferation regime had been built the discovery of a massive and largely unknown nuclear weapons development program in an NPT state, Iraq, changed another In this new environment the expectations are that with the diffusion of technology more states that are no longer under the watchful eye of the superpowers can engage in nuclear weapons development and that, because of security and political concerns no longer being subordinated to the superpower competition, some of these states well may seek to satisfy their political/security interests with nuclear arms

All of these factors have an impact on international institutions, not least the IAEA Most notably, the credibility of safeguards is now seen to be a function of their capacity to detect undeclared or clandestine nuclear activity And the measure of the IAEA is to be its willingness and capability to agree and implement a more intrusive verification regime -- a regime for which the basic authority is already essentially in place An underlying concern for some, as mentioned earlier, is whether an organization that simultaneously promotes and regulates nuclear energy can focus sufficiently and firmly enough on regulation to provide the necessary credibility, whether given the strong emphasis on confidence building in the past, it can apply rigorous verification

The effort to meet the new circumstances and new expectations has centered on re-examining existing safeguards authority and clarifying or building upon it as appropriate

The main focus has been special inspections, authority for which derives from the statute and the governing safeguards document, INFIRC/153. In February, 1992 the Board of Governors confirmed the Director General's conclusion that authority to conduct special inspections in full-scope safeguards states extended not only to other locations within an already declared facility, but also to facilities and locations other than those notified to the Agency by the state. It was also confirmed that a request for a special inspection could be based on plausible information from sources other than safeguards inspections, including information from national intelligence sources.

The authority to invoke special inspections is one thing; the willingness to do so, given its potential political ramifications is another. North Korea provided a testing ground for Agency determination. Faced with a discrepancy regarding how much plutonium may have been produced by the North Koreans when measured against findings derived from the procedures to establish an initial inventory pursuant to the North Korean safeguards agreement, and provided with corroborative non-safeguards information concerning the existence of undeclared waste storage facilities, the Director General called for a special inspection. When North Korea refused, this was reported to the Board of Governors which reaffirmed the need for a special inspection without further delay. North Korea's refusal to accede to this demand resulted in a finding and report of noncompliance to the United Nations Security Council. The IAEA acted with deliberation and decisiveness giving a clear indication that the new political environment was well understood, and that it was fully prepared to exercise its authority. Besides giving evidence of Agency will, this says something about the value of initiating challenges in a technical institution that is not encumbered with veto powers.

Other measures reinforcing the safeguards system have been taken including a Board of Governors decision requiring states, under a safeguards provision calling for design information to be submitted "as early as possible", to inform the agency at the time authorization to construct or modify a facility is given rather, than as has been the practice, no less than 180 days prior to introducing nuclear material into the facility. Together with a further Board decision calling upon states to adopt a policy of universal reporting of exports and imports of nuclear materials, sensitive non-nuclear materials and specialized equipment especially relevant to nuclear activity, the IAEA has moved to establish increasing transparency in the nuclear arena. The expectation is that as these early warning measures become institutionalized, the insight of the Agency into the world's nuclear programs will deepen and the proficiency of safeguards will increase.

Within the secretariat itself additional changes have been made. The inherent conservatism that prevailed in safeguards over the past two decades is giving way to greater political awareness about the linkage between safeguards and proliferation. The emphasis in reaching beyond declared nuclear activity is altering the mind-set of the inspectorate and organizational leadership is emphasizing the total nature of nonproliferation on a continuing basis. A system of country officers to consolidate all available information from all sources regarding the nuclear activities of states under safeguards and to assist in briefing and debriefing of inspectors has been established

These developments signify important progress in adapting to a changing international environment and to changing political expectations The process is dynamic, not a one time adjustment The actions and decisions taken thus far work to strengthen the ability of the IAEA to respond to the challenge of verification in new political circumstances Other measures are under consideration including adaptation of environmental monitoring and sampling techniques to increase confidence about the non-existence of undeclared facilities or activities, introducing institutionalized short-notice inspections and the like

These and other measures are valuable potential additions to the arsenal of capabilities at the disposal of the IAEA. What is necessary now is to consolidate the gains that have been made, to institutionalize new procedures, to build on what has been done and to identify and address remaining problem areas

There are some building blocks that need early attention and action Some of them are discussed in material I would like to ask the committee to incorporate in the record I will limit myself here to four points <u>First</u>, it is unequivocally clear that the ability of the IAEA to optimize its safeguards capabilities and to create the greatest probability for detecting clandestine activities depends to a substantial degree on the availability to it of sensitive information which only a limited number of states are able to provide The flow of relevant information to the IAEA should be regularized and institutionalized To my knowledge there has been little if any question raised about the ability of the IAEA to receive and utilize national intelligence information provided to it pursuant to its responsibilities under RES/687 There is every reason to take steps to ensure that information enhancing the IAEA's ability to carry out inspections or to request visits (a measure that is of recent vintage) in safeguarded states? The United States should take a lead in moving forward such regularization as well as ensuring any other operational or logistic support the IAEA might need to fulfill our expectations for its safeguards activities

<u>Second</u> it is a truism that international organizations lack meaningful enforcement power The exception is the United Nations Security Council which, if it invokes Chapter VII as it did in the case of the Gulf War can take ~~mandatory~~ action and pass mandatory resolutions binding upon member states The January, 1992 summit statement of Heads of State and Government of the Council declared that the proliferation of nuclear weapons constitute a threat to international peace and security which is the key to opening the door to Chapter VII and enforcement That same statement acknowledged the integral role of IAEA safeguards in implementing the NPT and asserted that "members of the council will take appropriate measures in the case of any violations notified to them by the IAEA " (UNSC, S/23500 January 31 1992) Given that the statement was made in the midst of a continuing crisis in Iraq and a then strong sense of unity of purpose on the Council it would be pertinent to strengthening the international consensus against safeguards or nonproliferation violations to codify this statement in a formal Security Council resolution This would

provide an important element of enforcement and enforceability to IAEA safeguards especially in view of the fact that by statute, the IAEA has direct access to the Security Council in cases of safeguards noncompliance

A third measure requiring political leadership and action is to ensure that the IAEA is adequately funded to meet the growing safeguards responsibilities with which it is confronted Studies are under way, and have been for some time, to ascertain whether and how increased efficiency can be built into the safeguards system without sacrificing quality of knowledge and an adequate basis for confidence in the integrity of the system Whatever streamlining might be achieved it stands as a stark reality that with Argentina, Brazil, and South Africa now under comprehensive safeguards and with former Soviet Union republics hopefully joining the NPT and negotiating comprehensive safeguards agreements with the IAEA added resources will be necessary if the agency is to operate a credible safeguards system This is all the more the case with enhanced safeguards that address problems of possible undeclared or clandestine nuclear activity

Fourth, the United States should take the lead with the Russian government, to make use of the IAEA to verify dismantled nuclear warhead material Such a measure would be a strong demonstration of confidence in the system and the openness it implies could have a potentially powerful precedent setting value The distinction between weapon and non-weapon states in so far as safeguards is concerned has long been an item on the agenda of the non-aligned, with support from other quarters The idea of applying comprehensive safeguards to all peaceful nuclear activities in weapon states is attractive in principle but costly in implementation. The consignment of verification responsibility for dismantled warhead material would at one and the same time be less costly and more useful It is a step that the United States government should take now

But the single most important element in strengthening the ability of the IAEA to meet the challenge of verification is the political will and political support of its member states and of the United Nations Security Council International organizations are creations of sovereign states, they lack sovereignty or independent political authority and are fundamentally dependent on the political will of their sovereign members Secretariats can influence, cajole and help to define collective interests, but it is the governing bodies of international organizations that are the repositories of political authority

Sovereignty is a vigorous and contradictory force against empowering international institutions with far-reaching authority But threats to international peace and security as nuclear proliferation is cannot be successfully addressed unilaterally, they require a collective action While international verification may have to be supplemented by regionally verified arms control and security arrangements it is something that cannot be done without it there is to be any confidence in the world at large regarding the status of national nuclear programs and the probable absence of clandestine nuclear activity That is why it is all the more important that governments like ours that are committed to effective international verification take whatever measures are possible to strengthen the hand of our chosen international instruments, in this case the International Atomic Energy Agency We and others have developed expectations for our international institutions, now we must ensure that the necessary authority, operational and financial support and political backing for vigorous implementation is available to them

One Hundred Third Congress

Congress of the United States

Committee on Foreign Affairs

House of Representatives

Washington, DC 20515

**Subcommittee on International Security,
International Organizations and Human Rights**

Iraq Rebuilds Its Military Industries

A Staff Report

prepared by Kenneth R Timmerman for the House Foreign Affairs Subcommittee on International Security, International Organizations and Human Rights

June 29, 1993

Letter of Transmittal

June 21, 1993

The Honorable Tom Lantos
Chairman, Subcommittee on International Security, International Organizations, and Human Rights, of the Committee on Foreign Affairs
U S House of Representatives
Washington, DC 20515

Dear Mr Chairman At your direction, I have prepared this staff report on the current status of Iraq's weapons manufacturing capability

While UN Council Resolution 687, which Iraq accepted, obligated the Baghdad government to renounce all production, stockpiling, and use of unconventional weaponry, Iraq has rebuilt many of the weapons plants damaged during the Allied air campaign, and has resumed the production of a very wide range of conventional weaponry Iraq has also succeeded in in returning to service most of the tanks, artillery, and combat aircraft damaged during Desert Storm If unchecked, the Gulf could face the threat of renewed Iraqi agression during this administration

In addition to published reports, mainly from the Iraqi press, information for this report was gathered from personal interviews with UN Special Commission staff in New York, with inspectors from the International Atomic Energy Agency in Vienna, and from a trip to Jordan in April 1992, prior to my joining the subcommittee staff Other interviews were conducted in Paris with French government officials, with German Customs officials in Cologne, and with German export authorities in Bonn and Eschborn At no time during the preparation of this report did the author have access to classified material

Some of the information on Iraqi procurement networks was developed by Jules Kroll, president of Kroll Associates, a private financial investigative firm on Wall Street under contract to the Kuwaiti government to identify hidden Iraqi assets abroad For material on Crescent Petroleum, I am indebted to British journalist Alan George My colleague Dennis Kane, of the House Banking committee staff, has generously made available some of the vast documentation he gathered while investigating the Atlanta branch of Italy's state-owned Banca Nazionale del Lavoro (BNL)

In addition, I would like to gratefully acknowledge the assistance of Kenneth Katzman and Zachary Davis of the Congressional Research Service

The conclusions drawn in this report are my own, and do not necesarily reflect the views of the Committee on Foreign Affairs or any member thereof

Sincerely yours,

Kenneth R Timmerman

Iraqi Weapons Plants

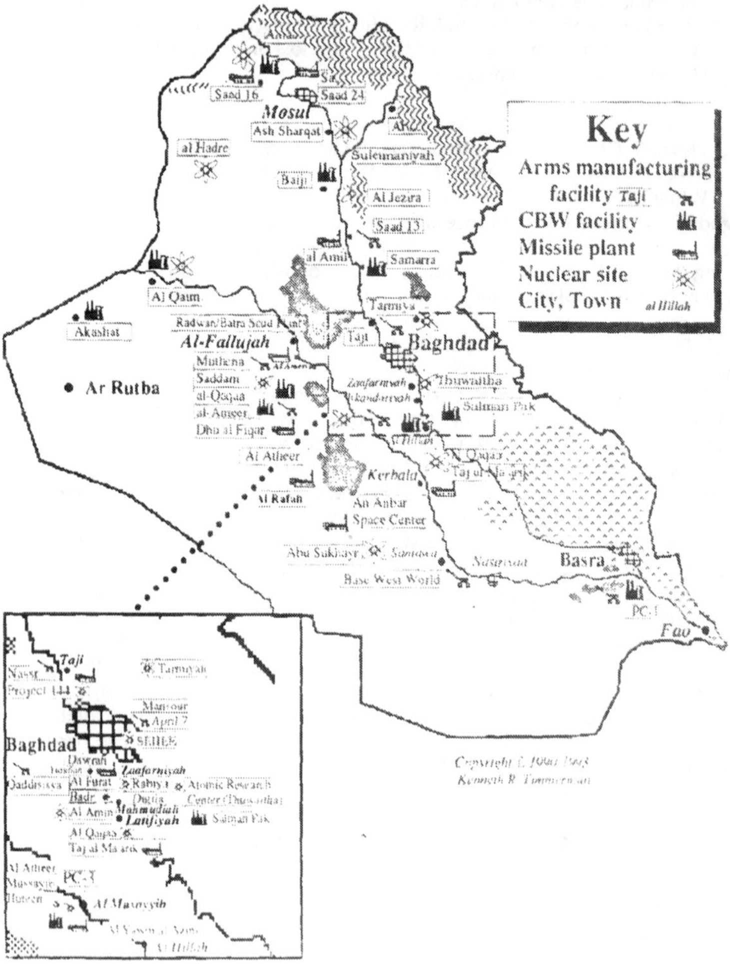

The weapons industry

The scope of Iraq's weapons industry was largely unknown before the invasion of Kuwait[1] More than forty major weapons-manufacturing complexes were built during the 1980s, most of which are beyond the scope of the UN inspections Many have already started operating again Little or no attention has been paid to these activities by Congress or the press

Saddam's son-in-law and cousin, Hussein Kamil al-Majid, who was the driving force behind the military industrialization of Iraq before Desert Storm, was officially rehabilitated in February 1992 after a brief fall from grace He is once again in charge of the weapons industries His principal technical assistants, Lt Gen Amir Hammoudi Al-Saadi (now Minister of Industry and Minerals), and Lt Gen Amir Rashid al-Ubaidi, continue to occupy positions of prominence Both are men of vision, and are extremely gifted in managerial skills They are assisted by a large number of experienced weapons designers and production technicians

Iraq announced in January 1992 that it had already repaired and tooled up more than 200 factory buildings associated with various military production lines[2] On May 4, 1992, Lt Gen Amir Al-Saadi announced that "more than 50 establishments" of the former Ministry of Industry and Military Industrialization had been put back into commission, using equipment taken out of the weapons plants and hidden before Desert Storm [3]

1The author of this Staff report chronicled the growth of Iraq s military industries in *The Death Lobby How the West Armed Iraq* (Houghton-Mifflin, 1991, Boston & New York) Information in this report is drawn from the author s previous experience in Iraq interviews with the directors of Iraqi weapons programs, and a broad range of government and industry sources in France, Germany, Britain, Israel, Egypt, Saudi Arabia, Sweden, and the United States, in addition to those sources mentioned in the letter of transmittal

2Middle East Defense News (MEDNEWS), March 9, 1992 Michael Eisenstadt, a military fellow at the Washington Institute for Near East Policy wrote in a March 1993 paper entitled 'The Iraqi Armed Forces since the Gulf War "Significant reconstruction activity has been observed at more than two dozen military-industrial sites and more than 200 buildings have been partially repaired Iraq has now reportedly resumed assembly of T-72 tanks and limited production of artillery, short-range missiles and rockets, ammunition and spares at some factories, although production is likely to remain limited as long as sanctions remain in place '

3 Minister Pledges Surprises in Industrial Output " Iraqi News Agency, May 4 1992

Among those facilities that have been "thoroughly reconstructed," accorded to inspection reports by the International Atomic Fnergy Agency (IAEA) are the notorious Saad 16 ballistic missile research and development center near Mosul, and the Al Rabiya plant in Zaafarniyah, which was bombed by Allied warplanes on Jan 17, 1993 [4]

Iraq has already reactivated many of its black market procurement networks to acquire spare parts for conventional weapons-manufacturing facilities Once United Nations sanctions are lifted, Iraq will be free to procure most of what it needs on the open market, to complete any gaps in technology

Speaking before the Washington Institute for Near East Policy on March 24, 1993, the Chairman of the UN Special Commission for the Disarmament of Iraq (UNSCOM), Ambassador Rolf Ekeus, said he believed Iraq fully intended to restore its military industrial base "The capabilities are there, the supply system including banks and payments is there The day the oil embargo is lifted, Iraq will get all the cash and that will be a great concern With the cash, the suppliers, and the skills they will be able to re-establish all the weapons programes," Ekeus said "It may grow up like mushrooms after the rain "[5]

It should be emphasized that Iraq's success in rebuilding its military-industrial base has occured despite the most rigorous international economic sanctions imposed on any nation since World War II, and despite intrusive inspections of certain weapons facilities by UNSCOM and the IAEA

Hidden Equipment

Iraq's industrial purchases from the West in the 1985 through 1989 ran to $14 2 billion - excluding armament The vast majority of this equipment went into Iraqi weapons plants and has not been found by the UN Special Commission It was purchased either directly by the Ministry of Industry and Military Industrialization (MIMI), which was run by Saddam Hussein's son-in-law, Hussein Kamil Hasan, or by entities directly reporting to that ministry

Production equipment found in Iraqi nuclear weapons plants has been catalogued in part by the IAEA Some has been placed under seal to prevent further use, other production tools have been slated for future monitoring, to

---

[4]IAEA 18th inspection report, page 5, released April 28, 1993
5Reuter March 24, 1993

ensure Iraq does not use them for its weapons of mass destruction Only a handful of state-of-the-art tools and application-specific fixtures have actually been destroyed, however The IAFA argues that Iraq should be allowed to retain production equipment that has a potential civilian use, since Iraq's nuclear weapons program has been fully dismantled Chief IAEA inspector, Maurizio Zifferero, has been arguing for months that Iraq's nuclear program "stands at zero now "[6] Few independent experts agree with this sanguine assessment Indeed, even IAEA director general, Hans Blix, has expressed his scepticism In a discussion before a non-proliferation study group in Paris on May 26, 1993, Blix acknowledged that Iraq has refused to allow the IAEA to establish permanent monitoring of its nuclear facilities

Throughout the 1980s, West Germany was Iraq's largest supplier of high-technology, with sales totalling $4 243 billion during the 1985-1989 period, or four times the level of U S sales

Iraqi purchases in Germany included

- $2 4 billion worth of heavy machinery and transportation equipment
- $1 3 billion worth of manufactured goods
- $425 million worth of chemicals, and
- $114 million worth of controlling instruments [7]

The vast majority of this equipment is still missing

Main-frame computers

Iraq's extensive purchase of mainframe, mini-supercomputers and process control systems provides an eloquent case of the type of supplier information the UN Special Commission would require in order to better identify and dismantle Iraqi unconventional weapons programs

It is widely acknowledged today in scientific circles that advanced computers give the edge to Third World countries such as Iraq, who seek to develop a nuclear device without going through the costly and political perilous process of a nuclear test Using high-speed computers and graphics work stations, it is now possible to simulate a nuclear blast, thus allowing design improvements to be developed in a matter of months that used to require long

---

[6] 'Iraq Nuclear Effort Is at Zero, UN Says, *International Herald Tribune*, Sept 3, 1992

[7] Figures derived from OECD monthly trade statistics Cf "Who s Been Arming Iraq,' Middle East Defense News (MEDNEWS), Paris, France, April 15 1991

The Men Who Built Iraq's Military Industries

Hussein Kamal Hasan al Majid,
former Minister of Industry and Military Industrialization, currently in charge of the Military Industries and head of clandestine procurement

Lt. Gen (Dr) Amer Hamoodi Al-Saadi,
the industrial mastermind.

Lt. Gen. Amer Rashid Al Obeidi,
the engineer

and arduous live testing The UN nuclear inspectors discovered documents in Iraq which proved beyond a doubt that Iraq was using mainframe computers in precisely this way, and had gone through five major design upgrades of a nuclear explosive device, without undertaking a live nuclear test

Most is known about U S high-tech exports to Iraq, although the United States was bottom on the list of Iraq's Western suppliers (a situation set to change had Iraq not invaded Kuwait) This is because intense pressure from the press and Congress forced the U S government to release detailed lists of export licenses requests for Iraq An analysis of Department of Commerce records shows that in the United States alone, Iraq received a total of 354 export licenses for computers and advanced scientific analysis equipment from May 1985 through August 1990, worth a total of $113,760,714

Of these licenses, at least 157, worth $57,792,275, were for advanced computing systems The most widely selling item were VAX machines from Digital Equipment Corp Other frequently sold items included high-speed oscilloscopes, radio-spectrum analyzers, integrated circuits, gas chromatography equipment, spectrophotometers, and a wide range of electronics manufacturing and test equipment All were used in Iraqi weapons plants, many in the manufacture of ballistic missiles and in nuclear weapons research and development Typical purchasers were the Iraqi Ministry of Industry, the Ministry of Defense, and weapons establishments including Saad, Huteen, Badr, and Nassr

Of the 157 computers, Iraq has acknowledged to possessing a single IBM 370 mainframe - just one - located at the Thuwaitha nuclear research center When the 8th UN nuclear inspection team demanded in writing a full accounting of all mainframe computers Iraq had purchased for use in its nuclear weapons program, this was the full text of the answer they received

"The Computer Office at Tarmiya was initially designed to accommodate the option of a large computer (mainframe) Due to the special circumstances in operating individual separators [ie, calutrons for uranium enrichment], it was discovered through experience that the best condition would be to connect the separators to small dedicated computers After achieving the steady operating conditions for the separators, the small computers would have been connected through a network located in the above-mentioned office This approach was adopted at Tarmiya It also applies to the design of the Computer Office at Ash-Sharqat, although computers were never introduced at this site

"At the Al Thuwaitha site, the large computer was an IBM-370, in addition there were a number of personal computers (PCs) including IBM PS/2 The approach adopted at Al Tuwaitha was to use the computer capability available in the country when needed in addition to the above-mentioned computers " [8th IAEA inspection report, p 13]

Iraq's consistent refusal to provide detailed supplier information is one of the most daunting problems facing the UN inspection teams Without detailed lists of equipment, suppliers, and the Iraqi purchasers, they have been hard put to penetrate the sophisticated shell game Iraq has been playing since April 1991, when the first inspections began, to hide its unconventional weapons capabilities In some cases, they do not even have the necessary data to ask the Iraqis the right questions

On Feb 12, 1992, UN inspectors demanded to visit computer centers in Baghdad, where they discovered six mainframe computers made by Digital Equipment Corp, IBM, and Hewlett Packard Three machines had been purchased by the Scientific Research Council (SRC), a procurement front run by Lt General Amer Rashid al-Ubaidi Iraq had never admitted to possessing any of them

Two of Iraq's major computer suppliers deserve to be singled out, since the scope of their deliveries puts them in a case all by themselves

Hewlett Packard received 57 licenses to export computer systems to Iraq from the United States, worth $3,147,608, from 1984 until 1990 HP systems can be found throughout the Iraqi nuclear weapons program, at Thuwaitha, at the Saad 16 research and development center, and at a variety of heavy engineering complexes that were manufacturing parts of uranium enrichment centrifuges and calutrons Hewlett Packard maintained an office in Baghdad throughout most of the 1980s, and was a major exhibitor in the yearly Baghdad international trade fair

The second company, International Computer Systems Ltd, was established in 1986 in the UK by a Jordanian of Palestinian origin, Esam Samarra ICS received 49 export licenses from the Department of Commerce in the United States to sell computers to Iraq, worth $16,377,132, in addition to extensive sales it made directly from Britain Samarra currently owns 70% of ICS

ICS serves as a distributor/front for Digital Equipment Corp (DEC) VAX and MiniVAX computers, which have proven their worth to weapons designers the world over It is no accident that ICS s clients were primarily Iraqi weapons establishments, including: Nassr, Saad 16, the Scientific Research Council, the Ministry of Industry and Military Industrialization, and the State Establishment for Heavy Engineering Industries (SEHEE), which was deeply involved in the manufacture of centrifuges and calutrons for uranium enrichment.

Esam Samarra subsequently set up a service company to maintain DEC computers in Iraq, called Computer and Communication Services Company (CCS), located in Amman, Jordan. Samarra told the author of this report during an interview in his Amman office in April 1992 that he had also been selling Iraq data systems made by McDonnell Douglas Computer Systems.

ICS was a major purveyor of VAX workstations to Iraq, importing equipment from the United States and from Great Britain, depending on where licenses could be obtained. It should be noted that during this same period (1985-1990), DEC only applied directly for four U.S. export licenses for Iraq.

Machine-tools

Machine-tools are the basic building blocks for any heavy industry, and are particularly critical for the weapons industry. Because of this, machine-tool sales were carefully regulated throughout the 1970s and 1980s by the Coordinating Committee for Multilateral Export Controls (COCOM), an informal group of NATO partners which attempted to prevent the sale of strategic technologies to the Soviet Union and its allies. In many countries, machine-tool exports required an export license regardless of the destination, because of the COCOM controls. This led Iraq to devise a particularly ingenious method for sidestepping controls, which has since become one of the hallmarks of Iraq's secret network.

In 1987, as plans to build an atomic weapon accelerated dramatically, the Iraqis decided to purchase a Western machine-tool manufacturer, Matrix-Churchill, as a means of securing unlimited supplies of advanced machine-tools and as Iraq's principal partner for establishing its own machine-tool industry. Matrix Churchill was purchased through a web of front companies controlled directly by Baghdad. The main procurement front was the London-based Technology and Development Group (TDG), run by Safa Habobi, a former director of the giant Taji weapons complex.

Once it became an Iraqi company, Matrix Churchill used its subsidiary in Solon, Ohio as a front to procure additional controlled technologies in the United States.

Key documents detailing the construction by Matrix Churchill and an American composite materials manufacturer, Glass International Incorporated, were uncovered during the investigation of the Atlanta branch of the Banca Nazionale del Lavoro, conducted by the House Banking Committee The ceramic and glass fiber plant was used by Iraq for the manufacture of uranium enrichment centrifuge rotors and possibley for missile nose cones None of this production equipment has been found by the UN Special Commission during its inspections in Iraq, although shipping documents and plant progress reports show that deliveries were virtually complete by July 1990 The plant appears to have functioned as a stand-alone unit at the Taji weapons complex in the northern suburbs of Baghdad, according to corporate site drawings

Similarly, little work has been done to date on the very large volume of industrial purchases by Iraq from Japan, Yugoslavia, China, and East European countries such as Czechoslovakia Sources in Prague, for instance, indicate that Czech state enterprises had a hand in Iraqi chemical weapon plants, while the IAEA has identified a Czech company as the source of the HMX explosives found at that were to be used in constructing nuclear bomb cores

A declassified U S Army intelligence document, obtained by privately funded Nuclear Control Institute in Washington, reveals that China was suspected of having built a top secret underground plutonium reactor in Iraq in the late 1980s, which the IAEA has sought to locate, without success So strong were IAEA suspicions that Iraq had built an underground reactor that in September 1992 plans were drawn up to begin long-range monitoring of Iraqi waterways, in order to detect the minute traces of radioactivity the operation of such a reactor would emit

Finally, much Japanese high-tech gear has been discovered by the IAEA in Iraqi nuclear weapons establishments, although procurement information has remained unavailable and unsolicited by the Japanese press

The UN Inspections

UN inspection teams have found only a portion of the dual-use manufacturing equipment known to have been purchased by Iraq in the mid and late 1980s

From April to June 1992, during its 11th and 12th inspection tours in Iraq, the IAEA catalogued 603 machine-tools that had been found in facilities related to Iraq's nuclear weapons program. However, approximately 2,000 machine-tools show up in Western export licensing records as having been sold to Iraq in the late 1980s, primarily from the UK, Germany and Italy. Because export controls on machine-tools were being relaxed at the same time, and because certain governments were seeking to expand their machine-tool exports to Iraq by decontrolling items that normally would have been controlled, it is impossible to estimate how many more machine-tools were actually delivered to Iraq without individually validated licenses. [8]

For instance, of the 603 nuclear-relevant machine tools found in Iraq, IAEA records showed that 502 were not licensed by exporting authorities. In the case of Great Britain, 49 of the 83 machine-tools found by the IAEA were subject to export licensing restrictions. However, British export licensing records, made available to Parliament as part of its inquiry into British arms sales to Iraq, show that the Department of Trade and Industry licensed 313 machine-tools to Iraq from 1987-1989 - and by all accounts, only a fraction of what was actually shipped[9]. By the most conservative estimate, therefore, at least 264 British tools are currently missing.[10]

In the two months preceding Operation Desert Storm, Iraq worked day and night stripping its manufacturing facilities of valuable production equipment, computers, records, and materials. According to a senior Jordanian official, interviewed in Amman in April 1992, this effort was supervised by Lt. General Amer Rashid al-Ubaidi, Undersecretary at the Ministry of Industry and Military Industrialization (MIMI). The Jordanian official was a frequent visitor to Iraqi weapons plants, ballistic missile tests, and research centers in the late 1980s, in his official capacity as a scientific and technical advisor to King Hussein. He claimed that General Amer boasted to him after the war of his success.

U.S. spy satellites photographed this activity only days before the air war began, leading one Operations intelligence officer interviewed subsequently to

[8]The U.S. Department of Commerce licensed only a handful of machine-tools; much production equipment was shipped without licenses. One example: 30-foot long boring machines intended for making long-range artillery tubes.

[9]"Exports to Iraq: Minutes of Evidence," House of Commons, Trade and Industry Committee, Tuesday, 26 Nov. 1991.

[10]An additional 94 Matrix Churchill tools were found in March 1993 during the 18th IAEA inspection at the Al Huteen State Establishment, bringing the total number of Matrix Churchil machine-tools found in Iraq to 148. See below.

observe that the Pentagon had "solid evidence" Iraq had been stripping its weapons plants in preparation for war[11]

Underground storage sites used to hide industrial equipment were not high-priority targets during the air war Besides, they were so numerous as to render a bombing campaign against them extremely costly After the Israeli bombing of the Osirak nuclear research reactor in June 1981 every government building in Iraq was constructed on top of large underground shelters Airbases and entire factory complexes were buried, with exact copies constructed elsewhere to fool enemy warplanes and reconnaissance satellites (so-called "potemptkin" facilities) This accounts in part for the difficulties in bomb-damage assessments during the air campaign

In mid-April 1992, following the destruction of the nuclear weapons design center at Al Atheer, Western intelligence photographed Iraqi trucks hauling equipment back into known manufacturing facilities This signalled Iraq's conclusion that it had reached the end of the intrusive UN inspections and was free to rebuild its weapons plants at will

Declarations in recent months by senior Iraqi leaders have only highlighted this intent On Jan 13, 1993, Lt Gen Amer Rashid boasted that Iraq had rebuilt its air defense network "better than before" Desert Storm[12] On Feb 7, Lt General Amir Hamoudi Al-Saadi announced that Iraq had succeeded in rebuilding the war-damaged Al Qaim industrial complex, which had been used to extract uranium from phosphates ore and for the manufacture of CW precursors Al-Saadi also hinted that Iraq had resumed production of main battle tanks "I think every country is entitled to produce what it can for its legitimate defence and Iraq is no exception," he said [13] Meanwhile, Russian ballistic missile expert Nikiti Smidovitch returned from an inspection tour to announce that Iraq had begun work on a new family of surface to surface missiles with a range just under 150 km [14]

---

[11] Confidential interview with the author, Nov 14 1991

[12] Iraqi News Agency, Jan 13, 1993

[13] Reuter, Feb 7, 1993

[14] Reuter Jan 29, 1992

The Ababil MLRS program

Photo copyright © Kenneth R. Timmerman, 1989

The Ababil is a multiple rocket launch system which Iraq developed jointly with Yugoslavia's Federal Directorate of Supply and Procurement. Two versions were built: a 50-km range launch vehicle, with 12 rocket tubes, and a 100-km range version, with 4 tubes. Both were designed to launch chemical as well as a variety of conventional warheads (cluster, hollow charge, HE, mine-laying), making it a powerful offensive weapon. Prototype launchers were put on display at the Baghdad International Arms Fair in May 1989 where they were photographed by the author. Contractual information obtained from sources in Yugoslavia shows that the first two unassembled launchers were shipped to Iraq in 1988 from Yugoslavia . The solid-fuel rockets and warheads were made in Iraq at the Saddam Engineering Complex (Saad 5), while most of the electronics were manufactured at the Salah-al-Din (Saad 13) plant. The Yugoslav designation for the system was M87.

The Limits of the UN Inspections

None of the UN Security Council resolutions concerning Iraq calls for the dismantling or future monitoring of Iraq's conventional weapons plants This is a loophole that has never been examined very closely in open fora

UN teams have inspected some of these plants, but only within the very limited framework of the contractual relationship between the facilities and Iraq's nuclear weapons complex or with the ballistic missile or CBW programs As one senior analyst with the UN Special Commission put it, "We can't be bothered with counting how many 155 mm shells the Iraqis can make, as long as they do not violate the terms of [UN Security Council Resolution] 687. We have too much to do as it is "

In other words, Iraq is fully allowed by the terms of the ceasefire to continue manufacturing conventional weapons and ammunition and whatever rate it desires, even in the same plants that have been identified for their relevance to the nuclear weapons program In theory, Iraq can even save equipment slated for disposal by the UN Special Commission by declaring that it will "only" be used for the manufacture of conventional weaponry Allowable activity includes the manufacture of artillery rockets and ballistic missiles with ranges of 150 kilometers or less. What is not allowed is research or production of weapons of mass destruction, defined as nuclear weapons, chemical or biological warfare agents, or ballistic missiles with a range greater than 150 kilometers

Iraq has tried to take advantage of this loophole to prevent the destruction of equipment used for the production of the Badr 2000 (Condor II), a 1000 kilometer-range ballistic missile believed to be far more accurate than Iraq's upgraded SCUDs (Its solid-fuel motors also make it easier to conceal and quicker to deploy) Starting in 1985, the United States government led a major Western campaign to prevent the sale of critical manufacturing equipment to the Condor II program, parts of which were being conducted jointly with Argentina and Egypt Before the UN inspections began in Iraq, it was widely claimed that halting the Condor II program was the largest single success of the Missile Technology Control Regime

UNSCOM ballistic missile teams soon discovered not one but four separate facilities in different parts of Iraq that were heavily engaged in the production of the solid-fuel Badr 2000 only days before the Allied bombing of Iraq began. One of the facilities, south of Fallujah, was also manufacturing liquid-fueled al Hossein and al Abbas missiles, Iraq's improved-range SCUDs.

All four missile plants appear to have been built by German and Italian firms, although the bulk of the solid fuel technology is said to have originated in the United States and to have reached Iraq via France and Italy. [15]

Nevertheless, in letters dated Nov 19, 1991 and Feb 28, 1992, Iraqi officials informed the UN Special Commission that they intended to "modify and alter the equipment for the Badr-2000 project with a view to its reuse... [for] the manufacture of civilian explosives [and] in the manufacture of 100 kilometer range Ababil missiles" - both of which were allowable activities.

In particular, the Iraqis wanted to save from destruction a series of solid fuel mixers, made by the Draiswerke company in Germany, installed at the Taj al-Ma'arik missile plant south of Baghdad. They argued that since the mixers could also be used for "allowable" activity, they should not be destroyed.

While UNSCOM rejected Iraq's reasoning in this particular case and began destroying Condor II manufacturing equipment in April 1992, it left the vast majority of Iraq's "dual-use" equipment untouched.

Thirty-one machine-tools were destroyed by the UN Special Commission during the March and April 1992 inspections Ten of these were designated as missile-related, the other 21 as nuclear-related. Twenty-five other pieces of production equipment were destroyed, most as part of Iraq's ballistic missile program (solid fuel mixers, induction furnaces, hot and cold isostatic presses, etc). Specialized jigs and mandrels were destroyed, as were calutron and centrifuge assemblies used in uranium enrichment. Isolated pieces of equipment have been rendered inoperational since then.

This extremely modest destruction of Iraq's unconventional weapons capability has left major military manufacturing programs virtually untouched

---

[15] "UN Inspectors destroy Condor II equipment," MEDNEWS, March 30, 1992.

The Zaafarniyah complex

The case of the Zaafarniyah industrial complex, located some 20 kilometers south of Baghdad, illustrates the limits of the inspection process as currently structured

Two distinct facilities were located on the same site, both of which were inspected by the IAEA because they had been producing parts for the nuclear weapons program The Digila electronics plant was inspected twice because it had produced electronic parts for the calutron uranium enrichment program The Al Rabiya heavy machining plant (aka al Rabee) was inspected on four separate occasions - twice by UNSCOM for missile activities, and twice by the IAEA

Like most Iraqi weapons plants, Al Rabiya was designed and operated as a dual-use facility, under the auspices of the Ministry of Industry and Military Industrialization Seventy-eight machine tools at this site were catalogued by the IAEA as related to the nuclear weapons program These included large German machines used to make the calutron casings Despite this known activity, the plant was never disabled by the IAEA, nor were these key manufacturing tools placed under any kind of monitoring that would have prevented their use in nuclear projects in the future Inexplicably, the IAEA eventually dropped it from its list of potential inspection sites

In January 1993, U S military planners concluded that Al Rabiya continued to operate, and that the Iraqis considered it a safe haven for illicit activity including the production of calutrons and uranium enrichment centrifuges assemblies

Confidential informants have told the Subcommittee staff that one Western government (not the U S) had urged the IAEA to destroy Al Rabiya prior to the U S air strike against the site on Jan 17, 1993 Despite the plant's clear relevance to both the calutron and centrifuge programs, however, the IAEA refused

Three days after the strike, Saddam Hussein vowed to rebuild the plant And on March 16, the head of Iraq's Military Industrialization Organization, Hussein Kamal Hasan, announced that reconstruction was not only complete but that the "enterprise is now operating even better than before "[16] In his

[16]Baghdad INA, March 16, 1993

announcement, Kamil renamed the plant the "al-Nida State Enterprise for Manufacturing Molds, Construction Works and Machines " Al-Nida is the codename for a project to build mobile missile launchers Indeed, al-Rabiya plant equipment was perfectly suitable for casting large steel and aluminium assemblies for missile launchers The reconstruction of Al Rabiya / Al Nidaa was documented during the 17th and 18th IAEA inspections

Another example, drawn from the 18th IAEA inspection report, is the notorious Saad 16 ballistic missile R&D plant near Mosul, built by Guildemeister and a consortium of German and Austrian companies in the mid-1980s By any interpretation of the UN ceasefire resolutions, this plant should have been thoroughly monitored and kept out of commission Just the opposite has occured According to the 18th IAEA inspection report,

"Al Kindi (SAAD 16) is a facility for military research and development, in particular, the pyrotechnics and propellants used in rockets The site has been thoroughly reconstructed after severe destruction during the Gulf War The facilities at the site have features that could be useful in development of small quantities of explosives such as those used in a nuclear weapons development program It has also some good quality machine shops for fabricating non-explosive materials, an electroplating capability and a primitive capability for the machining of high explosives The reconstruction effort has proceeded since the visit in November 1992 More buildings have been completed and additional equipment has last been installed No nuclear related activities prohibited under UNSCR 687 were observed "[17]

As a general rule, the IAEA has been loath to destroy dual-use equipment to avoid giving the impression it is seeking to prevent Iraq's scientific and technological development Rather than shut down an entire factory, the IAEA's approach has been to target isolated pieces of equipment spread across a number of sites This has left virtually untouched the largest military manufacturing base in the Arab world

Sometimes this has led to extreme cases Also during the 18th IAEA inspection in early March 1993, Chief inspector Dimitri Perricos chanced upon no fewer than 242 machine-tools, many of them potentially subject to UNSC 687 monitoring, in a single nuclear weapons facility, Al Huteen Earlier IAEA teams

---

[17] IAEA 18, April 28, 1993, page 5

had simply missed them 94 of these machine-machine tools were 3 and 4-axis turning machines manufactured by Matrix Churchill

The IAEA is unlikely to become more severe with Iraq, and indeed, can be expected to argue that Iraq should be allowed to retain its dual-use equipment and production facilities - indeed, even nuclear facilities During an extended conversation in Vienna earlier this year, the head of the IAEA inspection team, Professor Maurizio Zifferero, said he could see "no reason why Iraq should *not* be allowed to pursue legitimate civilian nuclear research again I can imagine the day where they might want to rebuild the Thuwaitha research reactor, or build nuclear power plants " Such activity, Zifferero believed, would be "legitimate and innocuous" since the IAEA has reduced the Iraqi bomb program "to zero "[18]

Since Zifferero's comments were publicized in the Wall Street Journal, he has backed away from this position in his public statements

Industrial strategy

Iraq has been steadily building up the industrial infrastructure necessary for a broad-based weapons industry since Saddam Hussein took charge of military procurements and security questions in 1974

At that time, Saddam set up a three-man Strategic Planning Committee that took charge of arms purchases, military-industrial planning, and the secret financial networks

In the early days, Saddam's partners on the three-man committee were his cousin, Adnan Khairallah (who went on to become Defense Minister in the 1980s before his death in a mysterious helicopter crash in May 1989), and Adnan Hamdani, Saddam's personal secretary Trained as a lawyer, Hamdani was in charge of contractual negotiations and financing, and went on to become Planning Minister [19]

---

[18]Comments reproduced in the *Wall Street Journal Europe*, "What the IAEA Hasn't Found in Iraq " Jan 28, a similar account of Zifferero's attitude toward dismantling Iraq s manufacturing capabilities can be found in Gary Milhollin, "The Iraqi Bomb," The New Yorker, Feb 1, 1993 Milhollin notes that Zifferero, who has been given the task of dismantling Iraq s nuclear weapons program, had sold Iraq plutonium reprocessing hot cells and other equipment in the mid-1970s as the lead Italian government official in charge of nuclear exports

[19]For more background, see chapters 1-4 of *The Death Lobby How the West Armed Iraq* op cit

Part of Hamdani's job was to slip strategic weapons projects into large contracts ostensibly devoted to developing Iraq's civilian manufacturing or agricultural potential, which in turn were buried in Iraq's Soviet-style Five-Year Plan Under the heading "agricultural development," for instance, Hamdani inscribed a little-noticed entry that called for "the creation of six laboratories for chemical, physiological, and biological analysis " To operate the laboratories, which were devoted to biological weapons research, the Plan called for the training by foreign companies of 5,000 technicians One of these labs was the now famous Salman Pak "baby milk' plant, identified by UNSCOM as Iraq's largest biological weapons facility

Every "civilian" plant Iraq built in the late 1970s and 1980s was also geared for military production Chemicals plants at Fallujah, for instance, also churned out precursors for poison gas Heavy engineering plants in the southern suburbs of Baghdad produced uranium centrifuge parts as well as machine-tools and railroad ties Steel plants were built so they could just as easily manufacture reinforcing bars for the construction industry as armor-plate for tanks To fully grasp the scope of Iraq's weapons-manufacturing capability, one must examine in detail Iraq's industrial base with an eye to dual-use This was the case before the UNSCOM inspections, and it remains the case today

The imbrication of military with civilian production made procurement of most materials an easy task throughout the 1980s Under the guise of building a $1 billion ' super-phosphates" plant at Al Qaim, for instance, Iraq also procured processing lines to separate uranium from phosphate ore As part of the gigantic steel complex at Taji, they purchased a foundry for tank barrels, or again, under the cover of electrical generating equipment they purchased large steel casings which were used for the uranium enrichment calutrons

Key Installations

While many Iraqi weapons plants were heavily destroyed during Allied bombing raids, extraordinary efforts have been spent over the past two years to get military production back up and running According to Israel's top private analyst on Iraq, Amatzia Baram, "Saddam must continue his military efforts, since his whole raison d'être over the past twenty years has been to transform

Iraq into the Prussia of the Middle East Arms manufacturing is built into his system Without it, Saddam will lose prestige, and perhaps lose power "[20]

Of the forty-seven main weapons plants listed in the Appendix, thirty-three have been cited by the IAEA for having contributed to Iraq's crash effort to develop an atomic weapon, ten were engaged in chemical or biological weapons production, twelve were involved in ballistic missile research, design, development, and manufacture, while twenty-four were making conventional armaments

Much remains of this vast industrial infrastructure As mentioned above, most production equipment was dismantled before the Allied bombings and was stored in underground bunkers or civilian industrial sites for the duration of the war Over one hundred pieces of production equipment from the Samarra poison gas works, for instance, were stored in the Mosul sugar factory, and discovered only by accident by UN inspectors It is not known how much of this equipment has been subjected to monitoring

The following is a brief summary by factory of the conventional weapons production capability still believed to exist in Iraq

• Al Ameen T-72 tank assembly, under Polish and Czech licenses, machine-tool assembly line

• Al Amil liquid nitrogen production

• Al Muthena (Fallujah chemicals plant) HMX, RDX explosives

• Al Qaqaa aerial bombs, TNT, solid rocket propellants

• Al Rabee precision machining

• April 7 proximity fuzes for 155 mm and cluster munitions

• Badr aerial bombs, artillery pieces, tungsten-carbide machine-tool bits

• Base West World major armor retrofitting center

• Digila computer software, assembly of process-line controllers for weapons plants, plastics casting

• Fao cluster bombs, fuel-air explosives

• Huteen explosives, TNT, propellants, potential for armored vehicle assembly

• Mansour defense electronics

• PC1 ethylene oxide for fuel-air explosives

[20]Interview with the author in Haifa in Feb 1992

• Saad 5 (Saddam Engineering Complex): 122 mm howitzers; Ababil rockets; tank optics; mortar sites

• Saad 13 (Salah al Dine): defense electronics, radars, frequency-hopping radios radios

• Saad 21: Nonferrous metal plant for ammunition cases

• Saad 24: gas masks

• Sawary: small patrol boats

• SEHEE: heavy engineering complex capable of a wide variety of military production (artillery, vehicle parts, cannon barrels)

• Taji: wheeled APCs (East European license); armor plate; artillery pieces.[21]

This very broad-based capability gives Iraq the possibility not only of refurbishing the 250 or more fighter aircraft and 2,500 main battle tanks that survived the war, but of expanding its military inventory in the very near future. Noting this development, the Chairman of the UN Special Commission, Rolf Ekeus, noted earlier this year that Iraq "considers its obligations ended once destruction of its weapons of mass destruction is completed, and has said it will not accept UN monitoring of any future arms buildup."[22]

UNSCOM believes that Iraq is systematically preserving its options in all four areas of unconventional weapons production - nuclear, ballistic missile, chemical, and biological. Furthermore, UNSCOM inspectors say they have seen no signs that Iraq has dispersed the teams of scientists that had worked on these weapons projects. Iraq has jealously guarded and protected its foreign suppliers network, and refuses to accept monitoring of its future capabilities, both of which constitute clear violations of the UN ceasefire agreements. Instead of cooperating with the UN, the Iraqis have tried to conceal as much production equipment as possible, redeploying it to "conventional" military production."

---

[21] "Rebuilding the Defense industry," MEDNEWS, March 9, 1992; "Does Iraq have the Bomb?," MEDNEWS, Jan. 25, 1993.

[22] Wireless File, USIS, Feb. 6, 1993.

Ongoing Procurement Efforts

Iraq continues to operate an extensive clandestine procurement network in Europe, the Middle East, and possibly in the United States Some of the most notorious agents who helped Iraq obtain sophisticated Western technologies for its long-range ballistic missile programs and its nuclear weapons effort are still at large Among these

• Safa Habobi, the President of Technology Development Group (TDG), London TDG led the Iraqi procurement effort in Europe, serving as the front for the purchase of the machine-tool company, Matrix Churchill Ltd British Customs inexplicably waited several months after the international embargo on Iraq and Iraqi assets was in place before raiding the TDG offices, allowing the Iraqis to cart of critical documents that might have exposed their network Habobi was allowed to leave Britain and return to the Middle East On September 27, 1992 he was involved in a non-fatal car crash and was identified in hospital in Amman, Jordan He is believed to have moved his procurement operations to Tunisia [23]

• Khaled Marzoumi, the former Commercial attaché at the Iraqi Embassy in Paris in the late 1980s, now operates out of the offices of the State Oil Marketing Organizaiton (SOMO) in Amman, Jordan, where the author briefly encountered him in April 1992 In 1988-89, he was instrumental in the operation of Babil International, an Iraqi front company registered in France that was controlled by Safa Habobi of TDG and was used for procurement and financial transactions on behalf of the Iraqi government

• Pierre Drogoul, the father of indicted BNL-Atlanta banker Christopher Drogoul Until recently, the elder Drogoul worked as a consultant for Babil International The French government has never closed Babil or seized its accounts, which are held at the Neuilly-sur-Seine branch of the Union des Banques Françaises et Arabes (UBAF) Drogoul continues to operate a trading company, Technique Materiel Commerce International (TMCI), in the Paris suburb of Garches

• Sam Namaan, aka Saalim Naman, served as Vice President of Matrix Churchill Corp, the U S branch of the British tool company that fitted out a

---

[23] Jim Hoagland, *International Herald Tribune* Oct 15, 1992

dozen Iraqi weapons plants in the late 1980s. Although the Solon, Ohio offices of MCC were raided by U.S. Customs agents in 1991 and Namaan was sought for questioning, he was reportedly allowed to re-enter the United States at Detroit on Oct. 10, 1992 on an immigration visa.[24]

• Anis Mansour Wadi, one of the original members in Europe of the Iraqi procurement network, established several companies in Britain and later in the United States that were used to purchase equipment for the nuclear weapons program. One of these, Bay Industries, of Century City, California, was searched and closed down by U.S. Customs agents on March 22, 1991. However, Wadi is believed to have continued operating in the United States.

German companies breaking sanctions

The investigative arm of German Customs, the ZKI (Zollkriminalinstitut), is currently investigating more than 150 German and Iraqi-owned companies based on German territory for possible breaches of the UN sanctions against Iraq. Among the companies on the "active" list, which was made available to the subcommittee by private sources in Europe, are some of Germany's largest industrial concerns, such as Thyssen, MAN, and Strabag Bau AG.

Some companies are familiar to investigators for their role in helping Iraq to develop its upgraded SCUD missiles, such as ABC Beaujean of Stuttensee. Others are under investigation for selling technologies with a potential nuclear end-use, including calutron magnets, and special piping for use in a centrifuge enrichment plant. This suggests that Iraq indeed intends to continue its nuclear weapons program, despite its commitment to UN Security Council Resolution 687.

Iraq-owned fronts constitute another category of companies on the ZKI case list. Among these are the Iraqi Shipping Lines in Bremen, and the German office of the Technology Development Group, known as TDG-SEG, Krefeld, which is believed to be purchasing machine-tools and other goods in Germany using fake Jordanian end-use certificates. Equipment purchased in this manner is shipped legally to Jordan, where it is subsequently diverted to Iraq by truck.

The German subsidiary of Minolta, based in Arensberg, is under investigation for a potential export of a flash x-ray camera. A similar item was discovered by the IAEA at Iraq's Al Atheer nuclear weapons lab, where it was

---

[24] John Fialka, *Wall Street Journal*, Dec. 11, 1992.

signing false end-use and embargo-compliance certificates Key to obtaining Jordanian support was the cutoff of U S aid to Jordan in 1991.

Jordan has been allowed, however, to continue purchasing Iraqi oil by the UN Sanctions Committee These purchases, estimated at 60,000 to 70,000 b/d, were specifically tied to the repayment of Iraq's debt to Jordan This debt stood at around $400 million when the initial waver was granted in August 1990 By all estimates, even at the reduced price of $16 per barrel, Iraq's oil deliveries should have wiped out the debt by late December 1991 However, the oil deliveries to Jordan continued on the same scale as before throughout 1992

According to Western diplomats interviewed in Amman, this is because the Central Bank of Jordan had been purchasing Iraqi debt from commercial banks, and reclassifying it as "official" debt Debt officers at the Central Bank of Jordan confirmed that the Iraqi government debt to Jordan still stood at around $400 million in April 1992, despite the oil deliveries, but refused to comment on how this had come about

Wall Street investigator Jules Kroll, who has been tracking Iraq's procurement effort in Jordan, alleges that the Iraqi government transferred $5 2 billion in government funds to the Arab Bank in Amman just as Operation Desert Storm was ending, to establish a new trading infrastructure for Iraq In addition to this, he alleges that the Central Bank of Jordan is laundering secret Iraqi government funds in Switzerland through commercial banks such as Jordan's Housing Bank, the Jordan Gulf Bank, and the Arab Financial Corporation

Oil and Arms

Already in March 1992, two French major oil companies, CFP Total, and Elf Aquitaine, acknowledged that they were engaged in active negotiations with the Iraqi government over future oil production-sharing agreements in Iraq [27] Since then, oil ministry and private businessmen from Russia, Italy, and Belarus have also attempted to renew contact

[26] "Jordan reverses embargo policy," MEDNEWS April 13, 1992

[27] *Le Monde* March 6, 1992

used to develop nuclear explosive "lenses " Minolta has strenuously denied accusations in the past of having supplied Iraq with dual-use equipment The IAEA in Vienna continues to look with great interest Iraq's suppliers of flash x-ray equipment Another unit was obtained from IMACON in Switzerland, apparently through the intermediary of a Geneva-based trading company, Bonaventure (Europe) Inc

In Hamburg, Stinnes Interoil AG is suspected by German Customs of having organized purchases of Iraqi oil, in contravention of the embargo It is not known whether they played the role of intermediary for foreign sales of Iraqi oil, or whether they imported oil into Germany itself As in all other cases cited, no criminal proceedings have been initiated.

Some new names appear on this latest list of German companies suspected of embargo-busting, including Krupp Atlas, of Bremen, and machine-tool manufacturers such as Condux Maschenbau, of Hanau, and Moller Maschinenfabrik GmbH, of Bekum Reman Enterprises-Raouf Mahdi, of Nurenburg, is suspected of having sold weapons Companies under investigation for unspecified embargo breaches include Allgemeine Nah-ost Handelsgesselshaft (Hamburg), Alloy Pipe and Metal (Rattingen), Benteller AG (Vienslacke), China Project and Investment (Hamburg), Comaco GmbH (Gellhausen), Commerce und Finance Service, Pan Trade GmbH (Bensheim), and Rotermund GmbH (Munich) None has been indicted [25]

Smuggling through Jordan

Until recently, Jordan had served as Iraq's primary conduit to the West Goods were imported for use in Jordan through the port of Aqaba, and shipped up through the desert to Baghdad on trucks operated by the Iraq-Jordan Land Transportation Company, which is owned jointly by the governments of Iraq and Jordan

Under intense pressure from the United States, and from public exposure of Jordan's role as a conduit for embargoed goods reaching Iraq, in early 1992 King Hussein ordered a crackdown on illicit activities, in an attempt to clear his country's name as an Iraqi ally However, it took several months before key Iraqi agents were weeded out of the Jordanian bureaucracy, where they had been

---

[25] German Companies Break Iraq Embargo " MEDNEWS, July 6, 1992

In March 1993, the State Department formally accused Iran of having violated the oil embargo on Iraq, after U S observation satellites detected what was described as a "large convoy of oil trucks" leaving Iraq for Iran Iran denied the charge, which was reiterated in the daily State Department briefing on March 30 by spokesman Richard Boucher

Unconfirmed reports from Kuwaiti sources warned that commercial contacts have intensified in recent months between major French defense exporters and Iraqi agents in Europe, in view of renewing the supply of spare parts for Iraq's fleet of Mirage F1 fighter-bombers The Franco-German Eurocopter consortium was also said to have been probing new sales Given the public support of the UN embargo by the French government, however, most foreign diplomats in Paris believe it highly unlikely that the French government would approve such sales One report, from a French source that claimed personal knowledge, alleged that a major French defense electronics company had established an office in Amman, Jordan for the sole purpose of servicing equipment sold to Iraq in the 1980s This has not been confirmed

What is certain is that the Iraqi Air Force Mirages have been performed training missions in recent months in an increasingly brazen manner, notably along the borders oaf the southern exclusion zone.

Furthermore, according to Andrei Volpin, a a Russian research fellow at the Washington Institute for Near East Studies, some 200 Russian military technicians remain in Iraq and are servicing Soviet-built equipment Russian officials from Oboronexport, the government's arms export agency, confirmed the presence of the Russian technicians in Iraq but insisted that they had been engaged on "private" contracts [28]

Crescent Petroleum

The Office of Foreign Assets Control continues to investigate a $700 million independent oil company, Crescent Petroleum Company International, on the suspicion it may be acting on behalf of the Iraqi government

Crescent operates out of the Emirate of Sharjah and is controlled by Hamid Dhia Jaafar, the brother of Jaafar Dhia Jaafar, the acknowledged head of Iraq's clandestine nuclear weapons program Jaafar Jaafar currently serves as senior

---

[28] Interview with Oboronexport officials at the Paris Air Show June 17, 1993

Undersecretary of the Ministry of Industry and Minerals, formerly known as the Ministry of Industry and Military Industrialization (MIMI), and is the principal interlocutor for International Atomic Energy Agency inspection teams investigating Iraq's nuclear weapons capabilities.

If Crescent has been acting on behalf of Iraq then its assets worldwide could be seized under the terms of UN Security Council resolutions. Crescent has a registered office at 5847 San Relipe, Suite 2150, Houston, Texas.

The allegations, which Crescent's owner of record, Hamid Jaafar, strenuously denied, revolve around the company's ties to MIMI. In 1989, Crescent was appointed sole agent on MIMI's behalf to negotiate the acquisition of technology for a large-scale aluminum smelter to be built near Nassiriyah in southern Iraq. In the "Chairman's letter" introducing the company's 1989-1990 Annual Report, Hamid Jaffar states that the project was halted by the UN embargo. In the 9th inspection report of Iraq's clandestine nuclear facilities, IAEA inspectors note that special aluminum parts used in Iraq's uranium enrichment centrifuges were melted down in May or June 1991 at the old Nassiriyah smelter, identified by the Iraqis as the "Ur Establishment" and described by the United Nations as "the only aluminum smelter in Iraq." Since then, the IAEA and the UN Special Commission have catalogued the Nassiriyah site as being "linked" to Iraq's clandestine nuclear weapons program.

Crescent appears to have been doing business directly with the head of Iraq's unconventional weapons programs, MIMI Senior Undersecretary Lt. Gen. (Dr.) Amir Hamoodi Al-Saadi. In an apparently unrelated deal, Al-Saadi empowered Hamid Jaafar to purchase financial interests in foreign oil refineries by using Iraqi oil as collateral. This led to an attempted purchase by Crescent of the entire Petrofina network of refineries and 3,000 filling stations in the United States, and would have vastly expanded the financial assets available to MIMI for weapons development.

While Crescent may not have been in the business of arms manufacturing or procurement per se, it was certainly linked to the principal Iraqi government organization that was. Crescent has repeatedly denied any wrong-doing. However, in a libel suit company lawyers brought against independent journalist Alan George for having written about Crescent's ties to MIMI, a London court ruled that no libel had been commited and awarded damages to Mr George.

Unconventional Weapons timetable

Former CIA Director Robert Gates put a timetable on the Iraqi rearmament effort, addressing Iraq's capabilities in the areas of nuclear technologies, chemical and biological weapons, and ballistic missiles in testimony before the U S Senate Government Operations Committee on Jan 15, 1992

The most immediate threat following the easing of UN sanctions would be from Iraqi biological weapons, because of the small amount of specialized production equipment required Iraq "could be producing BW materials in a matter of weeks of a decision to do so," Gates said

Some chemical warfare agents could also be produced almost immediately, since much of the hard-to-get production equipment was removed and hidden before Operation Desert Storm began However, heavy bomb damage to Iraqi CW plants and continued monitoring by the UN Special Commission will partially retard Iraq's effort to regain the CW capability it had previously enjoyed Gates believed that a full CW capability would take "a year or more" for Iraq to accomplish - a very short lead time, indeed

The CIA continues to estimate that Iraq has hidden away around 200 improved SCUD missiles (al-Hossein and al-Abbas variants, with ranges of 650 and 900 km respectively) - an estimate Ekeus reiterated recently [29] Added to this is a suspected capability to indigeneously produce liquid fuel for these missiles, making Iraq independent of outside sources or technology [30]

Iraq's nuclear program took the hardest hit, Gates claimed Even here, however, the CIA estimates the time Iraq would need to reconstitute its nuclear weapons program at "a few, rather than many, years "

Gates concluded "In our opinion, Iraq will remain a primary proliferation threat as long as Saddam remains in power " A similar view was expressed in a

---

29UPI, March 24, 1993

30The facility, code-named Al Amil, or Project 7307, is located approximately 6 km west of the Tarmiyah Electro-Magnetic Isotope Separation (EMIS) plant, and was inspected in 1992 by the IAEA The Iraqi authorities told the IAEA that while Al Amil was no longer doing work for the Iraqi nuclear program, production of liquid nitrogen - which can be used for liquid-fueled ballistic missiles - was continuing under German license Rebuilding the Defense Industry," MEDNEWS, March 9, 1992

recent Rand Corporation study on Iraq by former National Security Council staff member, Graham Fuller

To insist that Saddam Hussein's commitment to rebuilding the most powerful military machine in the region is an obstacle to peace, is not a "personalization" of the conflict between Iraq and the United States, it is merely a statement of fact

After World War I, Germany was banned altogether from rebuilding its military industries, and from moving troops into the Ruhr Valley The comparison with Iraq s current situation is illustrative While demilitarized zones have been created to protect Kurds in the north and Shiites in southern Iraq, no restrictions have been placed on Iraq's military industries beyond the ban on unconventional weapons development, manufacture, and possession Iraq has pumped all available resources into rebuilding its military plants, without a thought to international sanctions or to treaty restrictions As a result, Iraq is likely to reemerge as the predominant military power in the region in very short order

Machine-Tools Found in Iraqi Nuclear Facilities by UN Inspectors

The 11th and 12th Mission Lists

Source IAEA

Manufacturer	Country	Location	Quantity	Type Machine	Use
Ultradex	?	Badr	1	Plasma Cutting MDI (not CNC)	
Kunming	*China*	Saddam	6	Spherical Grinder 46mm Diameter	Gun Sights
Tos Hulin/Bosch	*CSSR Germany*	Daura	1	Turning VTL	Heat excha
Skoda/Phillips	*CSSR Netherlands*	Daura	1	Milling Boring	Heat excha
Skoda/Phillips	*CSSR Netherlands*	Daura	1	Milling Boring 150 mm spindle	Heat excha
Stenhoj Hydraulik	*Denmark*	Tuwaitha	2	Press vertical 1600kg	
Heckert WMW	*East Germany*	Badr	1	Gantry Mill	
Colly	*France*	Salah Al Din	9	Shear Press	
Fromat/Industio	*France*	Taji (Nassr)	1	Drilling/Boring	
HES	*France*	Salah Al Din	12	Milling not CNC	
HES	*France*	Salah Al Din	9	Milling (not CNC) ~400x250x150 mm	
Hure	*France*	Salah Al Din	1	Milling	
Petit Jean	*France*	Taji (Nassr)	1	Shear	
Petit Jean	*France*	Taji (Nassr)	2	Shear Press	
Sciaky	*France*	Al Rabiya	1	EB Welder	Cent
Renault HP/ Rennishaw-Probe	*France US UK*	Al Rabiya	1	CMM 1600mmx1300mm	
Renault HP/ Rennishaw-Probe	*France US UK*	Al Rabiya	1	CMM 1300mmx800mm	
Renault HP/ Rennishaw-Probe	*France US UK*	Al Rabiya	1	CMM 600mmx800mm	
	Germany ?	Iskandariya	1	Flowforming Horizontal (not CNC)	
Adolph Waldrich Coburg	*Germany*	Badr	1	Piano Mill not CNC	
Adolph Waldrich Coburg	*Germany*	Taji (Nassr)	1	Piano Grinder	
BHG Hermle/ Heidenhain	*Germany*	Al Rabiya	7	Milling	
Biller/ Heidenhain	*Germany*	Saddam	1	Turning ~10m	Gun/Barre
Blohm	*Germany*	Saddam	1	Grinding not CNC	
Deckel	*Germany*	Al Radwan	4	Milling	
Deckel	*Germany*	Badr	4	Milling	
Deckel	*Germany*	Salah Al Din	2	Milling	
Deckel	*Germany*	Taji (Nassr)	1	Milling	
Demag	*Germany*	Salah Al Din	1	Horizontal Press	
Donau	*Germany*	Badr	4	Milling Knee Type (not CNC)	GP
Dornes	*Germany*	Al Radwan	1	Turning VTL ~ 4m	EMIS
Dornes	*Germany*	Al Ameer	1	Turning VTL ~10m table	EMIS
Dornes	*Germany*	Al Rabiya	1	Turning VTL ~2 5m table	EMIS
Dornes	*Germany*	Aqua Bin Nafi	1	Turning VTL	EMIS
Dornes	*Germany*	Taji (Nassr)	1	Turning Vertical ~2 0m table	EMIS
Dornes	*Germany*	Taji (Nassr)	1	Turning Vertical ~2.0m table	EMIS
Dornes Siemens	*Germany*	Badr	1	Turning ~2m table VTL	EMIS
Droop & Rein	*Germany*	Badr	1	Milling	
ESAM	*Germany*	Aqua Bin Nafi	3	Flame Cutter	

Company	Country	Location	Quantity	Type Machine	Use
Frolich	Germany	Taji (Nassr)	1	Press	
Gerber/ Boehringer	Germany	Saddam	2	Turning	
Gildermeister	Germany	Al Atheer	1	Turning	
Gildermeister	Germany	Saddam	5	Turning	
H+H Metalform	Germany	Taji (Nassr)	4	Flowforming Vertical	Rotors
H+H Metalform	Germany	Taji (Nassr)	1	Flowforming Vertical	Rotors
H+H Metalform	Germany	Taji (Nassr)	1	Flowforming Verticle	Rotors
H+H Metalform	Germany	Taji (Nassr)	1	Flowforming Vertical	Rotors
H+H Metalform	Germany	Taji (Nassr)	1	Flowforming vertical	Rotors
H+H Metalform	Germany	Taji (Nassr)	1	Flowforming vertical	Rotors
H+H Metalform	Germany	Taji (Nassr)	1	Flowforming vertical	Rotors
H&H	Germany	Shuala	1	Flowforming	Rotors
H&H	Germany	Shuala	1	Flowforming	Rotors
H&H	Germany	Daura	1	Flowforming	Rotors
H&H	Germany	Daura	1	Flowforming Horizontal non CNC	
Hahn & Kolb	Germany	Aqua Bin Nafi	1	Milling	
Hahn & Kolb	Germany	Aqua Bin Nafi	1	Measuring	
Hahn&Kolb	Germany	Al Radwan	1	Milling	
Hennig/Siemens	Germany	Saddam	1	Milling	
Hermle/ Heidenhain	Germany	Al Rabiya	3	Milling	
Keilinghaus	Germany	Daura	1	Spin Forming non CNC	
Kieserling & Albrecht Siemens	Germany	Taji (Nassr)	3	Spinforming/flowforming	Warheads
Kuhlmann	Germany	Al Ameer	1	Milling	Electrodes
Kulhmann	Germany	Al Radwan	1	Milling	
Lieber	Germany	Tuwaitha	1	Turning non CNC	Uranium
Magdeburg	Germany	Taji (Nassr)	1	Turning	Shell Casin
Magdeburg	Germany	Taji (Nassr)	1	Turning	Shell casin
Magdeburg	Germany	Taji (Nassr)	7	Turning	Shell Casin
Magdeburg	Germany	Daura	1	Turning Special	Rotors
Magdeburg	Germany	Daura	1	Turning Special	Rotors
Magdeburg	Germany	Daura	1	Turning Special	Rotors
Maho	Germany	Aqua Bin Nafi	1	Milling	Weapons
Maho/ Heidenhain	Germany	Al Rabiya	4	Milling	
Maho/ Heidenhain	Germany	Al Rabiya	4	Milling	
Maho/ Heidenhain	Germany	Al Rabiya	3	Milling	
Maho/ Heidenhain	Germany	Al Rabiya	1	Milling	
Maho/ Heidenhain	Germany	Al Rabiya	1	Milling	
Maho Heidenhain	Germany	Tuwaitha	1	Milling	
Messer Gersheim Balzers	Germany	Al Radwan	1	EB Welder	
Peddinghaus	Germany	Taji (Nassr)	1	Press	
Petzing & Hartman	Germany	Badr	1	Cutoff Mach Bar	Prepare B
Petzing & Hartman	Germany	Badr	1	Cutoff Mach Bar	Prepare B
Petzing & Hartman	Germany	Badr	1	Cutoff Mach Bar	Prepare B
Pfauter Gildermeister	Germany	Badr	1	Gear Cutter	Maint
Ravensburg	Germany	Saddam	1	Turning ~15m long	Gun/Barr
Ravensburg	Germany	Saddam	1	Turning ~10m long	Gun Barre
Ravensburg/ Siemens	Germany	Saddam	2	Turning ~20m long	Gun/Barr

Company	Country	Location	Quantity	Type Machine	Use
Ravensburg/ Siemens	Germany	Saddam	2	Turning Vertiacl 1m table	
Ravensburg/ Siemens	Germany	Taji (Nassr)	4	Turning ~15m long	Gun/Barre
S H W	Germany	Al Radwan	3	Milling	
S H W	Germany	Al Radwan	2	Milling	
Scheiss	Germany	Al Ameer	1	Milling Boring 4 5 7 0 diam	EMIS
Scheiss Froreip	Germany	Al Ameer	1	Milling	
Scheiss Froreip	Germany	Aqua Bin Nafi	3	Milling Boring	EMIS
Scheiss Siemens	Germany	Al Radwan	1	Milling Boring ~150mm spindle moving column	
Sharmann	Germany	Al Ameer	1	Milling	
Sharmann	Germany	Al Ameer	1	Milling 150mm Spl	
Sheiss	Germany	Taji (Nassr)	1	Turning Vertical two heads ~6m table	EMIS
SHW	Germany	Taji (Nassr)	1	Milling	Weapons
SHW	Germany	Taji (Nassr)	1	Milling	
SHW	Germany	Taji (Nassr)	4	Milling	
SHW	Germany	Al Ameer	6	Milling	
SHW	Germany	Al Ameer	2	Milling	
SHW	Germany	Al Ameer	1	Milling	
SHW	Germany	Al Ameer	1	Milling	
SHW	Germany	Badr	2	Milling	
SHW	Germany	Badr	1	Milling	
SHW	Germany	Al Rabiya	1	Milling	
SHW	Germany	Al Rabiva	1	Milling	
SHW	Germany	Al Rabiva	2	Milling	
SHW	Germany	Al Rabiya	1	Milling	
SHW	Germany	Aqua Bin Nafi	1	Milling	Weapons
SHW	Germany	Aqua Bin Nafi	1	Milling	
SHW	Germany	Al Ameer	1	Milling	
SHW	Germany	Al Ameer	1	Milling	
SHW	Germany	Aqua Bin Nafi	1	Milling	
SHW	Germany	Taji (Nassr)	2	Milling	
SHW Siemens	Germany	Badr	1	Milling	
SHW/Heidenhain	Germany	Al Radwan	2	Milling	
SMS	Germany	Taji (Nassr)	1	Horiz Press	
Tiefbohrtenik	Germany	Taji (Nassr)	1	Turning/ Boring Mill	
Trennjagger	Germany	Taji (Nassr)	1	Press	
Trumpf	Germany	Al Rabiva	1	Laser Cutter	
VDF Wohlenberg/Siemens	Germany	Saddam	2	Turning ~20m long	Gun/Barr
VDF Wohlenberg/Siemens	Germany	Saddam	1	Turning ~5m long	Gun/Barr
Walter	Germany	Badr	1	Tool Grinder	Tooling
Walter Seigen	Germany	Al Radwan	1	Milling	Repair m
Walter Seigen	Germany	Al Ameer	1	Milling	Repair m
Walter Seigen	Germany	Al Ameer	1	Milling 20 m bed ~6m bridge	Repair M
Wanderer	Germany	Saddam	3	Milling	
Weiger	Germany	Daura	1	Shear Press	
Werner	Germany	Saddam	1	Milling	
Werner	Germany	Saddam	1	Milling Horizontal heads	
Wotan Siemens	Germany	Taji (Nassr)	1	Milling/ Boring	Weapon

Company	Country	Location	Quantity	Type Machine	Use
Wotan/Siemens	*Germany*	Saddam	5	Milling /Borng	
SHW/Aqua	*Germany Iraq*	Aqua Bin Nafi	3	Milling	
Maho/Phillips	*Germany /Netherlands*	Taji (Nassr)	2	Milling	
Maho/Phillips	*Germany /Netherlands*	Taji (Nassr)	1	Milling	
Maho/Phillips	*Germany /Netherlands*	Taji (Nassr)	3	Milling	
Maho/Phillips	*Germany /Netherlands*	Al Atheer	1	Milling	
Maho/Phillips	*Germany /Netherlands*	Al Atheer	1	Milling	
Maho/Phillips	*Germany /Netherlands*	Al Atheer	1	Milling	
Maho/Phillips	*Germany /Netherlands*	Al Atheer	1	Milling	
Maho/Phillips	*Germany /Netherlands*	Al Atheer	1	Milling	
Maho/Phillips	*Germany /Netherlands*	Al Ameer	1	Milling	Weapons
Maho/Phillips	*Germany /Netherlands*	Al Ameer	1	Milling	
Maho/Phillips	*Germany /Netherlands*	Al Ameer	1	Milling	
Maho/Phillips	*Germany /Netherlands*	Al Ameer	2	Milling	
Maho/Phillips	*Germany /Netherlands*	Al Ameer	1	Milling	
Maho/Phillips	*Germany /Netherlands*	Al Ameer	1	Milling	
Maho/Phillips	*Germany /Netherlands*	Badr	2	Milling	
Maho/Phillips	*Germany /Netherlands*	Al Rabiya	10	Milling	
Maho/Phillips	*Germany /Netherlands*	Al Rabiya	1	Milling	
Maho/Phillips	*Germany /Netherlands*	Al Rabiya	3	Milling	
Maho/Phillips	*Germany /Netherlands*	Al Rabiya	2	Milling	
Maho/Phillips	*Germany /Netherlands*	Al Rabiya	1	Milling	
Maho/Phillips	*Germany /Netherlands*	Al Rabiya	1	Milling	
Maho/Phillips	*Germany /Netherlands*	Al Rabiya	3	Milling	
Maho/Phillips	*Germany /Netherlands*	Al Rabiya	1	Milling	
Maho/Phillips	*Germany /Netherlands*	Al Rabiya	3	Milling	
Maho/Phillips	*Germany /Netherlands*	Al Rabiya	5	Milling	
Maho/Phillips	*Germany /Netherlands*	Al Rabiya	1	Milling	
Leitz/ HP/DEC	*Germany/ US*	Al Atheer	1	Coordinate Measuring (CMM)	Centrifuge i
Maho/Phillipes	*Germany/Netherlands*	Aqua Bin Nafi	1	Milling	
Maho/Phillips	*Germany/Netherlands*	Taji (Nassr)	1	Milling	
Maho/Phillips	*Germany/Netherlands*	Taji (Nassr)	1	Milling	
Maho/Phillips	*Germany/Netherlands*	Aqua Bin Nafi	1	Milling	
Maho/Phillips	*Germany/Netherlands*	Saddam	5	Milling	
Maho/Phillips	*Germany/Netherlands*	Saddam	3	Milling	
Maho/Phillips	*Germany/Netherlands*	Taji (Nassr)	1	Milling	
Boldrini	*Italy*	Daura	1	Press	
Carvaghi	*Italy*	Badr	1	Gantry Mill	
Ceruti	*Italy*	Badr	1	Milling horizontal	
DEA	*Italy*	Tarmiya	1	CMM	EMIS
DEA	*Italy*	Al Radwan	1	CMM	
DEA	*Italy*	Al Radwan	1	CMM	
DEA	*Italy*	Al Radwan	1	CMM	
DEA	*Italy*	Al Radwan	1	CMM ~7mx3 5m	EMIS
DEA	*Italy*	Al Ameer	1	CMM	EMIS
DEA	*Italy*	Al Ameer	1	CMM	
DEA	*Italy*	Al Rabiya	1	CMM ~2'x1'	
DEA	*Italy*	Al Rabiya	1	CMM 2'x1	
DEA	*Italy*	Salah Al Din	1	CMM	

Company	Country	Location	Quantity	Type Machine	Use
DEA	*Italy*	Saddam	1	CMM	
Famup	*Italy*	Salah Al Din	2	Milling	
Innocenti	*Italy*	Badr	1	Gantry Mill	Weapons
DEA/ DEC	*Italy US*	Al Rabiya	1	CMM 1000mm	
Fanuc	*Japan*	Salah Al Din	1	Turret Drill CNC	
Waida	*Japan*	Al Atheer	1	Jig Grinding (not CNC)	
Infratmena	*Romania*	Daura	1	Radia Drill	
Titan	*Romania*	Badr	1	Gantry Mill not CNC	
Sacem	*Spain*	Al Radwan	1	Milling	
Zaher	*Spain*	Aqua Bin Nafi	1	Milling	
Zayer	*Spain*	Al Ameer	1	Milling 5m bed	Weapons
Zayer	*Spain*	Al Ameer	1	Milling	
Zayer	*Spain*	Al Ameer	1	Milling	
Zayer	*Spain*	Al Ameer	1	Milling	
Zayer	*Spain*	Aqua Bin Nafi	1	Milling	
Zayer	*Spain*	Aqua Bin Nafi	1	Milling	
Zayer	*Spain*	Al Radwan	1	Milling	Weapons
Zayer/ Heidenhain	*Spain Germany*	Saddam	9	Milling	
Zayer Siemens	*Spain Germany*	Aqua Bin Nafi	1	Milling	Weapons
Zayer/Heidenhain	*Spain Germany*	Saddam	4	Milng	
Zayer	*Spain Netherlands*	Al Ameer	1	Milling	
Zayer/ Heidenhain	*Spain/Germany*	Al Radwan	1	Milling	
Zayer/ Heidenhain	*Spain/Germany*	Saddam	3	Milling	
Zayer/ Heidenhain	*Spain/Germany*	Saddam	1	Milling	
Zayer/ Heidenhain	*Spain/Germany*	Saddam	1	Milling	
Zayer/ Siemens	*Spain/Germany*	Taji (Nassr)	1	Milling	
Zayer/ Siemens	*Spain/Germany*	Al Radwan	3	Milling	
Aciera	*Switzerland*	Al Radwan	5	Milling	
Aciera	*Switzerland*	Al Radwan	2	Milling	
Aciera	*Switzerland*	Badr	2	Milling	
Aciera	*Switzerland*	Badr		Milling	
Aciera	*Switzerland*	Badr	3	Milling	
Aciera Phillips	*Switzerland*	Al Ameer	1	Milling	
Agie	*Switzerland*	Taji (Nassr)	1	EDM ram	
Agie	*Switzerland*	Al Atheer	1	Electrical Discharge	
Agie	*Switzerland*	Al Atheer	1	Electrical Discharge Ram type	
Agie	*Switzerland*	Al Radwan	1	EDM Wire	
Agie	*Switzerland*	Al Ameer	1	EDM	
Agie	*Switzerland*	Al Ameer	1	EDM	
Agie	*Switzerland*	Al Rabiya	2	EDM Ram	
Agie	*Switzerland*	Al Rabiya	1	EDM Wire	
Agie	*Switzerland*	Al Rabiya	1	DEM Wire	
Agie	*Switzerland*	Al Rabiya	1	Edm Ram	
Charmilles	*Switzerland*	Taji (Nassr)	1	EDM Ram	
Charmilles	*Switzerland*	Taji (Nassr)	1	EDM Ram	
Charmilles	*Switzerland*	Badr	3	EDM Ram	
Charmilles	*Switzerland*	Saddam	1	EDM Ram type	
Dixi	*Switzerland*	Salah Al Din	1	Jig Bore/ Mill non CNC	
Dixi	*Switzerland*	Taji (Nassr)	1	Jig Bore	

Company	Country	Location	Quantity	Type Machine	Use
Hauser	*Switzerland*	Al Radwan	1	Jig Grinding	
Hauser	*Switzerland*	Al Ameer	1	Jig Grinder	Tooling
Hauser	*Switzerland*	Al Rabiya	1	Jig Bore	
Hauser	*Switzerland*	Al Rabiya	1	Jig Grinder	Tooling
Hauser	*Switzerland*	Al Rabiya	1	Jig Bore	
Hauser	*Switzerland*	Badr	1	Jig Grinder	Tooling
Hauser	*Switzerland*	Salah Al Din	1	Jig Grinder	Tooling
Hauser	*Switzerland*	Saddam	2	Jig Grinder non CNC	
Kellenberger	*Switzerland*	Al Atheer	1	Grinding (not CNC)	
Kellenberger	*Switzerland*	Al Ameer	1	Grindind OD	
Mikron	*Switzerland*	Saddam	1	Milling	
Oerlikon	*Switzerland*	Taji (Nassr)	1	Milling	
Oerlikon	*Switzerland*	Taji (Nassr)	1	Milling	
Oerlikon	*Switzerland*	Saddam	1	Milling	
Reishauser	*Switzerland*	Saddam	1	Grinder	
Rigid	*Switzerland*	Iskandariya	1	Vertical Milling; 2 Spindle	
Schaublin	*Switzerland*	Badr	4	Turning	End Caps
Schaublin	*Switzerland*	Badr	2	Turning	End Caps
Schaublin	*Switzerland*	Badr	1	Turning	End Caps
Schaublin	*Switzerland*	Badr	2	Milling	
Schaublin	*Switzerland*	Saddam	13	Turning non CNC	
Schaublin	*Switzerland*	Saddam	12	Turning non CNC	
Schaublin Siemens	*Switzerland*	Al Rabiya	1	Milling	
SIP	*Switzerland*	Al Radwan	1	Jig Bore	Precision
SIP	*Switzerland*	Al Ameer	1	Jig Bore	Precision
SIP	*Switzerland*	Al Ameer	2	Jig Bore	Precision
SIP	*Switzerland*	Saddam	1	Jig Bore	
Studer	*Switzerland*	Al Atheer	1	OD/ID Crdng (not CNC0	
Studer	*Switzerland*	Saddam	4	Turning non CNC	
Tomos Bechler Sinumerix	*Switzerland*	Badr	1	Turning (Bar)	GP
Wahli	*Switzerland*	Salah Al Din	1	Milling	
EWAG	*Switzerland France*	Badr	2	Tool Grinding	Tooling
Mikron/Heidenhain	*Switzerland Germany*	Saddam	25	Milling ~250mm, 200mm. 150mm	
Mikron/Heidenhain	*Switzerland Germany*	Saddam	1	Milling	
Tarex/Bosh	*Switzerland Germany*	Saddam	8	Milling	
Schaublin	*Switzerland Japan*	Al Atheer	1	Turning	End caps
Matrix Churchill	*U K*	Taji (Nassr)	1	Grinding OD	
Cinn/Milacron	*UK*	Badr	1	Milling	
FMT	*UK*	Taji (Nassr)	1	Milling	
Harrison	*UK*	Badr	1	Turning	
Matrix Chruchill	*UK*	Al Radwan	1	Turning	End Caps
Matrix Churchill	*UK*	Taji (Nassr)	1	Turning	Ammo
Matrix Churchill	*UK*	Taji (Nassr)	1	Turning	Ammo
Matrix Churchill	*UK*	Taji (Nassr)	9	Turning	Ammo
Matrix Churchill	*UK*	Taji (Nassr)	22	Turning	Ammo
Matrix Churchill	*UK*	Shuala	1	Turning	End Caps
Matrix Churchill	*UK*	Al Ameer	2	Turning	End Caps
Matrix Churchill	*UK*	Badr	1	Turning	End Caps

Company	Country	Location	Quantity	Type Machine	Use
Matrix Churchill	UK	Badr	1	Turning	Cent
Matrix Churchill	UK	Aqua Bin Nafi	1	Turning	End Caps
Matrix/Churchill	UK	Taji (Nassr)	1	Turning	End Caps
Morgan Rushworth	UK	Tuwaitha	1	Shear Press	
Wickman	UK	Taji (Nassr)	17	Turning	Ammo
Wickman	UK	Taji (Nassr)	2	Turning	Ammo
Wickman	UK	Taji (Nassr)	2	Turning Bar type	Ammo
Colchester/ Fanuc	*UK Japan*	Badr	2	Turning	
Matrix Churchill/ Fanuc	*UK Japan*	Taji (Nassr)	1	Turning	End Caps
Matrix Churchill/ Fanuc	*UK Japan*	Taji (Nassr)	1	Turning	End Caps
Matrix Churchill/ Fanuc	*UK Japan*	Taji (Nassr)	1	Turning	End Caps
Matrix Churchill/ Fanuc	*UK Japan*	Taji (Nassr)	1	Turning	End Caps
Matrix Churchill/ Fanuc	*UK Japan*	Taji (Nassr)	1	Turning	Ammo
Matrix Churchill/ Fanuc	*UK Japan*	Al Rabiya	1	Turning	Piston Valve
Matrix Churchill/ Fanuc	*UK Japan*	Al Dijla	1	Turning	Cent
Matrix Churchill/ Fanuc	*UK Japan*	Taji (Nassr)	1	Turning	End Caps
Bridgeport/Heidenhain	*UK/Germany*	Taji (Nassr)	4	Milling Knee	
Bliss	*US*	Salah Al Din	2	Press (1 medium) (1 small)	
Pacific	*US*	Taji (Nassr)	6	Press	
Pangborn	*US*	Taji (Nassr)	1	Small Rolling Mill	
Hardinge	*US/UK (?)*	Al Atheer	1	Turning (not CNC)	Centrifuge
	USSR	Taji (Nassr)	1	Drilling	
	USSR	Al Radwan	1	Milling	
	USSR	Badr	1	Gantry Mill	
	USSR	Badr	1	Milling horizontal	
	USSR	Badr	4	Radial Drills not CNC	
Skoda	*USSR*	Daura	1	Turning Vertical	
	Yugoslavia	Saddam	1	OD Grinding not CNC Morpass Gaging	
Ivo Lola Ribar	*Yugoslavia*	Saddam	4	Milling	
Ivo Lola Ribar	*Yugoslavia*	Saddam	1	Milling	
Total machine-tools	605				

Iraqi Weapons Plants and Their Foreign Suppliers

Name.	**Abu Sukhayr**
Type:	Nuclear
Location:	Abu Sukhayr
Production:	Uranium prospection in the desert near Samawa
Foreign Contributors	NATRON (Brazil)

Name:	**Akashat**
Type:	CBW*
Location:	Akashat
Production:	Nerve agents and precursors from organic phosphorus compounds, UN says site of a second calutron uranium enrichment plant
Foreign Contributors:	Klockner Industries, Karl Kolb (Germany), Sybetra (Belgium)

Name.	**Al Ameen**
Type:	Conventional, Nuclear
Location:	Al Yusufiah
Production.	Headquarters of Auqba bin Nafi establishment and machining center for calutron ("Baghdadatron") parts Initially built for assembly of T-72 tanks on license from Poland and Czechoslovakia HQ located within the Badr complex Also made parts for hydroelectric power stations and assembled CNC machine tools (tool assembly resumed in 11/91) Most damage to the plant repaired
Foreign Contributors:	Polish and Czechoslovak state enterprises, Western machine-tool manufacturers

Name	**Al Amer**
Type:	Nuclear, Missile
Location.	Fallujah/ Amiriya
Production:	One of three turning/ machining centers of the Auqba Bin Nafi Establishment, dedicated at 70% to manufacturing

---

* Chemical and biological weapons

	assemblies for uranium enrichment calutrons and to al-Hossein and al-Abbas ballistic missiles Products included magnet cores, return irons, ion sources, and collector parts Al Amer had 2 large capacity turning and milling machines, plasma cutting machines for shearing metal sheets, jig-boring machines, and surface heat-treatment equipment used for improved SCUD missile casings
Foreign Contributors	Rexroth, Maho, Waldrich-Siegen, Dorries, Schiess-Frohripp, ABA, ESAB, DEMAG, Liebherr, Hahn & Kolb, Sharmann, SHW (Germany), DEA (Italy), Kaldyf, Zayer (Spain), Aciera, Agie, SIP-Hauser, Kellenberger, Kuhlmann (Switzerland), Raving Mayer (USA), Morris, Matrix Churchill (UK)
Name·	**Al Amil** (aka Project 7307)
Type	Nuclear, Missile
Location.	6 km west of Tarmiyah
Production:	Liquid nitrogen for EMIS diffusion pumps Other uses (rocket fuel?) also suspected Foreign-built No significant bomb damage, production continuing as of Nov 1991
Foreign Contributors.	Unknown
Name:	**Al Atheer** (PC3)
Type	Nuclear
Location	Al Musayyib
Production:	Nuclear warhead casting and assembly, co-located with PC2 Contained a Plasma coating facility (Powder building), a polymer lab, a carbide building (to make tungsten carbide for the Badr plant) Plant inaugurated by Hussein Kamil on 7 May 1991, blown up under UN supervision on April 14, 1992 Approximately 85 km south of Baghdad
Foreign Contributors.	ABRA, Hahn & Kolb, Maho, Gildermeister, Vakuum Technik GmbH,Plasmatechnik, Schaublin, Leitz (Germany), Philips (Netherlands), Hardinge Brothers (UK), Kennametal Matrix Churchill Corp, XYZ Options, Digital Equipment Corp, Hewlett Packard (US), Hamamatsu, NEC, Waida (Japan), Asea Brown Boveri Agie, Kellenberger, Studer (Switzerland)

Name:	**Al Furat**
Type:	Nuclear
Location:	An Walid
Production:	Industrial production of maraging steel centrifuges scheduled to start in mid-1991; German-built workshop to house 100-centrifuge enrichment cascade.
Foreign Contributors:	Interatom/Siemens (Germany)

Name:	**Al Hadre**
Type:	Nuclear
Location:	West of Mosul
Production:	Hydrodynamic studies and explosives testing for nuclear weapons program. Included open firing range for FAE and cluster bombs, and well equipped control bunker
Foreign Contributors:	Unknown

Name:	**Al Hakan**
Type:	CBW
Location:	Unknown
Production:	Biological weapons lab discovered by UN Special Commission, for production of unicellular proteins. Inspectors discovered virus strains imported from the US.
Foreign contributors:	US and German firms.

Name:	**Al Jezira**
Type:	Nuclear
Location:	Mosul
Production:	Uranium processing plant for industrial quantities of enrichment feedstock; UO_2, UCl_4 (for EMIS process); UF_6 for centrifuge. (Previously identified as located at Makhour, in the Jebel Qarachoq). Heavily bombed during Allied air raids. Inspected by the UN during 3rd and 4th IAEA teams.

Name:	**Al Mutasm**
Type:	Conventional weapons
Location:	Unknown
Production:	Towers for field observation posts; 4x120 mm rocket launcher, mounted on tracked AFV
Foreign Contributors:	Yugoslav state-owned defense establishments

Name:	**Al Muthena**
Type	Conventional, CBW
Location.	Al Fallujah
Production.	Naval mines, explosives HMX, RDX, CW precusors Identified by Iraq in 4/91 report to the United Nations Special Commission as a chemical weapons plant and depot
Foreign Contributors:	WET, Preussag, WTB Walter Thosti Boswau and numerous other West German companies

Name.	**Al Qadissiya**
Type:	Conventional, Nuclear
Location.	An Walid
Production:	Sniper rifles, optical sights, robotics R&D (for handling of nuclear materials), gun barrels
Foreign Contributors:	Unknown

Name.	**Al Qaim**
Type:	CBW, Nuclear
Location.	Al Qaim
Production.	Organic phosphorus compounds for chemical weapons, extraction of uranium from U-bearing phosphates ore (production capability 103 tons/year, according to UN inspection reports) Dual-use facility
Foreign Contributors:	Sybetra, Six Construct International Spie Batignolles (Belgium), Davie Power Gas (UK), Copee Rust (France) F R Schmidt (Denmark), Alesa Alusuisse Engineering Ltd (Switzerland)

Name.	**Al Qaqaa**
Type:	Missile, Nuclear, Conventional
Location	Al Hillah
Production.	Aerial bombs (500 kg), TNT filling, explosives, ammonium perchlorate for solid rocket propellant An explosion heavily damaged this plant on August 17, 1989 The Al Qaqaa State Establishment also maintains facilities at Al Fallujah and Karbala, variously identified as Project 395 or the Space Research Center and has been linked to the Iraqi nuclear weapons program
Foreign Contributors:	Multiple U S companies licensed by DoC, SNPE (France)? SNIA Bpd (Italy)?

Name:	**Al Rabee (Al Rabiya)**
Type:	Dual-use; Nuclear
Location:	Zaafarniyah
Production:	Precision machining; large-scale pieces in steel, stainless steel, and aluminium, including parts for calutron enrichment process. Run by MIMI; co-located with Digila plant
Foreign Contributors:	Agie, Hauser, Shaublin (Switzerland); BHG Hermle, Siemens, Maho, Dorries, Heidenhain (Germany); DEA (Italy); Digital Equipment Corp, Hewlett Packard, Rennishaw Probe (USA); Philips (Netherlands); Matrix Churchill (UK); Fanuc (Japan); Renault, Skiaky (France)

Name:	**Al Radwan**
Type:	Missile; Nuclear
Location:	Baghdad (Khandri)
Production:	Part of the Auqba Bin Nafi Establishment, dedicated at 70% to manufacturing assemblies for "Baghdadatrons" (Iraqi calutrons). Included five 6-meter diameter vertical turning machines to produce pole pieces for Tarmiyah separators. Also known as the Batra SCUD assembly plant. Inspected by 4th IAEA team and by UNSCOM 8.
Foreign contributors:	Waldrich Siegen, Doerries, Scharrman, Deckel, Hahn & Kolb, DEMAG, Liebherr (Germany); Goimendi (Italy); Sacem, SIP-Hauser , Aciera, AGIE (Switzerland); machine-tools from state suppliers in USSR, Bulgaria, and China

Name:	**Al Rafah**
Type:	Missile
Location:	At Taqtaqanah
Production:	Also known as the Al Shahiyat Liquid Engine Research, Development, Test & Engineering Facility, or as the Rufhah testing grounds. Located 135 km east of Kufa. Adjacent to this missile production site is a second facility, identified as Project 328, still under construction following Desert Storm, believed to be a missile test site for Silkworm and Russian "Volga" missiles.
Foreign Contributors:	Matrix Churchill (UK); Soviet, Chinese, and Bulgarian state companies; DEMAG (German: Baltimore Aircoil (USA)

Name	**Al Shaheed**
Type	Missile
Location.	Unknown
Production.	License of x-ray equipment from Great Britain in 1989, intended for "metallographical research"
Foreign Contributors	UK companies

Name:	**An Anbar Space Research Center**
Type	Missile nuclear
Location:	Karbala
Production.	Ballistic missiles, and dedicated missile testing range suspected location of nuclear warhead plant Run under the aegis of the Al Qaqaa State Establishment
Foreign Contributors:	Numerous German companies Consarc (U S), 600 Group (UK)

Name	**April 7** (Narawan fuze factory)
Type:	Conventional
Location:	Baghdad
Production:	Cardoen/ISC fuze factory for 155mm munitions
Foreign Suppliers	Industrias Cardoen (Chile), Matrix Churchill (USA), ISC (USA), Getplantrade, Switzerland

Name.	**Atomic Research Center**
Type	Nuclear
Location	Thuwaitha
Production:	Site of Osirak nuclear reactor, supplied by France and destroyed by Israel, Soviet 5 MW research reactor, nuclear fuel fabrication plant four hot cells pilot centrifuge plant for uranium enrichment, manufacturing site for calutrons production of trial quantities of UCl4 for EMIS enrichment Iraq's only nuclear site registered with the IAEA and partially subjected to international safeguards
Foreign Contributors	Snia Techint (Italy), Technatome, St Gobain Nucleaire, Framatome, CEA (France), Morgan Rushworth (UK), Maho, Heidenhain, Leybold Heraeus, Lieber (Germany), Veeco, Hewlett Packard (USA)

Name:	**Badr**
Type:	Conventional, Nuclear
Location:	Al Yusufiyah
Production.	Aerial bombs, artillery, tungsten-carbide machine tool bits A k a Badr General Establishment Contains the Al Amin workshop (qv)
Foreign Contributors	Skiaky (France), Centrifugal Casting Machines, American Bank & Trust, XYZ Options, Pratt & Whitney, Moore Special Tool, International Computer Systems/DEC, TI Coating Inc, Cincinnati Milacron (US), Aciera, Charmilles, EWAG , Schaublin, Tomos Bechler, Hauser (Switzerland), Waida, Fanuc (Japan), Adolph Waldrich Coburg, Donau, Deckel, Dorries, Siemens, Droop & Rein, Petzing & Hartman, Pfauter Gildermeister, SHW (Germany), Carvaghi, Cerutti, Innocenti (Italy), Colchester lathes, Harrison, Matrix Churchill (UK)

Name.	**Baiji**
Type:	CBW
Location:	Baiji
Production:	Chemical warfare agents Run under the aegis of the Arab Detergent Chemicals Company
Foreign Contributors	Technipetrole/TPL (Italy)

Name.	**Base West World**
Type:	Conventional
Location:	Samawa
Production.	Maintenance and retrofitting of Iraqi armored vehicles of Western origin Originally built using plans for a vehicle assembly plant provided by a West German consortium
Foreign Contributors	Weidleplan, Integral, and Kohlbecker (Germany), Giat, Sofma (France)

Name.	**Digila**
Type.	Conventional Nuclear
Location	Zaafarniyah
Production:	Computer software, hardware, process line controllers Plastics casting, using Matrix Churchill V2K machining centers licensed by the UK in 1989 United Nations inspectors found that it also made magnets and calutron parts for uranium enrichment Co located in suburb of Baghdad with Al Rabee
Foreign Contributors	HAL Computers, Matrix Churchill (UK)

Name	**Dhu Al Fiqar**
Type.	Missile
Location.	Fallujah
Production.	Condor II and upgraded SCUD missile cases Significant equipment slated for destruction by UN, 14 Feb 1992 A k a Project 124, Project 1728, Project 395
Foreign Contributors:	Werner & Plheiderer, Siemens, Hengstler, Lincoln GmbH, DEMAG (Germany), Carlo Banfi Rescaldina, Italargon, Generale Controlli, Galbadini, DEA, Torni Tachi, ECS, Resistanze Industriali, SNIA-BPD (Italy), Stankopromexport (USSR), Philips (Netherlands), Instom (UK), unidentified (Hungary)
Name	**Factory 10**
Type	Nuclear
Location:	Taji
Production:	Manufacture and assembly of gas ultracentrifuges for uranium enrichment Specialized workshop located within the Taji complex, foreign purchases organized by Nassr State Establishement for Mechanical Industries
Foreign Contributors.	H+H Metalform, MAN Technologie, Inwako, Export Union Dusseldorf GmbH (Germany) TDG, Euromac (UK)
Name	**Fao** [aka Saad 38]
Type·	Conventional, Missile
Location·	South of Baghdad
Production.	Future aircraft factory for advanced jet trainers, run by the Al Fao State Establishment, proximity fuzes, Cardoen cluster bomb plant, Fuel Air Explosives Identified in 7/91 House of Commons report as part of Project 395
Foreign Contributors·	Carlos Cardoen (Chile), Potain (France), Trebelan SA, Forjas Extruidas (FOREX) (Spain), Matrix Churchill (UK), ISC (USA)
Name	**Huteen**
Type	Conventional Nuclear
Location·	Al Iskandariyah
Production	Explosives, TNT, propellants fuzes tungsten-carbide machine-tool bits A very large facility with diversified output, possibly vehicle manufacture IAEA discovered high explosives testing for nuclear device at the Al Atheer firing

	bunker, within the Huteen walls. Foreign purchases by the Huteen General Establishement
Foreign Contributors:	Carlos Cardoen (Chile), TS Engineering (Germany); GTE Valenite, XYZ Options, Pratt & Whitney, General Industrial Diamond Co, Modern Machinery Associates, Moore Special Tool, Matrix Churchill Corp, Shalco, American Export Import (U.S.); Matrix Churchill Ltd (UK); Hertel (Germany); Sandvik (Sweden)
Name:	**Mansour**
Type:	Conventional
Location:	Baghdad
Production:	Transistors, linear integrated circuits (sister factory to Salah al Dine), run under the aegis of the Saad General Establishent. Foreign purchases also listed as intended for the Scientific Research Council and various University research projects
Foreign Contributors:	Thomson-CSF (France); multiple U.S. and UK companies
Name:	**PC1**
Type:	Dual-use; Conventional
Location:	Basra
Production:	Ethylene Oxide for fuel air explosives.
Foreign Contributors:	Multiple U.S., Germany, and UK suppliers
Name:	**PC2**
Type:	Dual-use; CBW; super-gun
Location:	Al Musayyib
Production:	Ethylene Oxide for FAE bombs; CW precursors. Foreign purchases handled by Technical Corps for Special Projects
Foreign Contributors:	Space Research Corp (Belgium, Switzerland); Walter Summers, Sheffield Forgemasters (UK); Bechtel , Lummus Crest (U.S.)
Name:	**Saad 16**
Type:	Missile; Nuclear
Location:	Mosul
Production:	Large ballistic missile research and design center, run by the Saad General Establishement
Foreign Contributors:	Consultco, Ilbau (Austria); SRC (Belgium); WTB International AG (Egypt); Sagem (France); Aviatest Blohm Maschinbau, Carl Zeiss, Degussa, Gildemeister AG, Heberger Bau,

Integral/Sauer Informatic/ICNE, Korber AG, MBB, MBB Transtechnica, Mauser-Werke, Scientific Computers GmbH, Siemens AG, Korber AG, TS Engineering, Water Engineering Trading (Germany), Snia Techint (Italy), IFAT Corp Ltd (Switzerland), Scientific Computers (UK), Electronic Associates Inc , Gould Inc , Hewlett Packard, Tektronix Inc , Scientific Atlanta, Wiltron (U S)

Name:	**Saad 21**
Type:	Missile
Location:	Mosul
Production:	Nonferrous metal plant for cartridge cases, Condor missile parts
Foreign Contributors	Steyr-Daimler-Puch (Austria)
Name·	**Saad 24**
Type	Conventional, CBW
Location:	Mosul
Production.	Gas masks, CBW protective clothing Major rubber and plastics plant Aka the Mosul Military Production Facilities
Foreign Contributors	Unknown
Name	**Saddam Engineering Complex** (Saad 5)
Type:	Conventional Nuclear, super-gun
Location:	Al Fallujah
Production:	122 mm howitzers, Ababil multiple launch rocket system possible site for supergun barrel manufacture Aka Kol 7 or Saad 5 Built by Yugoslav firms over a 9-year period (1980 1989 IAEA discovered manufacturing equipment for Type 1 (Beams) centrifuges The Saddam State Establishment for Optics, believed to be a sister organization, manufactures sniper rifles and optical sights for mortars and artillery
Foreign Contributors	Unisys, Dale Toler, RD&D International, Applied Systems, West Homestead Engineering, Kennametal, Matrix Churchill Corp (USA), Bratstvo, Zrak , Ivo Lola Ribar (Yugoslavia), Biller, Heidenhain, Blohm, Gerber, Boehringer, Gildermeister, Hennig, Siemens, Maho, Ravensburg, VDF Wohlenberg , Wotan, Werner, Wanderer (Germany), Zaver (Spain), Reishauser,Mikron, Schaublin, SIP, Studer, Tarex, Hauser, Charmilles (Switzerland) DEA (Italy) Kumming (China)

Name	**Salah al Dine** (ex Saad 13)
Type	Conventional (electronics) Nuclear
Location	Ad Dawr
Production.	Hybrid circuits, printed circuit boards and components, licensed production of battlefield computers, Rasit ground surveillance radars, Tiger G 2-D radar, Jaguar frequency hopping radars Bubble memory production planned Procurement by the Saad General Establishment, Scientific Research Council, and various University research projects
Foreign Contributors	Thomson CSF, CIMSA, Elno S A, Colly, HES, Hure (France), Deckel, Demag (Germany), Bliss (USA), Racal (UK), DEA, Fanup (Italy), Dixi, Wahli, Hauser (Switzerland), Fanuc (Japan)
Name	**Salman Pak**
Type	CBW
Location	Salman Pak
Production.	Chemical and bacteriological weapons research, United Nations inspectors in July 1991 discovered large-scale production facilities Virus fungi, and protozoa purchases made by the Iraqi Atomic Energy Commission
Foreign Contributors	Noske Kaeser, Thyssen Rheinstahl Technik, Identa Co (Germany), Atlanta Centers for Disease Control, American Type Culture Collection (U S), multiple UK companies
Name	**Samarra**
Type.	CBW
Location.	Samarra
Production:	Large-scale chemical weapons manufacturing site and research center run under the auspices of the State Establishement for Pesticides Production (SEPP), biological weapons, unit for manufacturing centrifuges for nuclear weapons Aka the Muthena State Establishment (sister plant in Fallujah)
Foreign Contributors	Karl Kolb GmbH, Preussag, WET, Ludwig Hammer GmbH Neuberger Wood and Plastics Industry, Ltd, Heberger Bau GmbH, Pilot Plant , Quast, Klaus Union (Germany), Protec SA, Carbone Lorraine, Le Vide Industriel, Pirep, Prevost, SVCM (France)

Name:	**Sawary**
Type:	Conventional
Location:	Basra area
Production:	Small naval patrol boats
Foreign Contributors.	Multiple U S companies
Name:	**Sharqat**
Type:	Nuclear
Location:	Ash-Sharqat
Production:	Site of calutron magnetic isotope uranium enrichment plant, still under construction when Allied bombing raids partially destroyed it in 1/91, under the control of the Iraqi Atomic Energy Commission Included dedicated 100 MW power plant Near the Jebel Makhour site, on western bank of the Tigris almost due west of Kirkuk
Foreign Contributors:	Unknown
Name.	**State Establishment for Heavy Engineering Equipment** (SEHEE)
Type.	Nuclear, Conventional, super-gun
Location:	Al Dura
Production.	Mechanical assemblies for super-gun, magnets and assemblies for calutrons and gas centrifuges, including vacuum chamber parts Production line to make components for the maraging steel Model 21 centrifuge (joint venture with Badr) Nuclear-specific equipment slated for IAEA destruction includes flow turning machine, expanding mandrel, electron beam welding chamber, 2 oxidation furnaces one MIG welder one brazing furnace, one heat treatment furnace, and 3 CNC machine-tools
Foreign Contributors:	ATI (Belgium), Destec International (UK), Destec Engineering B V , Philips (Netherlands), H+H Metalform Leybold Heraeus AG, Degussa, Magdeburg, Bosch (Germany), TechnoExport, Tos Hulin, Skoda (Czechoslovakia)
Name:	**Suleimaniyah**
Type:	Nuclear
Location	Suleimaniyah
Production:	Alleged site of centrifuge cascade for uranium enrichment
Foreign Contributors:	Unknown

Name.	Taj al-Ma'rik
Type:	Missile
Location.	Latifiyah
Production.	Solid fuel mixing plant for Condor II/Badr 2000, and Sakr 200 missile, casting of solid-fuel rocket motors and production of APC (ammonium perchlorate), under an Egyptian process Aka the "Soviet motor plant Located within the perimeter of the giant Al Qaqaa complex, but administratively part of the Bilat Ash Shuhadaa Establishment
Foreign Contributors	TMS, Draiswerke, Demag (Germany), Varian Linatron (USA), Consen group (Germany, Switzerland), Snia Techint (Italy), Abu Zaabal Specialty Chemical Co (Egypt)

Name	Taji (Nassr State Establishment)
Type	Conventional, nuclear
Location:	Al Taji
Production:	Artillery, T-72 tanks, production site for Gerald Bull's super-gun (Babylon Project) A k a Nassr State Establishement for Mechanical Industries, run by Safa Haboby Initial project called for 1,000 artillery pieces/year Very large, dual use facility, including steel rolling mills
Foreign Contributors:	ABB (Mannheim), Buderus Wetzlar, SHW, Wotan, Siemens, Magdeburg, H&H Metalform, Schloemann SIEMAG, Dango & Dienenthal, Ferrostaal AG, Graeser Technology Transfer GmbH, Hochtief (Essen), Klockner Industrie Anglage GmbH, Leifeld & Company (Leico), Leybold AG, LOI Industrie Anlagen, M A N , Machinenfabrtik Ravensurg, Maho, Dorries, Mannensmann Demag Huttentechnik, Blohm Maschinen, Thyssen Rheinstahl, Ravensburg, Rheinmetall, Ruhrgas, Saarstahl, Schmidt, Kranz & Co , Siemens AG, SMS Hasenclever, TBT Tiefbohrtechnik, Feld-Muehle, TuV, Zublin (Germany), Teco, Nassr State Enterprise for Mechanical Industries (Iraq), Danieli, Officina E Biglia, (Italy), HMT International Ltd (India), Georg Fischer Von Roll, Oerlikon & Shaudt, Schmeidemeccanica (Switzerland), Bull Oak Tool & Gauge, Gerber Systems Technology, Pacific, Pangborn (USA), International Computer Systems, Matrix Churchill, FMT, Wickman Bennett, Bridgeport (UK), Petitjean, Fromat (France)

Name:	**Tarmiyah**
Type:	Nuclear
Location:	At Tarmiyah
Production:	Site of calutron uranium enrichment plant Heavily damaged during Allied bombing
Foreign Contributors:	Unclassified technologies provided by Hypotronics and other U S companies

بسم الله الرحمن الرحيم

الجمهورية العراقية

وزارة الصناعة والتصنيع العسكري

هيئة التصنيع العسكري

العدد / ح / ١ / ٩٥٩

التاريخ ١٤ / ٥ / ١٩٨٩

٩ / شوال / ١٤٠٩ هـ

REPUBLIC OF IRAQ

MINISTRY OF INDUSTRY and
MILITARY MANUFACTURE

BAGHDAD

14th May 1989

Mr. Hamid D. Jafar
Chairman and Chief Executive
Crescent Petroleum Company International Limited
P. O. Box 2222
Sharjah, United Arab Emirates

<u>International Downstream Integration</u>
<u>Petroleum Industry</u>

Dear Mr. Jafar:

This letter is to confirm the establishment of the Joint Venture between the Ministry of Industry and Military Manufacture of the Republic of Iraq and Crescent Petroleúm Company International Limited ("Crescent"), for the purpose of acquisition of joint ownership interests in international petroleum refining, marketing and petrochemical assets outside of the Republic of Iraq.

Crescent is hereby authorized to contact the owners and/or managers of appropriate companies in order to discuss and negotiate the potential purchase or participation of the Joint Venture in such companies and/or in the appropriate petroleum assets.

Crescent is also authorized to discuss with the aforementioned owners/management the terms for provision of Iraqi crude oil to such assets on a long term basis in support of such transactions. The formal contract negotiations and execution will be undertaken by the relevant Agency of the Government of Iraq.

If the parties which are contacted by Crescent should require direct confirmation from the Ministry of the authority hereby vested in Crescent they may contact the undersigned at the Ministry in Baghdad on telex number 213670 "SAFAN IK", or telefax (9641) 538 4634.

Yours sincerely,

Lt. Gen. Dr. Amir H. Al-Saadi
Senior Deputy Minister

THE NEW YORKE
FEBRUARY 1, 1993

THE NEW ARMS RACE

THE IRAQI BOMB

Because the International Atomic Energy Agency is ineffectual Saddam Hussein will continue to outwit U.N. inspectors.

BY GARY MILHOLLIN

LAST week, as the United States and its coalition partners sent cruise missiles crashing into a nuclear ite near Baghdad, the message to addam Hussein was clear: Don't interere with international inspectors—let nem look anywhere, any time, and at nything, in accordance with the United Nations resolutions. The allies know nat Saddam is still hiding part of his tom-bomb program, and they're eager or the inspectors to find it. What the ales did not say is that, even though addam has now allowed the U.N. uclear inspectors back in, they probably von't find what he is hiding. They are eing thwarted by their own managenent as well as by Saddam Hussein.

The inspection trips are a constant est of nerves. The inspectors usually stay t the Sheraton Ishtar Hotel, in Baghad. "It is unlike any other Sheraton in ne world," one of them told me. "The nost gruesome thing is the dove. It's on poster in the lobby, stretched out on a ross—crucified—with blood dripping own. And on the top of the cross is vritten 'U.N.'" This inspector is disouraged, and so are many others. For lmost a year, they have found practically othing new. The Iraqis are outfoxing nem at every turn, harassing them, and naking it more and more likely that addam Hussein will wriggle out from nder the current embargo with large arts of his A-bomb effort intact. In

ings—apparently left there by mistake. These finds produced invaluable leads, which, if they had been followed aggressively, might have unveiled the essentials of the Iraqi nuclear program. The opportunity was lost, many inspectors believe, because of the timidity of the International Atomic Energy Agency, an arm of the U.N. based in Vienna. The I.A.E.A. was created in 1956 with two conflicting goals: to encourage the proliferation of atomic energy and, at the same time, to insure that the civilian nuclear projects it spawned did not make atomic bombs. After the Gulf War, the Security Council created a Special Commission to uncover the Iraqi missile, nuclear, and chemical-and-biological-weapon programs, but left control of the nuclear inspections in the hands of the I.A.E.A. The Special Commission and the I.A.E.A. immediately began to feud.

It is the Special Commission that gets intelligence about Iraq from the United States and other governments; it then designates sites for the I.A.E.A. to inspect, and it controls the inspection budget. The Special Commission also persuades friendly governments to supply technical experts, who are used to augment I.A.E.A. inspection teams. But the I.A.E.A. runs the inspections in the field, and it tends to rely on Iraqi disclosures, as it does in its civilian inspections. It also hoards any information it finds. The Special Commission does have in-

Vestern suppliers," and he
ie whole effort to stop the
on of nuclear weapons de-
making the I.A.E.A. much
ise than it has been to date."
he inspectors I've spoken
of whom insist on anonym-
r of finding anything more in
g as the I.A.E.A. remains in

now one inspector describes a
al in Iraq: "You fly in from
a C-160 Transall, operated
man Air Force—the Luft-
sit on canvas seats made for
s, and it gets cold. You take
it with you—food, water,
ipment, even tires. You need
replace the slashed tires on
les. You land at Habaniya,
bout sixty miles from Bagh-
first thing you see is a di-
us, in the green-and-white
aqi Airways. It's low-slung,
and stinking. It
to the operations
ere you get your
. Then you load
on another bus,
you to Baghdad.
is you meet your
hese are the Iraqis
be your hosts
ways with you,
u go. You assume
ugged.
otel, everything is
he lobby, the res-
e hallways, the
locatch. The ho-
bugged. In the
e is an enormous portrait of
oking down on everything.
the power of the dove. This
first notice the security guys.
t the same as the minders.
around the lobby and watch
Most of them wear dark
y are also in the hallways up-
out seven in the evening, you
st team meeting, in a confer-
off the lobby. The whole
y has one or two dozen in-
hom are from the I.A.E.A.
te from the U.N., but most
al experts lent by friendly
s. The chief inspector breaks
p into subgroups, and each
different mission. After the
ng, you meet the Iraqis—or

their representatives. These are your counterparts—the technical guys who are the experts. They ask you where you're going. They want to know, because they're going with you. They provide your security and arrange your visits. You tell them about the routine inspections—the ones where you go back to sites you've already been to—but you don't tell them about the surprise inspections, where you go to new sites. You save these until the next morning, at the last minute."

The I.A.E.A. chief inspector for Iraq is Maurizio Zifferero, a sixty-two-year-old nuclear chemist from Italy who is a specialist in plutonium processing. He was asked to join the I.A.E.A. in 1980 as a deputy director-general—a high post for which he needed his government's backing. Several U.N. inspectors condemn his conduct of the entire inspection operation and cite a string of incidents involving him which, they claim, have enabled the Iraqis to stay ahead of the game. Last week, I gave him an opportunity to comment on these incidents in a telephone conversation with him at I.A.E.A. headquarters in Vienna.

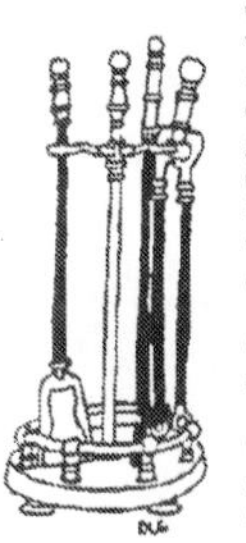

Two U.N. inspectors who were present at secret pre-inspection discussions last February in Baghdad say that they believe the Iraqis were alerted to several surprise inspections because Zifferero discussed them in areas the Iraqis had bugged. The result, a United States official says, was that on one "surprise" inspection, the Iraqis were waiting for the inspectors with coffee and doughnuts. Rejecting this charge of careless talk, Zifferero told me, "I assume that everything is bugged in the hotel, and I never mention sites in meetings." The inspectors insist that it happened, and that United States intelligence and several inspectors warned Zifferero beforehand that the areas were bugged.

The same U.N. inspectors say that Zifferero has been lax about the security of documents. Inspection-team members are supposed to keep their backpacks with them at all times, but they say they saw Zifferero relaxing in the hotel without his backpack, which at the time contained line drawings of Iraqi nuclear sites based on recent American intelligence photographs. Again, Zifferero disputes the charge. He told me he always wears his backpack and always keeps his documents in it. The seriousness of the Iraqi effort to find out what the inspectors know manifests itself outside the country. In New York, Marjatta Rautio, Finland's representative to the Special Commission, got a shock in her hotel room when she emerged from the bathroom to find a man who had been let in by the bellboy going through her wastebasket. The U.N. inspectors assume he was an Iraqi agent.

The anxieties about Zifferero's performance go beyond concern over his carelessness. He is also charged with "spoiling" fresh intelligence. A few months ago, documents seized in Iraq revealed that the Iraqis had been doing secret research on plutonium metal. Some thirteen pounds of this substance destroyed Nagasaki in 1945. Although plutonium can fuel nuclear reactors, there is no real use for plutonium metal other than in atomic bombs, so the fact that the Iraqis were working on it proved their dedication to bomb-making. It was assumed that Zifferero, as the I.A.E.A.'s chief inspector, would use the tip as a lead and do additional research. That might have produced enough detail to force the Iraqis to reveal more leads, or might have brought about a surprise inspection. Instead, to the dismay of his colleagues, Zifferero merely took the information to the Iraqis and asked for an explanation. They calmly replied that they were planning to study neutrons. This was not credible technically, but Zifferero simply quoted the Iraqi reply, without comment, in his December 10th inspection report, which did not even note that Iraq was experimenting with bomb material. Last week, Zifferero told me that the I.A.E.A. didn't consider the matter closed, and might pursue it further.

Zifferero's behavior has not escaped the eye of the United States Congress. Senate Intelligence Committee staff members have specifically requested information about Zifferero from the C.I.A. The committee should have been told, among other things, that in the mid-nineteen-seventies Zifferero, who was then working for the Italian Atomic Energy Commission, went to Baghdad to, as he put it to me last week, help "negotiate a bilateral agreement" for Italy to sell plutonium-production equipment to Iraq The equipment was essential to Iraq's plan for the bomb, and would complement a reactor that France was preparing to build there the Italian equipment would extract plutonium after the French reactor irradiated uranium Other Italian equipment, also part of the deal, would fabricate uranium into reactor fuel rods suitable for irradiation Iraq had bought a complete plutonium-production line

"We raised hell about the Italian deal," a senior American official who opposed it at the time told me Zifferero says that in 1976 he visited an Iraqi radiochemistry lab to help Iraq determine whether it could do "fuel-cycle research"—plutonium research—in its existing facilities He says that he never went back to Iraq—and never visited the facilities that were using the Italian equipment—until he was sent by the I.A.E.A. after the Gulf War

The Israelis, who were not fooled by Iraqi promises of peaceful use, destroyed the French reactor with precision bombing in 1981 But the Italian equipment survived In fact, it lived on to become the hottest topic of conversation during the I.A.E.A.'s fourth inspection, which began in late July of 1991 Before a shocked group of inspectors, a senior Iraqi official calmly revealed that Iraq had used the Italian equipment to extract plutonium in violation of Iraqi promises to the I.A.E.A.

This was a watershed for the I.A.E.A. It was the first time in history that a country was known to have broken its pledge to report all work with plutonium to agency inspectors Thus the very equipment that Zifferero helped supply was used to break the promise that he is now responsible for enforcing To make matters worse, the Iraqi official was himself a former I.A.E.A. inspector He told his outraged ex-colleagues that his I.A.E.A. experience had made it easier to dupe them "He really rubbed their noses in it," said David Kay, a former inspector and I.A.E.A. employee, who has led several inspections in Iraq and was present at the meeting

The Italian equipment was not

"Before we get started, are we showing ponytail or not?"

• •

U.N. inspectors believe that Israel's bombs also missed the French reactor's control panels, instrumentation system, and computers. These are vital components, and the Iraqis would have a hard time replacing them if they decided to build a second reactor. Some U.N. inspectors think they have tried to build a new, underground reactor; otherwise, the plutonium research makes no sense. The inspectors have searched for this reactor with no success.

The French components were yet another lead that was not followed up. The components are on an I.A.E.A. list of sensitive nuclear items that the inspectors know the Iraqis have, and which the Iraqis are required to account for, but when Zifferero asked where the components were, the Iraqis refused to produce them (while admitting that they existed). Zifferero accepted this refusal without challenge. Last week, when I pressed Zifferero about the components, he said, "This is a lead that will be followed up soon. It may have been an oversight not to follow it up earlier."

Senate Intelligence Committee staff members are still puzzled about Zifferero. The committee asked the C.I.A. months ago about his background, but still has no answer. Some senior officials at the Pentagon say they have been complaining about Zifferero for months, but they say the State Department has done nothing to have him removed. Our government is divided on this issue. Officials in at least one other major Western government also have doubts about him. According to a well-placed official, its intelligence analysts find his behavior inexplicable.

An inspector described to me a typical day in the field: "The loudspeakers in the mosques come on at 5 A.M. with the first call to prayer, so you don't need an alarm. You assemble in the lobby by seven. If you are driving, you go in a bus or a van, usually a blue-and-white Toyota. All the vehicles are Toyotas, usually with broken windows. Behind you is a U.N. vehicle driven by a U.N. medic or radio operator. It's loaded with water, communication equipment, medical kits, and food. The Iraqis provide all the other vehicles, including the one you ride in, and the drivers. In front, there's an Iraqi police car—an Olds Cutlass Ciera, with a blue light on top. If you get caught in traffic, the Iraqi police stick their arms out the windows and wave their guns. Then everybody gets out of the way."

The teams always take along a portable IMARSAT—International Marine Satellite dish. The size of a big suitcase, it beams its signal up to an IMARSAT over the Indian Ocean, enabling team members to talk to the U.N. in New York. If a team is going to a new site, its leader shouldn't tell the Iraqis where until the team actually gets in the car. Then the Iraqis radio ahead. This usually gives the site a half hour to an hour's notice. And, of course, the Iraqis can drive slowly. The site is usually protected by a high fence and anti-aircraft guns. Team members go first to the headquarters building to meet the director-general in his office. In many of the factories, there is a model of the site after it was bombed, showing every piece of damage in detail. Next to it is a model of the new site—rebuilt to the highest standards. (As they approached one site, team members saw huge piles of debris that the Iraqis had bulldozed to clear the way for a new building. The Iraqis told the team that they had taken all the machines out of the site to escape the bombing. They hid them between people's houses, and after the war they moved them into the new building.)

The team leader will ask the director-general for a history of the plant, whether it made any nuclear equipment, and other questions. The Iraqis always deny everything. The interview takes twenty or thirty minutes. Then the team tours the plant, looking for proscribed activities and for equipment on Annex 3—the list of items that Iraq is not allowed to possess under U.N. resolutions. It also looks at the plant's potential for going back into weapons production. Team members can take notes, or samples, or photographs.

The inspector says, "Normally, you don't find anything. After two or three hours, you eat lunch. Usually it's American M.R.E.s—meals ready to eat—and bottled water. Then you go to the next site. By the end of the day, you're tired, because it's hot and you've walked so much. Everybody is also demoralized, because you haven't found anything. You do this every day for about ten days"—the usual duration of a team's tour. "Back at the hotel, you have the team meeting, which is a debriefing. The subgroups report on what they did, but you can't be very specific, because the room is bugged. Then you shower, eat dinner, and go to bed."

BEFORE the war, I.A.E.A. inspectors had visited Iraqi nuclear sites twice a year for a decade. Their job was to verify that Iraq was keeping its promise not to make an atomic bomb. As late as 1990, they rated Iraqi coöperation as "exemplary." But all that time Saddam was running a vast A-bomb program under their very noses. The inspectors spent their time at a huge complex called Al Tuwaitha, where they visited only the buildings that Saddam designated; they never looked at what was going on next door. If they had, they would have found laboratories busily engaged in research on both plutonium and uranium for atomic bombs. In the words of an American official, "the I.A.E.A. missed the Iraqi bomb before the war, and now it's missing it again."

One U.N. inspector accuses the agency of "playing information games." The process of gathering information about Iraqi activities is fairly complex. The Iraqis are watched by satellites, by U-2 spy planes, and by U.N. helicopters flying out of Baghdad. They are also being informed on by a number of defectors. Most of this intelligence pours in to the C.I.A., which sifts it and prepares a package of promising sites to visit. The package then goes to both the State Department and the Pentagon, which together decide what sites to propose to the Special Commission. The British, French, German, and Russian intelligence agencies do the same. The Com-

sile and chemical-and-biological inspections, but it hasn't worked for nuclear inspections. When the missile inspectors, who work independently of the I.A.E.A., find something—a rocket-engine diagram, say—they immediately inform the governments that provided the leads. The governments then funnel the data back to their missile experts, who evaluate it and provide more leads. The Special Commission's missile inspectors thus get the benefit of concerted expert analysis, which they could never provide themselves. Each inspection builds on the previous one.

The I.A.E.A. doesn't work that way. It deems the results of its inspections confidential, and puts only a fraction of what it knows in its written reports; it gives data to the Special Commission only upon specific request. The Special Commission's inspectors complain that they don't know what to ask for, because they don't know what the agency has. Nor does the agency generally report its findings back to the governments that have supplied its intelligence leads. The result is a gap in the information loop, isolating the nuclear inspectors from competent intelligence work. The agency has no expertise in nuclear weapons, because since its inception it has inspected only civilian nuclear plants. Most of its employees are from countries without nuclear weapons, and they lack security clearances. "Your typical I.A.E.A. inspector wouldn't know a nuclear-weapon part if it fell on him," says one American bomb expert who was an inspector in Iraq. The agency has no photo interpreters—essential for understanding data from satellites. Its few available analysts cannot possibly match the power of the American, Russian, British, and French nuclear-weapon laboratories. (Incidentally, the I.A.E.A.'s practice of including as many nationalities as possible on the inspection teams allows inspectors from countries without nuclear weapons to learn in Iraq what machines are needed to build them, where to get the machines, and how to avoid detection.)

ONLY two of a total of sixteen nuclear inspections in Iraq have produced major intelligence leads, and in second inspection, the inspectors were giving the Iraqis between six and twelve hours' notice before each site visit. This was the rule laid down by I.A.E.A. headquarters in Vienna. The Iraqis understood the rule far too well; they were moving equipment from one site to another during the notice period. In June, as American satellites watched, the Iraqis went to hiding places in the desert, dug up giant machines for processing uranium, loaded them on trucks, and drove them to a site called Abu Gharib, to which the inspectors had been denied entry. Then the satellites saw the trucks move the equipment from Abu Gharib to a second site, at Al Fallujah.

David Kay, the American who led the team, says that he got this information in Iraq at about 3 A.M. He then called together six inspectors "for a long walk in Baghdad," during which they could talk without being bugged. They agreed to do a zero-notice inspection at Al Fallujah that morning, despite the policy of giving six to twelve hours' notice. Kay told the Iraqis that he was going "in the direction of" a site the team had already toured—a site that happened to be on the road to Al Fallujah. Kay managed to get his vehicle in front of the column and went right by the first site. The Iraqis "went crazy," Kay says. "They turned on red lights, pulled us over, and argued with us, but we got to Fallujah anyway." There they were denied entry, but they managed to photograph trucks leaving through another gate, while the Iraqis fired bullets over their heads.

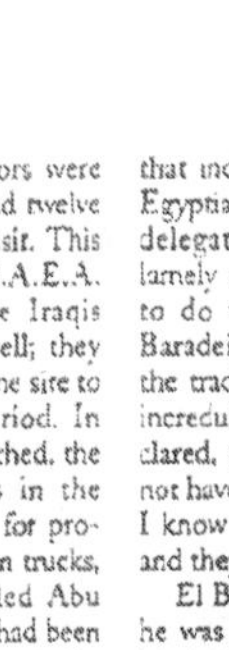

The moment was dramatic: the inspectors had the first clear proof that Saddam was trying to make a bomb. The equipment included huge seventeen-foot magnets, weighing more than fifty tons, which could be used only for enriching uranium—raising it from its natural state to nuclear-weapon grade. Kay saw it as a vindication of the team. "We all pulled together and it worked," he said. "Even though we had to break I.A.E.A. rules to do it."

The I.A.E.A. then sprang into action. It and the Special Commission rushed to Iraq a high-level delegation that included Mohamed El Baradei, an Egyptian on the I.A.E.A legal staff. The delegation found the Iraqis arguing lamely that the equipment had nothing to do with uranium enrichment. El Baradei, fresh on the scene, embodied the tradition of the I.A.E.A. Before an incredulous group of inspectors, he declared, as Kay recalls it, "The Iraqis do not have a uranium-enrichment program. I know so, because they are my friends and they have told me that they don't."

El Baradei was wrong, of course. But he was following the line laid down by his I.A.E.A. superiors. If they had had their way, Kay's inspection might never have occurred. After the first inspection, in May, Iraq had accounted for all the imported nuclear material it had previously informed the I.A.E.A. about, which balanced the agency's accounts.

"The I.A.E.A. was lucky," a former inspector who was on the first team says. Kay and this inspector say that Zifferero and his boss, Hans Blix, the director-general of the I.A.E.A., wanted to put out a report at the end of May concluding that everything was fine. But a minority of inspectors, mostly Americans, wouldn't go along. They couldn't understand why the Iraqis had left some of the bombed buildings untouched while razing others, even tearing out foundations as far as several metres down. The Americans thought that the Iraqis might be concealing nuclear-weapon work, and they wanted the report to say so. "It all looked very suspicious," the inspector said. "But the I.A.E.A. wasn't interested. It wanted to pasteurize our language and put the report out anyway." The I.A.E.A. was saved from humiliation by a defector, who turned up just before the report was to be released and told Western intelligence about the equipment. A few weeks later, Kay succeeded in finding and photographing it.

Kay also led the only other team that produced major intelligence leads. After arriving in Baghdad late in the afternoon on September 22, 1991, the team set out early the next morning. Kay pointed toward the Al Rashid Hotel, and told the Iraqis simply to "drive that way." By 6 A.M., the team was searching a nine-story building in Baghdad from the top down. It turned out to be where the Iraqis were designing facilities for their first atomic bomb. When they reached the basement, a few hours later, the team found trunkfuls of classified documents from the Iraqi Atomic Energy Commission.

This discovery sparked an intense confrontation. The Iraqis kept the team in the parking lot until 7 P.M., confiscated the documents until 2 A.M. the next day, and then gave only some of them back. What the Iraqis didn't know was that the inspectors had spirited out two reports marked "Top Secret." These crucial papers contained the bomb design. The design was crude but workable, and would have produced a weapon with nearly twice the power of the Hiroshima bomb.

EARLY on the morning of September 24th, Kay's team began a search of two other buildings, using the same tactics. These buildings turned out to be the headquarters of the entire Iraqi A-bomb program, code-named Petrochemical 3. The team turned up personnel lists and procurement records, and four hours later there was another confrontation. The Iraqis demanded that the team surrender its records, its photographs, and its videotapes. When the inspectors refused, the Iraqis held them at the site. This was the celebrated "parking-lot incident"—a four-day standoff in the scorching Baghdad heat. The team lived near its immobilized bus until the Iraqis finally backed down.

Eventually, the team hauled out pay records, computer files, and more than sixty thousand pages of documents, including the two top-secret reports on bomb design. The reports were a gold mine of intelligence nuggets: they revealed numerous aspects of Saddam's bomb-manufacturing effort and still constitute the primary evidence of how close he was to the bomb when the war broke out.

The aggressive tactics required for this breakthrough did not please the I.A.E.A. Zifferero, who was not in Iraq at the time of that inspection, later told an inspector who was there that the episode was "one of the worst things that ever happened." And, according to Kay, Hans Blix reacted by saying that Kay was not going to be assigned to any more inspections in Iraq. Kay then resigned from the agency. He and another American inspector who was in the parking-lot standoff maintain that "everybody associated with the parking-lot incident became persona non grata" at the I.A.E.A. As for the sixty thousand pages of documents, only about fifteen per cent of them have been translated from the Arabic, although summaries of most documents have been completed. The titles alone show that the documents are rich in procurement data and other leads. The I.A.E.A. has farmed most of them out to coalition governments for translation, but none has committed the resources to do the job effectively. Thus, the inspectors are like treasure hunters who can read only scraps of a map.

Acting on an intelligence tip from a United States ally, Zifferero finally had a chance to lead his own team into the Petrochemical 3 headquarters last December. The team was an unusual combination. It had Special Commission inspectors from New York, who were looking for missile and chemical-and-biological-weapons documents, and I.A.E.A. inspectors who suspected the Iraqis of having moved nuclear documents back into the building. On this particular trip, I'm told, Zifferero appeared to observe security precautions more closely. Nevertheless, the difference in methods and attitudes between the I.A.E.A. and the Special Commission was striking.

When Zifferero gave the order to begin, the Special Commission's "document-exploitation team" fanned out quickly to surround and occupy the building. Zifferero, however, had no experience with rapid engagement. "As team leader, he had to be ready to order teams to go here, go there—immediately—and to order Iraqi escorts to go with them," a missile inspector later said. "But he was totally unable to do that—he couldn't keep up."

The result was a breakdown in command and control. The Special Commission and I.A.E.A. inspectors started to debate procedures in front of the Iraqis, and the Iraqis themselves began to move documents. One threw a bundle out a window, and another picked it up and ran with it to a city bus. A Special Commission inspector dashed in front of the bus to stop it, but had to leap out of the way to avoid being run over. (The Iraqis later returned what they said were the documents.) In this instance, the I.A.E.A. procedures were probably harmless, because Petrochemical 3 had been turned into a fundamentalist seminary with low security, making it an unlikely hiding place for sensitive information. The intelligence tip from the allied government was probably a dud.

To put the blame on Zifferero or Hans Blix for the I.A.E.A.'s attitude and its unwillingness to run intrusive inspections is to miss the point. Many inspectors don't see Zifferero as a villain. They say that he is simply the wrong man for the job. One inspector sums it up this way: "Zifferero has poor organizational skills in the field, and he is out of his element when it comes to getting things done if the opposition doesn't want you to." Other inspectors agree that he doesn't have the temperament for confrontation. The fundamental problem is the I.A.E.A. itself. "The agency's charter didn't have in mind the amplitude of inspections called for by the U.N. resolutions" on Iraq, says Gerard C. Smith, who was Ambassador at Large for Nonproliferation Matters in the Carter Administration and represented the United States on the I.A.E.A.'s board of governors. The agency was established in the glory days of nuclear power, when people thought that electricity from the atom would be "too cheap to meter." It was given the job of spreading nuclear technology to developing countries, mostly by promoting exports from advanced countries. At the same time, it was supposed to inspect the exports to make sure they weren't used to make atomic bombs. The conflict of interest is obvious: if the agency catches somebody making bombs, it means that the nuclear exports were too dangerous to have been sold in the first place, and should not have been promoted.

Iraq is the perfect example. The I.A.E.A. gave Saddam a clean bill of nuclear health for a decade before the invasion of Kuwait. Why would the agency now want to find even more evidence of how badly it was duped? "It's against the I.A.E.A.'s culture to find anything," says an American expert who was on one of the early inspection teams. Only this "culture" can explain Zifferero's statements to the press. Just a year ago, in February, he told Reuters that "practically the largest part of Iraq's nuclear program has now been identified—probably what is missing is just details." He made this statement after his team's tenth inspection trip—the one during which he is said to have discussed surprise-inspection sites in the bugged hotel.

On September 2nd, Zifferero told Reuters that Iraq's nuclear program "is at

"I'm behind on my carrots."

zero now," and that the Iraqis "have stated many times to us that they have decided at the higher political level to stop these activities." He also made the spectacularly improbable statement "This we have verified." Even the I.A.E.A. had to disavow that; it put out a statement the next day blaming the press for giving "a misleading impression of his understanding of the situation," and saying that it is "too early to conclude" that Iraq's entire nuclear program had been uncovered. Zifferero, undeterred, reiterated the same day that "there is no possibility of a substantial organized [nuclear] program going on in Iraq now." And, for good measure, he said a few days later, "I don't believe in the existence of an underground reactor."

When I asked Zifferero about these statements last week, he insisted, "The Iraqi program is now dormant. Iraq has other priorities, and now has no labs in which to continue the program."

ZIFFERERO stated in his latest report that the inspection team "was not harassed." If that was the case, it was unique. On most trips, the inspectors tell me, the harassment is unrelenting. "The Iraqis start calling about 1 A.M.," one of them said. "They threaten you or they just dial to wake you up. You also get notes under the door." The Special Commission inspectors say the notes are often death threats. Some of the German members got notes saying that what the United States did to Iraq during Desert Storm was the same as what the United States did to Germany during the Second World War, so the Germans shouldn't cooperate with the "American" inspections.

Another inspector says, "They also come into your room, whether you're there or not. You have to put everything valuable in your backpack, and you have to assume that if you don't sleep with it tied to you, you'll lose it. This creates a lot of tension and makes it hard to sleep." Team members are also harassed in restaurants, another inspector adds. "Somebody will stop at your table, pick up your plate, and dump your food in your lap. This is always a young, well-dressed, physically fit Iraqi male."

On two occasions, while groups of inspectors were standing in the hotel atrium, someone threw a light bulb terrified everybody, because when it hit the floor it sounded like a rifle shot. A Special Commission inspector says, "They even came up to one of our people in the street and threw diesel fuel on him." Another inspector tells me that "after two weeks of this, you're exhausted. Nobody is sad on the trip back to the airport. When the plane takes off, everybody applauds."

THE Special Commission flatly rejects Zifferero's rosy picture of Iraq's nuclear status. In its reports to the Security Council, the Commission accuses the Iraqis of "non-coöperation, concealment and sometimes false information" in all areas that are being inspected, and goes as far as to say that they have "actively falsified the evidence." The Special Commission's inspectors still want to find (1) parts of the giant machines that the Iraqis used to raise uranium to nuclear-weapon grade, to learn how much progress they made; (2) the identities of Iraqi nuclear personnel, to learn what those people are doing; (3) records of test explosions, to learn the status of the Iraqi bomb design; (4) other records of the nuclear-weapon program, to learn whether all its components have been discovered; (5) Iraq's foreign sources of technical advice, to cut them off; and (6) Iraq's network of foreign equipment suppliers, to make sure that the network does not revive as soon as the embargo is lifted.

These inspectors also fear that Saddam may be hiding experimental centrifuges used to raise uranium to weapon grade, and an underground reactor that could secretly make plutonium for bombs. They are not likely to find any of these things under the aegis of the I.A.E.A. Zifferero's press statements alone have undermined his credibility. Can he plausibly search for something that he says doesn't exist? The solution to the problem, these inspectors argue, is to transfer authority for the nuclear inspections to the Special Commission, which would require a U.N. resolution. The I.A.E.A. knows how to do only one thing: visit declared sites. In civilian inspections, a country tells the agency what it is doing and invites it in, and then the agency inspects only agreed-upon items at agreed-upon sites. It closes its eyes to anything else. And, worse, it usually doesn't reveal what it finds. But no bomb-builder ever admits what he is doing, let alone where he is doing it. And Saddam Hussein is certainly no exception. (However, some United States government analysts think that Saddam is likely to make a spectacular offer soon to President Clinton. It will probably contain a dramatic revelation about one or more of the weapon programs and will probably include information—and disinformation—about Western companies that provided crucial help. Saddam's goal will be to drive a wedge into the Gulf War coalition by convincing some of its members that he has finally come clean, and that the embargo should be lifted.)

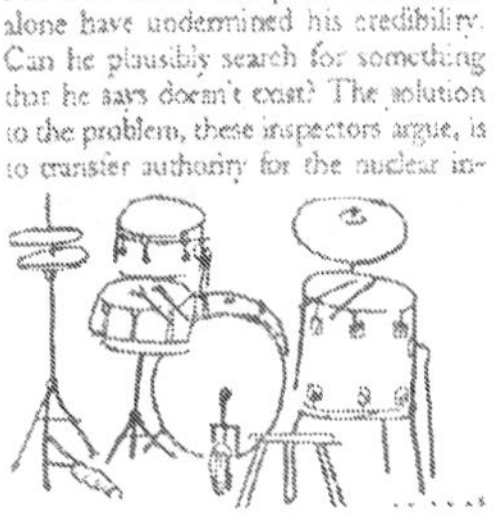

There are still two big jobs to do in Iraq: find the rest of Saddam's bomb program and prevent him from gaining control of resources already found and reconverting them to bomb-making. To accomplish the first task, the inspectors need to change tactics. "We have diplomats when we should have detectives," a knowledgeable American official says. "This is a shell game, and you have to stop the other guy from moving the shells." The inspectors are reluctant to go into government ministries, universities, and private homes, but that is their best chance of finding the nuclear-bomb program. United States intelligence is convinced that the program is on computer data bases. Only a data base could keep track of the design, manufacturing, testing, and procurement data essential to continuity. The computers are believed to be at universities or in the homes of key members of the nuclear program. "We think that if the inspectors went into these places they would find some important stuff," says an informed United States official.

The United States government has also proposed that the Special Commission adopt an "area strategy," in which the Commission would pick an area and search every building and every cave be-

"You know you have my support on pork and bears, but where do you stand on chicken and dumplings?"

• •

are only a few places where Iraq has the people communications and infrastructure to continue to run the program," an American official says, "so you can designate the areas." The goal is to freeze Saddam's shells in place so that any moves by the Iraqis could be detected.

This strategy would require more inspectors. The United States proposes that a score or more move into Iraq permanently. The plan is that they would work in prefabricated bug-free quarters flown in from America, enabling them to talk to New York without Iraqi ears bent over their telephones. When new intelligence develops, they could strike quickly, hitting two or three areas at a time, thus overwhelming Saddam's disinformation specialists.

The United States proposal was submitted to Rolf Ekeus, of Sweden, the head of the Special Commission. Ekeus has been a tenacious leader of the Special Commission inspectors, but, with the exception of the proposal for secure prefab quarters, he has rejected the American plan, out of concern that the U.N. might lose control of the inspections in the field. The inspectors would be mostly British and American, and he fears that once they began to generate hot intelligence leads which would be analyzed in London and Washington the U.N. could be pushed out of the information loop. He also points out that Saddam would have more ammunition for his charge that the inspections are really an Anglo-Saxon operation.

It may be that Ekeus can no longer afford these qualms. The information tug-of-war between the C.I.A. and the I.A.E.A. has reached a deadlock. As David Kay describes it, "The I.A.E.A. is saying, 'Tell us where to go,' and the C.I.A. is saying, 'Do something to get something moving so we can see it.'" The C.I.A. has the better argument: some action is needed to flush Saddam's nuclear covey from its hiding place.

The other big job in Iraq is to guard what has been found. By mid-November, the I.A.E.A. had compiled a list of six hundred and ninety pieces of sensitive equipment, of which eighty-four have direct nuclear-weapon applications. Virtually all the equipment was imported, and most of it is "dual use"—capable of making either civilian products or weapons of mass destruction. The U.N. must decide whether to destroy it, monitor it, or release it to the Iraqis.

The United States wants the inspectors to destroy any item that was either used to make nuclear weapons or intended for such use. The I.A.E.A. doesn't want to go along with that proposal. It argues that Iraq would still have many machines—some still in their crates—equivalent to the ones destroyed, and therefore destruction would not really derail the Iraqi bomb program but would only be punitive. The I.A.E.A. would rather let the Iraqis use the machines under its monitoring.

But Iraq smuggled many of those machines out of Western countries illegally, and it falsely promised to confine others to peaceful use. For example, in the late nineteen-eighties the Iraqi government secretly took over a British machine-tool maker called Matrix Churchill, which apparently lied to British customs about the uses to which its exports would be put in Iraq. According to a U.N. report, Matrix Churchill supplied thirty-three machines with nuclear-weapon potential. Matrix Churchill also sold Iraq nineteen additional machines, which were found in damaged condition. Letting Iraq keep these machines rewards Iraqi fraud.

If the inspectors were allowed to destroy any sensitive equipment not bought honestly, they would catch most of the machines now in dispute. Iraq is already supposed to disclose its supplier network, to comply with U.N. resolutions. But that network is one of its most important secrets. If Iraq won't say where it got the machines, the inspectors should assume that it got them dishonestly. To leave the machines in Iraqi hands, one inspector says, would be folly, for "Iraq already has the people and the know-how, and it will still have the dual-use equipment, so if the world gets tired of monitoring Iraq is back in business."

Without new leadership and protection, the inspection effort will die by demoralization. The stakes are enormous. An American A-bomb expert who served on one of the inspection teams says that if Saddam had not invaded Kuwait "he could have had a first crude device by now, deliverable with great accuracy in a Ryder truck." There is no evidence that any of Saddam's nuclear scientists have been laid off, and unless the inspectors find the rest of his nuclear program and neutralize it the world will face the same uncertainty about the Iraqi bomb in 1993 that it faced before the war. •

The New York Times

MONDAY, APRIL 26, 1993

Iraq's Bomb — an Update

By Diana Edensword
and Gary Milhollin

WASHINGTON

Soon, possibly this week, the U.N. will report that its inspectors in Iraq have found yet another cache of [illegible] equipment for making nuclear weapons. [illegible] the International Atomic Energy Agency, [illegible] He [illegible] in September that President Saddam Hussein's nuclear weapons program was "neutralized" and "at zero." He even said that Iraq had "decided at the highest political levels to stop [illegible]"

Saddam Hussein never told the I.A.E.A. about the newly discovered equipment, as required by U.N. resolutions. And he continues to [illegible] the inspectors, indicating that he has more to hide. In March 1992, Iraq's Deputy Prime Minister, Tariq Aziz, told inspectors that Iraq had not relinquished the right to build weapons of mass destruction.

Before his army marched into Kuwait in August 1990, Saddam Hussein had a [illegible] bomb design, more [illegible] a multi-billion dollar nuclear manufacturing base and a global supply network able to [illegible] its Western export controls, especially those in Germany. His Western-trained scientists had produced small amounts of plutonium and enriched uranium, the fuels in the bombs that destroyed Nagasaki and Hiroshima. They [illegible] the I.A.E.A. inspected regularly.

If Saddam Hussein had left Kuwait alone he might have had his first bomb by now. He still has his scientists on the payroll and has [illegible] of many of his [illegible] suppliers. He has even started to get European and American [illegible] on future oil sales [illegible] dollars for a renewed bomb effort.

[illegible] of nuclear related equipment in Iraq today. It draws on [illegible] records and reports by inspection teams. The names of manufacturers who may not have shipped their products directly to Iraq, are given where known. Iraq claimed the equipment was for civilian use. The U.S. Government [illegible] of the material destroyed. The I.A.E.A. [illegible] under the agency's monitoring. [illegible] that failed to detect Iraq's bomb program in the first place.

Diana Edensword is a research [illegible] of the Wisconsin Project on Nuclear Arms Control. Gary Milhollin is the director of [illegible]

Found but Not Destroyed or Removed

These items have been tagged for possible destruction, monitoring by the I.A.E.A. or [illegible] to Iraq:

- [illegible] tons of natural uranium (Brazil, Niger and Portugal).
- 1.7 tons of enriched uranium (Italy).
- 255 tons of HMX, a high explosive for detonating atomic bombs.
- 69 machines that shape metal into centrifuge parts, by [illegible], Kaltenbach & Albrecht, Leifeld and [illegible] (Germany), Matrix Churchill (Britain) and Schaublin (Switzerland).
- Mass spectrometers to monitor bomb-fuel production, by Finnigan-MAT (U.S., Germany).
- Two electric frequency converters to power atomic bomb fuel production, by [illegible] (Switzerland).
- More than 200 valves that can process atomic bomb fuel, by Balzers, VAT (Switzerland) and Nupro (U.S.).
- Two coordinate-measuring machines to [illegible] centrifuge production, by DEA (Italy).
- 76 mixer-settler units to extract [illegible] by [illegible] AB (Sweden).
- Machines for milling metal by [illegible], SHW and [illegible] (Germany), [illegible] (Italy) and [illegible] (Spain).
- Two assembly presses and two balancing machines to make centrifuges.
- One resin-mixing and [illegible] machine to support electromagnetic uranium enrichment by [illegible]
- [illegible] machine [illegible] to make centrifuge motors by Arburg (Germany).
- One [illegible] hydraulic press to shape explosive atomic bomb parts.
- One mainframe computer used to process nuclear atomic bomb codes by NEC (Japan).
- Two [illegible] furnaces for making centrifuge parts by Degussa (Germany).
- One electron beam welder to assemble centrifuges, by Sciaky (France).
- Tantalum metal sheets for making crucibles to cast atomic bomb cores.

Still Missing

These items are suspected or known to be in Iraq, but have not been found or accounted for:

- More than $1 million worth of computers, electronic testing machines, computer graphics equipment and frequency synthesizers licensed for shipment to atomic bomb builders by Hewlett Packard (U.S.).
- More than $7 million worth of computers licensed for shipping to atomic bomb builders by International Computer Systems (U.S.).
- Nuclear reactor control panels, instruments and computers salvaged from a damaged reactor by the [illegible] Cerbag (France).
- Computers and instruments capable of analyzing metals and powders for atomic bomb manufacture, licensed for shipping to an atomic bomb builder by Siemens (Germany, U.S.).
- $42,000 worth of computers for a nuclear weapon testing site, licensed for shipment by EZ [illegible] (U.S.).
- $30,000 worth of electronic and computing equipment to measure neutrons and gamma rays, licensed for shipping by Canberra Industries and Canberra Elektronik (U.S., Germany).
- Five frequency converters capable of powering centrifuges, by [illegible] (Switzerland).
- Parts that collected enriched uranium in electromagnetic enrichment machines.
- One [illegible] machine to make centrifuge motors, by Arburg (Germany).
- One powder press suitable for compacting nuclear fuels, by [illegible] (U.S.).
- $1.5 million worth of [illegible] presses, by [illegible] (Germany).
- $2.2 million worth of computers licensed to be shipped to an atomic bomb builder by Unisys (U.S.).
- $200,000 worth of computers and electronic and photographic equipment for nuclear weapons laboratories [illegible] by [illegible] (U.S.).
- $[illegible] worth of computers licensed for shipping to an atomic bomb builder to run its machine tools, by [illegible] (U.S.).
- [illegible] plant to [illegible] by [illegible]
- More than [illegible] mixer-settler units to extract [illegible] by [illegible] AB (Sweden).
- Centrifuge [illegible] to enrich uranium.
- Underground reactor and [illegible] plutonium.
- Records of Iraq's foreign sources of expertise on uranium enrichment, foreign equipment suppliers and explosive tests of atomic bomb components.
- Records revealing identities and current activities of Iraqi nuclear personnel, including those trained by [illegible] [illegible], Leybold, [illegible] and PSI (Germany), Balzers [illegible], Chemator (Finland), [illegible] and [illegible] (Britain).
- A computer database showing scope and extent of the entire nuclear weapons program.

The New York Times

OP-ED FRIDAY, APRIL 24, 1992

Iraq's Bomb, Chip by Chip

The U.S. Commerce Department licensed the following strategic American exports for Saddam Hussein's atomic weapon programs between 1985 and 1990. Virtually all of the items were shipped to Iraq; all are useful for making atomic bombs or long-range missiles. United Nations inspectors in Iraq are still trying to find most of them. The list is based on Commerce Department export licensing records; the dollar amount of each transaction is as claimed by the exporting company. It was compiled by Gary Milhollin, a law professor at the University of Wisconsin and director of the Wisconsin Project on Nuclear Arms Control, and Diana Edensword, a research analyst at the project.

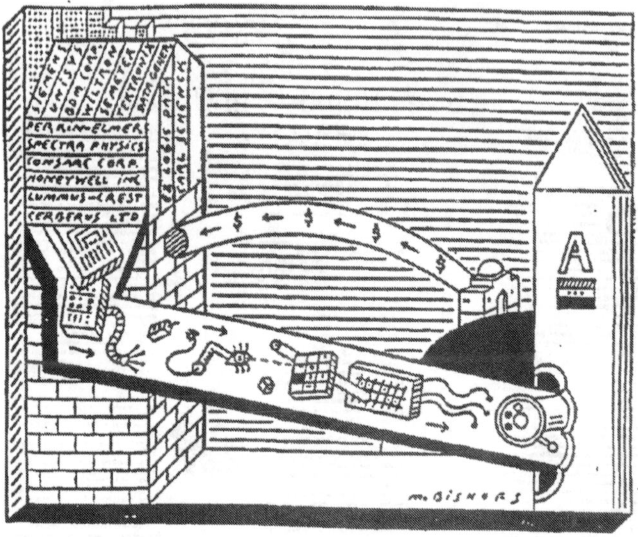

Atomic Bomb Builders

Sales to Iraqi Atomic Energy Commission, the main atomic research laboratory; Badr and Doura sites, where bomb fuel was made; Al Qaqaa site, where detonators were made

Canberra Elektronik: computers for measuring gamma rays and fast neutrons — $30,000
Cerberus Ltd.: computers — $55,181
Hewlett Packard: computers, electronic testing, calibration and graphics equipment — $25,900
International Computer Systems: computers useful for graphic design of atomic bombs and missiles — $1,500,000
Perkin-Elmer: computers and instruments useful for quality control of bomb fuels — $268,000
TI Coating Inc.: equipment for coating metal parts, useful for bomb production — $215,708

Atomic Bomb and Missile Builders

Sales to Ministry of Industry and Military Industrialization, which ran the atomic bomb, missile and chemical weapon factories; Nassr state enterprise, where equipment for enriching atomic bomb fuel was made; Salah Al Din site where electronic equipment for missiles and atomic bombs was made; Ministry of Defense, which oversaw missile and atomic bomb development

Axel Electronics: capacitors — $84,000
BDM Corporation: computers; computer-assisted design equipment — $33,000
Canberra Elektronik: computers for computer-assisted design — $31,551
Carl Zeiss: microcomputers for mapping — $184,545
Consarc Corporation: computers to run machine tools capable of manufacturing atomic bomb parts (this sale was stopped by Presidential order in June 1990) — $515,550
Data General Corporation: computers for mapping — $334,005
Gerber Systems: computers to run machine tools capable of manufacturing atomic bomb and missile parts — $187,438
Hewlett Packard: computers for making molds; frequency synthesizers and other equipment useful for operating secured military communications systems — $1,015,500
Honeywell Inc.: computers — $253,123
International Computer Systems: computers for manufacturing, tool design and graphics — $1,497,700
International Computers Ltd.: computers — $581,856
Leybold Vacuum Systems: computer controlled welder used by Iraqis to produce centrifuges for making atomic bomb fuel — $1,400,000
Lummus Crest: radio spectrum analyzers, design computers, computers for factories producing mustard gas ingredients — $250,000
Rockwell Collins International: equipment for navigation, direction finding, radar communications or airborne communications — $137,508
Sackman Associates: computers and instruments capable of analyzing metals and powders for atomic bomb and missile manufacture — $80,500
Siemens Corporation: computers and instruments capable of analyzing metals and powders for atomic bomb and missile manufacture — $78,000
Spectra Physics: lasers, detection and tracking equipment for lasers — $18,000
Unisys Corporation: computers — $2,500,000
Wild Magnavox Satellite Survey: computers for processing satellite images that are useful for military mapping and surveillance — $270,000
Zeta Laboratories: quartz crystals for military radar — $1,195,000

Missile Builders

Sales to Saad 16, the main missile research site; State Organization for Technical Industry, the procurement organization for missile sites that bought most Scud missile parts and equipment

BDM Corporation: computers, superconducting electronics — $28,885
Carl Schenck: computers — $18,228
KZ Logic Data: computers — $27,500
Finnigan MAT: computers that U.N. inspectors believe monitored uranium enrichment for atomic bomb fuel — $483,000
Hewlett Packard: electronic testing equipment, computers, frequency synthesizers, radio spectrum analyzers — $599,232
International Computer Systems: computers — $1,315,000
International Imaging Systems: computers for processing satellite data, infrared equipment capable of aerial reconnaissance and military surveillance — $888,000
Lummus Crest: computers to aid factory design — $88,725
Perkin-Elmer: computers — $26,560
Scientific Atlanta: equipment for producing radar antennas — $820,000
Semetex Corporation: computers — $5,129,781
Spectral Data Corporation: satellite data processing equipment — $25,000
Tektronix: high-speed electronics useful in developing atomic bombs and missiles, radio spectrum analyzers for developing microwave equipment — $133,000
Thermo Jarrell Ash Corporation: computers for testing materials — $230,545
Unisys Corporation: computers for production control — $7,795
Veeco Instruments Inc.: computers for factory design — $4,616
Wiltron Company: equipment for testing radar antennas — $49,557

The New York Times Magazine
MARCH 8, 1992
30–36

BUILDING SADDAM HUSSEIN'S BOMB

BY GARY MILHOLLIN

"ABOUT THIS BIG" HIGH IN THE UNITED Nations building in New York, a U.N. official is holding his arms out in a circle, like a man gripping a beach ball. "About a yard across, weighing about a ton."

This is the Iraqi bomb — slightly smaller than the one dropped on Hiroshima, but nearly twice as powerful — packing an explosive force of at least 20,000 tons of TNT. The official is dramatizing a drawing he has made in his notebook, based on documents seized in Iraq. He is sure that the bomb, if built to the specifications in the drawing, will work.

At the bomb's center is an explosive ball of weapon-grade uranium. Around this is a layer of natural uranium to boost the yield and a second layer of hardened iron to keep the core from blowing apart prematurely. If the bomb is to detonate properly, these parts must have just the right dimensions, and there must be a firing circuit accurate to billionths of a second. Documents in the United Nations' possession show that the Iraqis have all the right dimensions and the necessary firing circuit.

This is the bomb that, according to U.N. estimates, Saddam Hussein was 18 to 24 months from building when the gulf war started. It is the bomb he is still likely to build, despite the war and the most intrusive nuclear inspections in history, unless the United Nations changes its tactics.

"They are pouring concrete as we speak," says a U.N. official at the next desk. Saddam, he says, is rebuilding the bombed nuclear sites in plain view of U.N. inspectors. "He is even planting trees and re-landscaping," he adds, "to boost employee morale." Another U.N. official has a similar story. During a visit to the Iraqi nuclear weapon testing site at Al Atheer, he says, his Iraqi hosts looked him in the eye and said, "We are waiting for you to leave."

Since the inspections started last spring, the Iraqi disinformation specialists who serve as guides have done their best to baffle the inspectors. In one instance, the Iraqis hid reactor fuel by loading it on the back of a truck and driving it around the reactor site, always staying about 200 yards in front of the inspection team. The fuel contained weapon-grade material.

Perhaps the most notorious confrontation occurred when inspectors followed an intelligence tip to a cache of sensitive documents. In an attempt to elude the Iraqis, each of the 44 team members hid a stack of papers inside his clothing. Rather than strip-search the inspectors before video cameras, the Iraqis simply forbade them to leave, leading to a four-day standoff in a Baghdad parking lot under a scorching summer sun. Only after a unanimous vote of support by the Security Council did Iraq finally relent.

That spirited encounter is now as much a part of history as the brief triumph of the 100-hour war. Under the cease-fire terms, inspectors for a U.N. Special Commission were charged with the "destruction, removal or rendering harmless" of Iraq's nuclear weapon potential. But after months of chasing increasingly fruitless intelligence leads, morale on the Special Commission is scraping rock bottom.

The Iraqis know it, too. "They've started laughing at us," one U.N. official says, adding that the Iraqis have even threatened individual inspectors. "They have basically told our people that they know where we live," he says in exasperation.

The problem is that the inspectors have exhausted their information. The first inspections were fueled by leads from Iraqi defectors and the chance discovery of the sensitive documents in Baghdad. But that luck has run out just as the Iraqis have organized their resistance to the inspections. Recently, in fact, they told the inspectors that "you won't find any more documents in this country."

That remark came after a U.N. team had charged into several suspected reactor sites, following intelligence leads that turned out to be duds. "All we found were empty warehouses, cement factories making real cement and prisons with real prisoners," one inspector says. The inspectors believe they have reached a dead end.

The inspectors' defeat raises a chilling prospect: In the absence of a major new U.N. effort, Saddam Hussein is still likely to get the bomb. Thus, Iraq has become a test case for nuclear proliferation. If war and a full-court press by the United Nations cannot stop an outlaw nation like Iraq from making the bomb, what will it take to stop countries like Iran, North Korea and Libya?

In a sense, what is being played out in Iraq is the first battle of a new cold war, fought with spies, international pressure and export controls. The West may have won the first cold war against the Soviet Union, but it is losing the second to Iraq and other nations that want to get the bomb.

SADDAM HAS HAULED HIMSELF UP THE

Gary Milhollin directs the University of
[illegible]

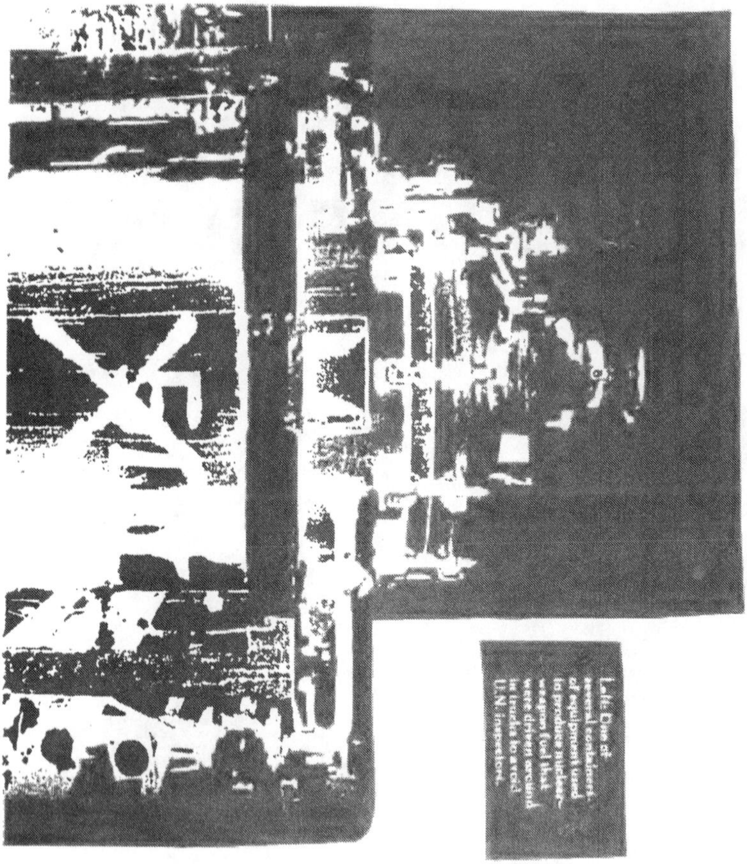

Left: One of several containers of equipment used to produce nuclear-weapon fuel that were driven around in trucks to avoid U.N. inspectors.

trying to find them. Other similarly favored nations could easily follow Saddam's example, given existing export laws. Iran and Libya are now maneuvering into this position.

Iraqi scientists know, for example, how to cast uranium metal into bomb parts in a vacuum furnace. The vacuum prevents molten uranium from burning in air. At Al Atheer, U.N. inspectors found vacuum furnaces made by a German firm, Arthur Pfeiffer Vakuum Technik. The inspectors rejected Iraq's claim that the furnaces were for scientific research.

The inspectors also found a large "isostatic" press, made by a Swedish-Swiss firm, Asea Brown Boveri. This, too, the Iraqis claimed was for research. But the U.N. team thinks the machine was for shaping the high-explosive charges that set off a nuclear chain reaction. These specially shaped charges are wrapped around the bomb core and set off simultaneously, creating a shock wave that travels inward, "imploding" and compressing the core. When the core is compressed to sufficient density, the nuclear chain reaction begins.

How did the Iraqis learn to use such specialized equipment? In large part from the United States Government. In August 1989, the Pentagon and the Department of Energy invited three Iraqis to attend a "detonation conference" in Portland, Ore. Financed by American taxpayers, the meeting brought together experts from around the world to explain to the Iraqis and others how to produce shock waves in any desired configuration. There were even lectures on HMX, the high explosive of choice for nuclear detonation, and on flyer plates, devices that help produce the precise shock waves needed to ignite A-bombs. Both HMX and flyer plates have turned up at Al Atheer, which should surprise no one. The three Iraqis who attended the conference came from the laboratory that eventually provided Al Atheer with its first shaped charges.

To design a successful bomb, the Iraqis also needed computing power to solve the hydrodynamic equations that predict the behavior of shock waves. The inspectors discovered that Iraq was running the equations on a mainframe computer from the Japanese company NEC. Another Japanese firm, Hamamatsu, sold Iraq two "streak cameras," sensitive instruments that can photograph a high-speed shock wave as it implodes. The inspectors confiscated both cameras after determining that they were rapid enough for nuclear weapon work.

Altogether, the Iraqis carried out 20 detonation tests before May 31, 1990 — the date of the last Iraqi progress report on Al Atheer found by the United Nations. The Iraqis [illegible] the weapon's total weight from one ton in the first version to about half a ton in the last — light enough to go on a missile.

After May 1990 the Iraqis worked unimpeded at Al Atheer for eight more months. No one knows how much more they achieved. The Iraqis started relocating vital equipment before allied bombing began in January 1991, and as late as last summer tore out concrete floors to prevent inspectors from determining which machines were used there. They even ripped out electrical hookups to hide power usage. Now that Al Atheer is "sanitized," inspectors fear the bomb work has moved elsewhere.

Wherever the work is going on, the Iraqis still have plenty of equipment. During the late 1980's, Baghdad bought machines by the factory load, few of which have been found. The purchases included additional vacuum furnaces, from the German firm Leybold; plasma-coating machines, which could be modified to coat the surfaces of the molds into which molten uranium is poured, from the American company TI Coating; high-speed oscilloscopes, needed to develop firing circuits for nuclear weapons and for nuclear tests, from the American company Tektronix; and two X-ray diffraction systems, capable of analyzing weapon-grade uranium during production, from the German firm Siemens. TI Coating sold directly to an Iraqi factory charged with making A-bomb fuel; Tektronix sold to an Iraqi procurement agent for a string of nuclear and missile sites; Siemens sold to the Iraqi Ministry of Industry and Military Industrialization, which set up Al Atheer.

These purchases followed Iraq's policy of "parallel sourcing." The Iraqis never buy just one machine or build a single plant. If the item is important, they buy or build two. So if one vital machine or plant is bombed or surrendered to inspectors, they almost always have another.

The inspectors found out one other thing about the Iraqi bomb — it is highly unstable. The design calls for cramming so much weapon-grade uranium into the core, they say, that the bomb would inevitably be on the verge of going off — even while sitting on the workbench. "It could go off if a rifle bullet hit it," one inspector says, adding: "I wouldn't want to be around if it fell off the edge of this desk."

Even a "fizzle," when the bomb explodes too soon to get a full chain reaction, would be serious. The minimum blast effect would be equal to filling 20 semitrailers full of TNT, parking them side by side and setting them off simultaneously. The full yield would be like setting off 1,000 semitrailers of TNT.

WITH A WORKABLE AND MOST- [illegible] grade uranium fuel. Iraq started producing this precious substance before the war, but never got close to making enough for a bomb. Whether it finally succeeds will depend on its foreign suppliers.

The key will be the centrifuge. By spinning uranium gas at high speeds, centrifuges separate light, unstable uranium isotope that explodes in an atom bomb from the heavy, stable one that doesn't. A spinning tube called a rotor propels the heavy isotope to the outside wall and leaves the light one at the center. As the gas is run through a series of centrifuges called a cascade, the concentration of the light isotope is gradually raised from less than 1 percent in natural uranium to over 90 percent in uranium of nuclear weapon-grade. This technically demanding process is called enrichment.

Iraq's centrifuges are based on German designs and were built with German help. Iraq somehow got German blueprints in the 1980's. By 1988 it was already running experimental models. When one model developed a hitch in late 1988, Iraq summoned Bruno Stemmler, an ex-employee of M.A.N., the German company that makes centrifuges for the German national enrichment effort. After studying Iraq's illicit blueprints, Stemmler removed the hitch.

Iraq's next goal was mass production. It takes from 1,000 to 2,000 German-style centrifuges to produce a bomb's worth of enriched uranium each year. German firms again obliged. From H & H Metalform — a company subsidized by the German Government — came "flow forming" machines that are specially adapted to produce rotor tubes, the most difficult part of the centrifuge to make. From Leybold's American subsidiary came a giant electron beam welder, equipped with custom-made fixtures for welding the rotors to their necessary end caps. From Dr. Reutlinger & Sohne came machines to balance the rotors vertically and horizontally. From Neue Magdeburger came other specially adapted machine tools. And from Degussa came an oxidation furnace to treat the surfaces of parts so they could withstand corrosive uranium gas.

After surveying this glittering array, the U.N. inspectors concluded that Iraq would be able to produce more than 2,000 centrifuges a year, enough for a full-fledged bomb program. From a recent inspection, we know that Iraq [illegible] many parts were actually delivered, or how many centrifuges Iraq may have made.

The U.N. teams have now destroyed all the centrifuge parts it could find. But the inspectors don't know how many more centrifuge parts there are, because they don't know how many were sold to Iraq by Western companies. They are especially worried about a "missing cascade." They assume that Iraq would not have built a plant to mass-produce centrifuges without first being able to connect them in an experimental cascade. No cascade has been found. As the inspectors warn in their report, Iraq "may still have an undisclosed program."

The inspectors are also worried about a possible cache of weapon-grade uranium. Last July, they found four traces of this material in samples taken from Tuwaitha, Iraq's primary nuclear site. Because of the possibility that the samples were contaminated after they left Iraq, however, the evidence was not considered conclusive. New samples were taken in October, but the test results are still not in. Thus, the U.N. inspectors cannot pursue the lead.

There is also the matter of a hidden reactor. Western intelligence sources believe that the Iraqis have at least started to build one, but the inspectors have not been able to find it. Even a small, 20-to-40-megawatt reactor would be large enough to fuel a few nuclear weapons a year.

And, finally, the inspectors are worried about outside suppliers.

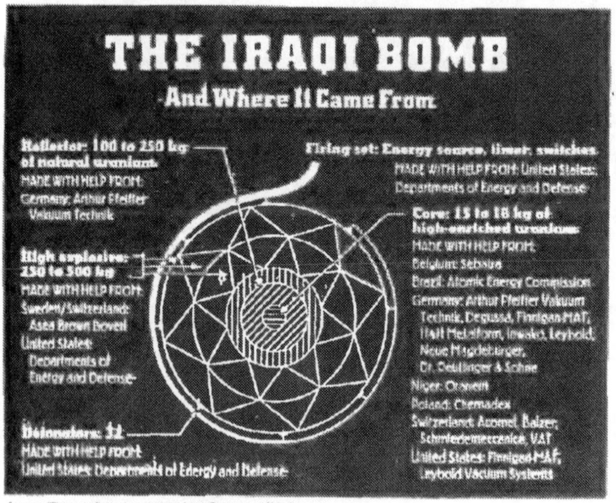

Sources: Wisconsin Project on Nuclear Arms Control and U.N. Inspection reports

This is the actual Iraqi bomb design described in secret documents seized in Baghdad. Saddam was within 18 to 24 months of producing this bomb before the gulf war.

Saddam permanently there must be "strict maintenance of export controls by the industrial nations." But nothing in recent history suggests that the industrial nations will exercise such restraint.

In the five years before the Persian Gulf war, for example, the Commerce Department licensed more than $1.5 billion of strategically sensitive American exports to Iraq. Many were for direct delivery to nuclear weapon, chemical weapon and missile sites. Companies like Hewlett-Packard, Honeywell, International Computer Systems, Rockwell and Tektronix sold high-performance electronics either to Saad 16, Iraq's major missile research center; to the Ministry of Industry and Military Industrialization, which set up Al Atheer; to the Iraqi Atomic Energy Commission, responsible for atomic-bomb research; or to Nasr State Enterprise, in charge of Iraq's missile and nuclear procurement. Honeywell even did a feasibility study for a powerful gasoline bomb warhead, intended for an Iraqi-Egyptian missile.

The computer giant Sperry and its successor, Unisys, also benefited. They got licenses to sell multimillion-dollar computers designed to handle a "personnel data base." The powerful machines — ordered by Iraq's Ministry of the Interior, which houses the secret police — are ideally suited to tracking and suppressing civilians.

The Commerce Department approved all these exports despite strong warnings from the Pentagon, the first coming in November 198[illegible]

ertheless permitted the sale of hundreds of thousands of dollars' worth of sensitive computers and electronics to Saad 16, all after the warning.

And there was the strange case of the Badr General Establishment, a factory outside Baghdad. In the summer of 1989 it wanted to buy a computer-controlled lathe from Cincinnati Milacron and a high-accuracy measuring system from Brown' & Sharpe. Badr said the equipment would make "crankshafts, camshafts, and gears" for automobiles. But the Pentagon was skeptical. Commerce therefore agreed to a "pre-license check," in which an American official would actually visit the site.

After a 30-kilometer trip out from the capital, two embassy officials toured Badr with its production manager, Salem Fadl Hussain. The verdict was unanimous. The American Ambassador, April Glaspie, cabled the good news to Commerce on Sept. 13: "We believe that Badr General Establishment is a reliable recipient of sensitive United States origin technology and technical data." We now know that Badr and another organization were jointly in charge of all the centrifuge production in Iraq.

As bad as the American record is, Germany's is worse. Germany supplied more of Iraq's mass-destruction machinery than all other countries combined. Germany not only sold Iraq most of its centrifuge equipment, it also furnished an entire chemical weapon industry and was Iraq's greatest supplier of missile technology, including a flood of parts that enabled Iraq to extend the range of its Scud missiles. During the Persian Gulf war, enhanced Scuds hit Tel Aviv and a United States Army barracks in Saudi Arabia, killing 28 sleeping soldiers.

To develop an even longer-range missile, Iraq turned to the German armament giant Messerschmitt, now doing business as MBB (Messerschmitt-Bolkow-Blohm). MBB supplied the know-how for a 600-mile nuclear-capable missile called the Condor II that Iraq tried to develop jointly with Egypt and Argentina before the war. The missile's range and configuration are similar to that of the American Pershing, which MBB worked on at the Pentagon. The same MBB employee who worked on the Pershing at the Pentagon also represented MBB in Iraq for the Condor, and thus was in a position to transfer American missile technology to Baghdad.

SINCE THE INSPECTIONS BEgan, critics have questioned wheth-

United Nations inspectors uncovering weapon-grade reactor fuel in a pit near Tuwaitha, Iraq's primary nuclear site. The fuel had been hidden to avoid allied bombing during the Persian Gulf war.

Above: A United Nations inspector, Douglas M. Englund, chief of operations of the Special Commission, confronts the hosts of a ballistic missile inspection at Taji. One U.N. inspector was told, "We are waiting for

der United Nations inspectors could eradicate Iraq's weapons of mass destruction That question has now been answered Despite great courage and enthusiasm the inspectors still have not found the hundreds of Scud missiles Iraq is known to be hiding or the headquarters of the centrifuge program or exposed the supplier network Nor have they solved the mystery of the weapon grade uranium Obviously, stronger methods are needed

First, the United Nations has to change tactics "We have diplomats when we should have detectives says a knowledgeable United States official It s like looking for an escaped murderer You question everybody who might have a lead and you keep on asking until you get answers

In other words shift to police style investigations. Only the Iraqis know where their nuclear treasure is buried only they can reveal it To make headway, the United Nations will have to deploy inspectors by the hundreds station them in Iraq instead of New York, and use soldiers as well as civilians The inspectors must be free to interrogate every Iraqi scientist or engineer who might have relevant information and to follow up the leads immediately. And they must have the power to push aside Saddam Hussein s disinformation specialists

The inspectors also need to know exactly what Iraq has bought So far though, not a single country has been willing to tell the inspectors what its companies sold Only Germany has provided leads, and when it did the inspectors quickly turned up centrifuge parts As long as other suppliers sit on their export data the inspections will be reduced to fishing expeditions with the Iraqis steering the boat

The United Nations must also put its own house in order While the Special Commission has run the missile and chemical inspections with great zeal the nuclear inspections are assigned to the International Atomic Energy Agency the equivalent of an oxcart with its brakes on

In late September for example the agency seized more than 60,000 pages of Iraqi documents many of them describing the supplier network Five months later practically no translations have been done

The agency is also timid about destroying illicit equipment While the Special Commission is destroying every machine it can find that the Iraqis bought built or used to make chemical weapons or missiles the Atomic Energy Agency has been willing to destroy only small parts of the machines used to make nuclear weapons For example Iraq bought a giant electron beam welder to fabricate centrifuges but the agency destroyed only the small fixture that holds the centrifuge in place leaving the giant welder intact This means that if the Iraqis have extra fixtures — which is likely, given their parallel sourcing plan — they can go back into the bomb business with the same machines

Assuming the United Nations does manage to eradicate Iraq s nuclear chemical and missile programs it still faces the problem of preventing Baghdad from starting over One solution is to expose Iraq s supplier network, which is still intact The United Nations has compiled lists of the companies in the network and what they sold but it has furnished them only to the involved governments The United States is reported to favor making the lists public but Germany and France are said to be resisting

Another way to defeat the network is to toughen export laws Most of what Saddam bought was licensed Governments knew he was getting dangerous equipment but hated to see their companies lose a sale The resulting debacle should have taught the world a lesson but Western export controls are no stronger now than they were before the gulf war In fact with the end of the cold war the NATO countries and the European Community have been easing export controls

The outcome in Iraq is now in the hands of President Bush and his gulf war allies If they are willing to turn the United Nations into a vehicle for curbing the spread of the bomb the battle in Iraq can still be won If not Iraq s bomb maker will pick up where they left off and the new world order will fail its first important test ■

Written statements submitted by the International Atomic Energy Agency (IAEA) at the hearings jointly held by three sub committees of the Committee of Foreign Affairs of the 103rd Congress of the United States - Washington
29 June 1993

Question

How successful have the efforts of the international community since the Gulf War been in identifying and rendering unusable Iraqi resources and capabilities to develop and produce weapons of mass destruction?

Answer

Insofar as UN Security Council resolution 687 [1991] assigns to the UN Special Commission the tasks related to ballistic, chemical and biological weapons, these remarks will be limited to the Iraqi nuclear weapons programme

The IAEA has been successful in identifying, destroying, removing or otherwise rendering harmless the key components of a hitherto secret and broadly-based Iraqi programme aimed at the acquisition of nuclear weapons capabilities

1 Identification

The identification of the various elements of the clandestine Iraqi programme was largely completed at the end of September 1991, i e six months after the adoption by the Security Council of the cease-fire resolution Charting the map of this programme has entailed a number of difficulties, including dramatic confrontations on several occasions between Iraqi authorities and IAEA inspection teams The Iraqi government has employed a strategy of obstruction and delay in its efforts to conceal the real nature of its nuclear projects, while, on the other hand, demonstrating a level of co-operation in some less sensitive areas

As to the completeness of the picture obtained, it is the considered opinion of the IAEA, based on the results of nineteen inspection missions, the analyses of thousands of samples, the evaluation of several hundred documents confiscated in Iraq, the assessment of procurement and other information obtained from Member States of the IAEA, that the essential components of the clandestine program have been identified Even if the picture lacks detail in some areas, the efforts in identifying the scope of the

Iraqi nuclear weapons programme have been successful

While leaving the summary description of the Iraqi nuclear weapons programme to a fact sheet appended to this statement this is maybe the appropriate occasion to place on record that success in the rapid identification of the secret Iraqi program is due, in no small measure, to the support extended to the IAEA by its Member States through the provision of intelligence information and of experts who expanded the competence of the IAEA inspection teams in particular areas The combination of intelligence information and experts with rapid and intrusive field inspections to verify and follow up intelligence leads has proved to be the most powerful tool in achieving success This is an important lesson learned from the Iraqi experience

2 Destruction

The second main task laid upon the IAEA by resolution 687 concerns the destruction, removal or rendering harmless of the essential ingredients of the Iraqi nuclear weapons development programme including the nuclear-weapons-usable material known to have been in Iraq in the form of safeguarded reactor fuel

Extensive destruction of Iraqi nuclear installations occurred during the Gulf War as a result of the air raids by Coalition forces Additional destruction of equipment and material was carried out by the Iraqi army at the end of the war and prior to the start of IAEA inspections, in an attempt by Iraq to remove evidence of its secret programme Also, important equipment, machine tools instrumentation, spare parts, stock materials and components were salvaged and hidden by Iraqi personnel An important exception was Al Atheer, the site where weaponization activities (i e , activities relevant to weapons design development and assembly, as distinguished from activities for the production of nuclear-weapons-usable material) had been planned Facilities at this site were still under construction at the time of the war, which is probably one of the reasons it went practically unscathed through the conflict The association of this site as well as several others to the clandestine Iraqi programme were not known at the time of the Gulf War to either national or international authorities The role of these facilities was only uncovered through the inspection process Since September 1991, i e when the scope of the clandestine Iraqi programme came into focus, the IAEA has been supervising a systematic destruction of facilities, technical buildings, equipment and other items proscribed under UN Security Council resolution 687, which had escaped destruction or which had been only slightly damaged Details on the destruction activities may be found in the attachment to this statement This process cannot yet be considered complete as the possibility of finding more items cannot be ruled out and surprises are always possible As to the quantities of weapons usable nuclear material (highly enriched uranium in the form of reactor fuel elements) known to have been in Iraq under IAEA safeguards, these were found untouched and have been fully accounted for The removal operation has involved extensive negotiations with Member States, who have recently agreed to accept this material The task has entailed a complex technical effort by Iraq to clear part of it from the rubble of a bombarded research reactor The removal of this material will be completed by February 1994 if funds, in the order of US$20 million, are made available

3 Is the job finished?

By no means The IAEA and the Special Commission are facing increasing resistance by the Iraqi authorities to compliance with Iraq's obligations under resolutions 687, 707 and 715 in two areas which bear particular importance for future monitoring activities aimed at preventing a resurgence of the of activities proscribed by the cease-fire resolution

Since the beginning, Iraq has refused to disclose the names of foreign suppliers and intermediaries, including the network of front companies established abroad, which provided materials, equipment and technical know-how essential to Iraq's weapons programme This information is necessary to permit verification of the completeness of available declarations and information, to provide adequate basis for the long term monitoring activities and to ensure that any loopholes in export regulation are identified and closed The persistent refusal of Iraq to disclose the sources of supplies is a breach of its obligations under the Security Council resolution 707

A second important obstacle that must be overcome is the refusal of Iraq to accept resolution 715, which approved the plans for long term monitoring of compliance by Iraq with the limitations imposed under resolution 687

Resolution 715 also established the rights of the IAEA and of the Special Commission which are deemed essential for effective application of this long term monitoring

Effective measures on Iraq applied by the UN Security Council has, in the past, played a decisive role in modifying the attitude of the Iraqi Government when it has refused or resisted compliance with its obligations These measures should be maintained until full compliance with all of Iraq's obligations is obtained

Question

How well has the International Atomic Energy Agency accomplished the tasks in Iraq that were assigned to it by the United Nations Security Council?

Answer

In response to this question, it might be more appropriate to recall that full satisfaction with the IAEA's activities in Iraq under UN Security Council resolution 687 has been expressed on a number of occasions by members of the Security Council and by IAEA Member States' Governments

Some considerations may assist the Congressional Sub-Committees which are holding these hearings in formulating their own judgment of the effectiveness of the IAEA's response Nine days after the adoption of the cease-fire resolution by the Security Council (6 April 1991), the IAEA established an Action Team, reporting directly to the Director General of the IAEA, to implement the tasks assigned to the IAEA by the Security Council under that resolution The team is composed of five senior and experienced professionals of the IAEA, headed by a former Deputy Director General of the IAEA and is empowered to draw on any necessary IAEA resources on a priority basis to discharge its duties The first on-site inspection team was ready to enter Iraq as of 1 May 1991, less than four weeks after the adoption of the cease-fire resolution To date, 19 inspections have been conducted for a total of over 2000 inspector days (the 20th inspection team is at this moment in the field) Appropriate links and close co-operation have been developed with the UN Special Commission The Security Council and the IAEA's Board of Governors are kept constantly informed of the results of inspection activities as they develop Assistance has been sought and obtained from a large number of IAEA Member States Intelligence information has been shared with the Agency on an unprecedented scale

The tasks entrusted by the Security Council to the IAEA are essentially threefold search, destroy and prevent any reconstitution The IAEA has searched, has found and has destroyed The basis has been established for preventing a reconstitution of the Iraqi nuclear programme Effective control of future Iraqi activities can be put in place if adequate measures are maintained at the political level and sufficient resources continue to be provided

Question

What steps can be taken in the future, to strengthen the ability of the IAEA in dealing with such challenges in Iraq and elsewhere?

Answer

The events in Iraq have not only highlighted the need to strengthen the IAEA safeguards system - and, in fact, the non-proliferation regime as a whole - but also have heightened the readiness of Governments to contribute to these improvements

During 1992 and 1993, the IAEA Board of Governors supported proposals for strengthening safeguards and increasing the ability of the safeguards system to detect the existence of, and gain access to undeclared nuclear activities in States with comprehensive safeguards agreements The proposals relate to

- access to carry out special inspections at any location which the IAEA has reason to believe it needs to visit to obtain additional information relevant to safeguards,

- the early provision of design information about new facilities or modifications to existing facilities as soon as the decision is taken to construct or modify the facility The IAEA's authority to verify design information is a continuing right that extends throughout the facility life cycle,

- the reporting of exports, imports and production of nuclear material as well as exports and imports of certain equipment and non-nuclear material which could be relevant to a weapons programme

The use of environmental sampling as a tool to help assess the completeness of a State's declaration regarding its nuclear activities has been implemented in particular situations (including Iraq) and its applicability in the broader safeguards context is being considered Additional changes involving increased intensity of safeguards in countries with more than a significant quantity of highly enriched uranium and/or plutonium distributed among small facilities is being implemented

These measures are intended to improve and broaden the scope of the existing safeguards system This system has worked well in verifying the non-diversion of declared nuclear material at declared nuclear installations The system was not geared to provide assurance that no undeclared nuclear installations existed Although the safeguards system as originally designed, provided for the legal authority to do this, the Secretariat lacked the information needed to implement this authority Therefore, it was not timidity but the lack of information about undeclared sites meriting inspection that prevented the discovery of Iraq's clandestine programme This situation is being corrected through actions by the Secretariat with the support of Member States

The discoveries in Iraq highlighted the importance, for effective safeguards, of three types of access to information, to sites and to the Security Council of the United Nations

In using inspections as a tool for verification, the first basic requirement is for information regarding locations which might have undeclared nuclear-related items or facilities, requiring inspection In this context the IAEA gathers much information of its own from its general verification activities, from States themselves, through in-depth analysis of information about nuclear activities obtained from the media and other open literature and, now, through more detailed reporting by States on nuclear material, equipment and relevant non-nuclear material Additionally, the IAEA now receives information obtained by its Member States through national intelligence means The IAEA is of the view that no information relevant to safeguards, whatever its provenance may be ignored but all information must be critically analyzed to determine its credibility

The second basic requirement is for unlimited right of access for inspectors to locations which the IAEA considers to be relevant to safeguards even at short notice Where IAEA access to information and to sites is not forthcoming, then access to the Security Council becomes of particular importance The Relationship Agreement of 14 November 1957 between the United Nations and the IAEA contains provisions allowing for prompt interaction between the United Nations, including the Security Council, and the IAEA If a State fails to comply with its safeguards agreement, the IAEA is obliged to refer the matter to the Security Council which may decide to take enforcement action to induce a State to accept inspection

In its statement of 31 January 1992, the Security Council emphasized not only the integral role of fully effective IAEA safeguards in implementing the NPT, but also its readiness to take "appropriate measures in the case of any violations notified to them by the IAEA" All this attests to the fact that the Security Council is conscious of the risks inherent in proliferation It is also sensitive to two specific requirements that IAEA safeguards must be sufficiently effective to detect any breach or concealment with a high degree of probability, and that the international community needs to be able to continue to trust in the credibility of the safeguards system.

IAEA Action Team for Iraq
(Attachment to the written statements submitted by the IAEA)

FACT SHEET
25 June 1993

The IAEA Action Team was created to manage the UN Security Council Resolution 687 as it relates to Iraq's nuclear weapons programme This resolution mandates the destruction of all weapons of mass destruction in Iraq The IAEA has the sole responsibility under this resolution to destroy, remove, or render harmless all nuclear weapons and prohibited precursor materials

RESULTS TO DATE

19 IAEA nuclear inspection teams have visited Iraq to inspect facilities, interview key personnel, inventory nuclear materials, identify prohibited items and carry out destruction and removal operations

The Iraqi Nuclear Weapons Programme consisted of eight dedicated sites There were dozens of major processing buildings that represented an investment (in US equivalent) of several billion dollars Most of these buildings have been destroyed by the war or under inspection team supervision The remaining facilities consist of offices, warehouses and light industrial buildings with no unique capabilities

The programme involved millions of dollars in specialized equipment Much of this equipment has been destroyed by the war, by inspection teams, and by the elements as the equipment is left outdoors or moved around The teams have inventoried hundreds of pieces of equipment that may fall into prohibited or monitorable categories

The clandestine Iraqi nuclear programme consisted of a tremendous and well-financed approach to redundant and multiple paths of production of highly enriched uranium (HEU) The Gulf War and the subsequent inspection effort stopped this production effort well before any significant amounts of such material was produced. All known activities related to fissile material production were destroyed or rendered harmless either during the War or under the supervision of IAEA Inspection Teams

Significant quantities of HEU in the form of fresh or unirradiated fuel were in Iraq under IAEA safeguards and there was concern in some quarters that this material could have been diverted to produce a nuclear explosive Pre-war estimates that Iraq could produce a nuclear explosive within a few months explicitly assumed that this material would be diverted It was not All of this material has been accounted for by the IAEA The fresh fuel has been removed from Iraq and the removal of the irradiated fuel is imminent

Another concern is a possible clandestine stockpile of illicitly obtained HEU or plutonium This has neither been reported nor uncovered The existence of such an undeclared stockpile would, however, be a major concern It was a major consideration in deciding to destroy facilities and equipment that could fabricate HEU or plutonium into a nuclear explosive

All of the comments regarding times to completion of an explosive device are based on the assumption that the program would have continued along the same lines, keeping its original goals This would have taken several more years to complete because much of the program was just being put together and many pieces were missing It does not appear that these pieces were coming together in a well-organized way Even before the embargo began, it appears that the program had a long way to go both in terms of organization and technical progress

Actually, the facilities and plants are suggestive of a grandiose and over-designed program If a political decision were taken today to produce a crude weapon (source of fissile material unspecified), it could be done without many of the specialized facilities that had been built for weaponization Good equipment would be needed, however, and much of what Iraq had acquired has been destroyed

The theoretical aspect of the program is the largest worry under the current sanctions regime This is an ideal time for the low visibility theoretical work to progress It could lead to a more efficient experimental program in the future if, for any reason, Iraq were to resume While more visible activities, such as fissile materials production, fabrication studies and testing, are impeded or deterred by the inspections, improved codes and design efforts could run on small computers even today

The key remaining element is the technical experience that has been gained to date If this expertise is held together, the design and organization process, and possibly small scale research activity, may continue with a low probability of being rediscovered These are low signature activities not likely to be revealed to inspectors without extraordinary luck or the defection of knowledgeable Iraqi personnel

The key to monitoring and inspecting Iraq's programme must be preventing access to fissile materials, either by diversion or purchase It is also important to prevent any reconstitution of indigenous programmes for uranium enrichment or plutonium production Such programmes are high profile in terms of cost, visibility, and foreign procurements All require continuing observation

Appendix A
STATUS OF FACILITIES AND EQUIPMENT USED IN THE IRAQI NUCLEAR PROGRAMME

Tuwaitha Nuclear Research Centre - Headquarters of the programme and site of many R&D functions This site was devastated and much of the equipment on this site was destroyed during the war Little additional destruction was necessary

Al Qaim uranium concentration plant - Destroyed during the war

Al Jazirah feed materials plant - This plant manufactured UO_2 and UCl_4 to the EMIS[1] programme The buildings were destroyed during the war Most equipment has been accounted for and has been destroyed or is in very bad condition

Tarmiya EMIS Plant - This site was largely destroyed during the war The electromagnetic separators were destroyed by the Iraqis in attempts to conceal them The inspection teams supervised the destruction of the remaining process building (the beta calutron building) the utility system and a few other structures so that the site cannot be used for its original purpose

Ash Sharqat EMIS Plant - This was a twin of Tarmiya that had not yet been completed when it was heavily bombed during the war The IAEA teams requested and supervised additional destruction along the lines of that carried out at Tarmiya No process equipment had been installed yet at Ash Sharqat

Al Atheer Materials Centre - This was a partially completed nuclear weapons development and production site It was virtually untouched by the war The eight specialized process buildings comprising some 350,000 square feet of lab space were blown up by Iraqi demolition teams under IAEA supervision A significant quantity of high quality fabrication equipment which had been installed or stored there was destroyed

Al Rabiyah Manufacturing Plant - This was a plant with large mechanical workshops designed and built for the manufacture of large metal components for the Iraqi EMIS programme The main function had been to support the EMIS programme The plant had high quality but not unique, machine tool capabilities The IAEA inventoried the plant and has been inspecting it regularly Several pieces of equipment in the plant will be monitored under the

[1]EMIS = ElectroMagnetic Isotope Separation

terms of the on-going monitoring plan. The plant was severely damaged by a cruise missile attack in 1993.

Dijila Electronics Plant - This plant supported electronics fabrication activities for the IAEC. It has almost no unique pieces of equipment. The plant was not damaged, and will continue to be monitored by the IAEA .

A ninth site was under construction close to Al Walid to house the centrifuge manufacturing facility of the Al Furat project. This was also the site where Iraq had planned to establish its first pilot cascade of 100 centrifuges, scheduled to start operations in mid-1993. At the time of the Gulf War most of the key buildings at this site were still in an early construction stage.

A number of other manufacturing workshops were contracted by the Iraqi Atomic Energy Commission for the production of components relevant to the weapons programme. All these workshops have been identified and are subject to IAEA monitoring.

APPENDIX B
ASSESSMENT OF THE STATE OF CRITICAL TECHNOLOGY AREAS

Nuclear materials: All highly enriched uranium in Iraq under pre-war safeguards has been accounted for. About one third, in the form of fresh reactor fuel, has been removed from Iraq and the balance, contained in irradiated fuel, is awaiting removal. A contract for removal has been signed and an approximately eight-month effort to remove the irradiated uranium fuel has begun.

About 500 tonnes of natural uranium has been identified and tracked through the Iraqi uranium processing system. Teams are currently reviewing whether the Iraqi declaration of uranium is complete and credible. The IAEA removed six grams of plutonium produced in Iraq (roughly two-thirds of which had been produced illegally).

Assessment: Hundreds of tons of low value nuclear feed materials are under IAEA seal. There remains, however, accountability problems which make it difficult to conclude that all known nuclear materials in Iraq have been discovered or reasonably accounted for.

Electromagnetic Isotope Separation This clandestine program was discovered early in the inspection process. Most of the now known EMIS equipment was damaged in the war. The IAEA inventoried EMIS items, destroyed the remaining pieces, and verified quantities through suppliers. Several facilities that had not been completely destroyed during the war were destroyed by Iraq under IAEA supervision. Equipment utilized in the manufacture of EMIS components remains under seal. A cruise missile attack on the Al Rabiyah facility in January did additional damage to equipment which could have been used in the future to reconstitute EMIS. Reconstitution of this programme seems unlikely insofar as it was a large programme that had relied on a blind spot in Western intelligence to get as far as it did.

Assessment: The EMIS program is completely destroyed. It was an indigenous approach to isotope separation that escaped detection. The program was facing serious difficulties in start-up and implementation due to a lack of technical depth among Iraqi technicians. It would have been several years before it produced enough uranium for military purposes.

Centrifuge Program: Iraq declared its facilities and much of the centrifuge equipment in July 1991. Two centrifuge prototypes had been tested with some success in test bed experiments. All known centrifuge components and specialized tooling were destroyed in 1991. Other specialized, but dual use, equipment is now under IAEA seal. The Iraqi government has made a political decision not to name suppliers of sensitive equipment and materials. This complicates verification, but should not prevent it. Suppliers of carbon fiber centrifuge rotors have recently been discovered by German authorities. Iraq eventually admitted that the Rashdiya facility has had a design role in the centrifuge program. This disclosure came after over a year of pressure from the IAEA.

Assessment: The Iraqi centrifuge program was in a very early stage, using clandestinely obtained European designs and illicitly obtained materials to build a few research machines. The procurement of hundreds of tonnes of specialty metals and components, enough to build thousands of machines, was discovered. These materials have been seized and destroyed.

Uranium Ore Concentration: The ore concentration plant at Al Qaim was completely destroyed during the war.

Assessment: No capability to indigenously process uranium ore now exists in Iraq. The Iraqis have taken no steps to rebuild this plant.

Nuclear Material Conversion: The nuclear materials feed plant at Al Jazirah was completely destroyed during the war.

Assessment: This key capability is completely destroyed at the production plant level. No back-up capability is known or suspected.

Nuclear Reactors and a Plutonium Program: The two nuclear reactors at Tuwaitha were totally destroyed in the war by aggressive bombardment. They cease to exist. Suspicions of the existence of an underground reactor have existed since before the war. All information specific enough to be checked out have proven to be negative.

Assessment: While suspicions of an underground reactor are vague and seem to be premised on circularly repeated rumors, the IAEA continues to search for any evidence for an underground reactor and the requisite peripherals such as irradiated fuel reprocessing and nuclear waste handling. No information of any verifiable quality exists at this time to support the existence of such a facility.

Nuclear Weapons Design: A program to assess a nuclear weapon design existed in Iraq before the war. It consisted of a plan to investigate all of the practical elements of designing and building a prototype nuclear weapon. A number of specialized facilities, including buildings for high explosives testing and radioactive materials handling, had been built at Al Atheer to support this programme. These facilities have all been destroyed by Iraq under IAEA supervision. The Tuwaitha nuclear research site was largely destroyed during the war as well. Continued speculation about the existence of a plutonium program in Iraq is uninformed, given the complexity, high visibility and difficulty of the plutonium route.

Assessment: The Iraqi nuclear weapons design effort was at an early stage and consisted of a broadly based study of all aspects of producing a uranium core implosion weapon. Sophisticated concepts for the future were under consideration. A practical design had not been achieved as a number of problems remained to be overcome. The hardware and facilities to support this program have been destroyed, but the concepts remain.

Programme Documentation and Personnel: One of the early IAEA inspection teams seized about 50,000 pages of documents from the IAEC. A substantial fraction of this material consisted of technical progress reports. Correspondence found in this material indicated that other documents had been taken away and hidden by the Iraqi security services just before the team arrived. The Iraqis claim that all programme documentation had been destroyed much earlier. Virtually all of the scientists associated with the nuclear programs remain in Iraq. Captured documents show layoff records for hundreds of people whose work places were destroyed in the war.

Assessment: Iraq could reconstitute a weapons program faster than another state that had never tried. The capable scientists remain. How they are currently employed is difficult to ascertain because they have been dispersed. It seems highly probable that a set of documents about the program remain safely hidden away. The important physical facilities are all destroyed, however, and would have to be rebuilt at great cost, in order to revive the weapons programme.

LONG TERM MONITORING

The Action Team will monitor equipment and facilities that remain after the war and Inspection Team destruction activities. The first phase of a waterway monitoring programme has been completed with the cooperation of the Iraqi government. This programme is sensitive enough to detect very small quantities of radionuclides and other chemicals used in the nuclear industry. The first series of results show that no unknown nuclear facility has been operating in Iraq in the last couple of years Based on verification activities and available information, it is reasonable to conclude that Iraq is not operating clandestine nuclear facilities, especially a reactor, or a reprocessing plant

An essential prerequisite for effective implementation of the Agency's long term monitoring plan, is the unconditional acceptance by Iraq of UN Security Council resolution 715 [1991], which determines the rights of UNSCOM and IAEA inspectors and the corresponding obligations of Iraq Iraq has so far refused to formally accept this resolution

Outstanding Tasks

Remove the highly enriched irradiated uranium still in Iraq

Aggressively follow-up any serious reports of clandestine facilities, especially nuclear reactors and their required support such as fuel reprocessing

Resolve remaining accountancy differences in the nuclear material balance

Continue periodic surveys of the waterways monitoring program and phase in gradually other elements of the long term monitoring plan

Identify suppliers and middlemen

- centrifuge components
- explosives
- dual use equipment
- materials

Resolve issues of dual-use industrial equipment in Iraq

NUCLEAR CONTROL
INSTITUTE

June 24, 1993

Representative Tom Lantos
Chairman, Subcommittee on Arms Control,
International Security and Science
House Foreign Affairs Committee
2401A Rayburn House Office Building
Washington, DC 20515-6129

Dear Mr. Chairman:

Since I will not be testifying as originally planned at your hearing on June 29, I wanted to share with you an exchange of correspondence I have had with IAEA Director General Hans Blix concerning his misleading statements about the effectiveness of the Agency's safeguards on Iraq's bomb-grade uranium prior to the Gulf War.

In preparation for my testimony, I wrote to Dr. Blix, asking him to correct these misstatements and to set the record straight so that I could insert our exchange of correspondence into the record of your hearing. Enclosed you will find that correspondence, which I submit for the record.

The Nuclear Control Institute has long sought to direct attention to the severe limitations on what IAEA safeguards on bomb-grade nuclear material can deliver in problem NPT states like Iraq. In our view, the principal lesson of Iraq (and more recently of North Korea) is the danger of allowing highly enriched uranium and separated plutonium into civilian nuclear programs on the grounds that IAEA safeguards are adequate to detect and deter misuse of these materials in nuclear weapons.

So long as the agency misleads the public into believing that its safeguards on these materials "work"---precisely the twaddle that Dr. Blix and his spokesman put forth in the context of Iraq---it will be all the more difficult to eliminate these materials from civil nuclear programs, for which they are uneconomical and unnecessary, in any event.

Export controls and other nuclear non-proliferation undertakings become wasting assets in the face of growing stocks of safeguarded, "peaceful" bomb-grade nuclear materials. Civilian nuclear power and research programs run quite well without these materials. With them, these programs pose an undeniable proliferation threat because the materials can be converted into nuclear weapons in a matter of days or weeks This is true in major industrial states as well as nuclear threshold states Nonetheless, the IAEA continues to perpetuate the myth that its safeguards on these materials are effective

The most glaring proof that these materials are fundamentally unsafeguardable came at the time of the Gulf War when Iraq secretly removed most of its supply of HEU research reactor fuel from the Tuwaitha facility near Baghdad and hid it Iraq, in direct violation of its safeguards agreement under the Non-Proliferation Treaty (NPT), did not inform the IAEA for over three months---ample time to convert this material into one or two first-generation fission weapons As I wrote to Dr Blix, the fact that Iraq chose not to attempt to use its hidden HEU in weapons should not be twisted into proof that safeguards "worked"

Dr Blix still refuses to acknowledge that Iraq's relocation of the HEU fuel was a safeguards violation and he insists that any diversion of the HEU to non-peaceful uses would have been "immediately discovered" Given that IAEA did not even know of the fuel's relocation for months, this claim borders on the absurd He also stands by his statement that the IAEA never gave the Iraqi nuclear program a "clean bill of health" despite the comment of the Agency's safeguards chief that Iraq s cooperation with the IAEA had been "exemplary"

Since Dr Blix s spokesman has pronounced "this particular exchange of correspondence closed" without acknowledging or correcting any of Dr Blix s misstatements I hope you will pursue the specific matters I raised with him when you question witnesses from the IAEA and other witnesses that defend IAEA safeguards on bomb-grade materials as effective

Also attached to this letter are some articles I have written on the subject of Iraq, the IAEA and the NPT In addition I have enclosed the testimony I presented to the House Foreign Affairs Committee over 10 years ago on "what steps are needed and being taken to ensure that our safeguards goals can be met" As you will see from this earlier testimony things haven t changed much our safeguards goals are still not being met and there remains a need for forceful leadership such as you can provide on Capitol Hill

I appreciate your interest in these urgent matters

Sincerely

Paul Leventhal

Enclosures

NUCLEAR CONTROL
INSTITUTE

June 4, 1993

Dr. Hans Blix
Director General
International Atomic Energy Agency
Vienna, Austria

BY FACSIMILE: 011-431-234-564

Dear Dr. Blix:

I am writing to ask that you correct certain statements you made at a press briefing sponsored by the Atlantic Council in Washington on May 20. It is important that the public record be set straight on Iraq's violations of IAEA safeguards.

At the press briefing, you stated that during the 1991 Persian Gulf War, Iraq "did not touch" the highly-enriched uranium (HEU) fuel for its research reactors, or violate IAEA safeguards on that fuel. This is quite similar to the following statement you made the previous month to the Japan Atomic Industrial Forum concerning Iraq's HEU fuel: "What had been placed under safeguards inspection had been left untouched presumably in the awareness that any violation in this regard would have been reported immediately and led to some international reaction." (Dr. Hans Blix, "IAEA Verification of Non-Proliferation," Panel on Non-Proliferation, JAIF Meeting, Yokohama, April 16, 1993, p. 3)

In fact, Iraq moved almost all of its HEU fuel--enough for about two weapons--in January 1991, in anticipation of coalition air strikes. Some of the fuel was secretly relocated within the Tuwaitha site, and some was removed from the site entirely. In a letter to Mauricio Zifferero, leader of the IAEA Action Team, dated April 27, 1991, the Iraqi government confirmed that "nuclear material has been shifted during the war from the locations known to the Agency to nearby locations ..." Further, the Iraqi government refused to disclose the location of this safeguarded material to the Agency for several weeks, insisting upon guarantees that the fuel would not be subject to further attack.

Iraq's failure to inform the Agency promptly of the movement of the HEU fuel or of its new locations violated the safeguards requirement of "[i]nventory change reports showing changes in the inventory of nuclear material. The reports shall be dispatched as soon as possible and in any event within 30 days after the end of the month in which the inventory changes occurred or were established ..." (INFCIRC/153, paragraph 63a).

Further, the fifth IAEA inspection in Iraq under Security Council Resolution 687 reported that "[d]uring item-counting of the fresh [HEU] fuel, two of the Soviet-type fuel assemblies were found to have had the top and bottom inert parts cut off" (Report on the Fifth IAEA On-Site Inspection in Iraq Under Security Council Resolution 687 (1991) 14-20 September 1991 p 4) The Iraqis insisted that the cuts were made in a panicked attempt to fit the fuel elements into shipping containers prior to coalition air strikes However, according to the fifth inspection report, "[t]he evidence is inconclusive as between the Iraqi explanation and the hypothesis that the cutting was a preliminary to removal of the highly enriched component of the assembly" (ibid) Regardless of the purpose of the cuts, however, you cannot accurately claim that the Iraqis "did not touch" the HEU material during the Gulf War

In addition you said that the IAEA had never given the Iraqi nuclear program "a clean bill of health" prior to the Gulf War, rather that it had only certified that all materials under safeguards were accounted for This claim ignores the statement by Jon Jennekens, then-director of the Agency s Safeguards Division made soon after Iraq's invasion of Kuwait Mr Jennekens stated that the cooperation of Iraqi officials with IAEA had been 'exemplary,' and that they "have made every effort to demonstrate that Iraq is a solid citizen" in the nonproliferation regime ("No Bomb-Quantity of HEU in Iraq IAEA Safeguards Report Indicates ' NuclearFuel, August 20 1990, p 8) This assertion, made by the Agency s top safeguards official certainly gives the appearance of a "clean bill of health" for Iraq by the IAEA

I hope you will promptly correct the above-cited statements as they have the unfortunate effect of misleading the public about the effectiveness of Agency safeguards I have been invited to present testimony to a Congressional subcommittee hearing late in June on the lessons of Iraq for the IAEA safeguards system I would appreciate receiving a response from you in time so that I may insert our exchange of correspondence into the record of the hearing

Thank you for your attention to this matter Copies of all materials cited above are attached to this letter

Sincerely

Paul Leventhal

Attachments

INTERNATIONAL ATOMIC ENERGY AGENCY
AGENCE INTERNATIONALE DE L'ENERGIE ATOMIQUE
МЕЖДУНАРОДНОЕ АГЕНТСТВО ПО АТОМНОЙ ЭНЕРГИИ
ORGANISMO INTERNACIONAL DE ENERGIA ATOMICA

15 June 1993

Dear Mr. Leventhal,

Your letter of June 4 to our Director General has been passed to me for reply.

You ask for comments essentially on two points. The first is a remark reportedly made to an individual journalist by the IAEA's former Deputy Director General for Safeguards, Mr. Jennekens, in August 1990. The second is the Director General's reference to highly enriched uranium (HEU) fuel elements in Iraq as being "untouched" when speaking in Washington on May 20 this year

I will not comment on the personal quote attributed to Mr. Jennekens I would point, however, to the prudent line of the IAEA in its public pronouncements on safeguards inspections in Iraq After inspections conducted in both April and November 1990, for instance, we issued carefully worded press releases (attached) stating, in November, that "based upon the information collected during these inspections it has been concluded that no change has taken place in the status of nuclear material under safeguards in Iraq since the last inspections At that time it was concluded that all nuclear material under safeguards was accounted for " No more, no less

As for the Director General's remarks, I do not think it reasonable to try to construct a case concerning the failure of the safeguards system, on the grounds that the IAEA was not "promptly informed" of the movement of HEU fuel to a hurriedly improvised location, ignoring the highly dramatic context of aerial raids in which this took place. It is also capricious to interpret the Director General's reference to the HEU having been "untouched" as implying that none of it had been physically moved, when what he clearly meant was that none of it was ever diverted to non-peaceful use

Mr Paul Leventhal
President
Nuclear Control Institute
1000 Connecticut Avenue N W
Suite 704
Washington D C. 20036

fax 202 452 0892

As you know well, all the HEU supplied to Iraq was and is accounted for. The fresh fuel was removed from Iraq in November 1991 and the irradiated fuel is expected to follow in the second half of this year.

By way of further clarification, let me correct your statement that Iraq moved almost all of its fuel "in anticipation of coalition air strikes" (third paragraph of your letter). The transfer of part of the fuel occurred _after_ the first bombardment of the Tuwaitha Centre (17 January 1991), which resulted in the destruction of the Russian supplied IRT 5000 research reactor with fuel inside. It is worth noting that when the first air raid against Tuwaitha occurred during the night of 17-18 January 1991, the IRT reactor was in full operation, indicating that no coalition air strikes were expected. Removal of the irradiated HEU fuel elements from their original location at the Tammuz 1-Tammuz 2 complex to an improvised location nearby, was carried out under continuing air raids in which bombing might have caused serious radioactive contamination of the area at any time.

As to the episode of the two Soviet-type fuel assemblies which were found without top and bottom fittings, and irrespective of the explanations for this unusual operation, the fact remains that the HEU contained in the two assemblies in question was still there and had not been diverted to non-peaceful uses.

Yours sincerely,

David R Kyd
Director
Public Information Division
IAEA

NUCLEAR CONTROL
INSTITUTE

June 23, 1993

Dr. Hans Blix
Director General
International Atomic Energy Agency
Vienna, Austria

BY FACSIMILE: 011-431-234-564

Dear Dr. Blix:

I am writing with regard to David Kyd's letter of June 15, responding to my letter of June 4 to you.

I had written you in the hope and expectation that you would correct certain misstatements and set the record straight concerning the serious shortcomings of IAEA safeguards in Iraq prior to the Gulf War. Based on Mr. Kyd's response, I find it remarkable that the Agency seems incapable of acknowledging specific, significant limitations to what its safeguards on bomb-grade nuclear material can deliver in problem NPT states like Iraq.

On the issue of whether the IAEA gave a "clean bill of health" to the Iraqi nuclear program, Mr. Kyd declines to comment on former Director of Safeguards Jon Jennekens' November 1990 statement that Iraq's cooperation with the IAEA was "exemplary" and that Iraqi nuclear experts "have made every effort to demonstrate that Iraq is a solid citizen" in the NPT regime. In Mr. Kyd's words, this was a "personal quote" and presumably not of the same weight as two Agency findings that year in Iraq that "all nuclear material under safeguards was accounted for."

An on-the-record comment made by a high-level Agency official to a leading nuclear trade journal cannot be dismissed in this fashion. Mr. Jennekens made his statement just after Iraq's invasion of Kuwait, when world attention and concern was focused on the Iraqi nuclear program. In this context, Mr. Jennekens was surely aware his statement was bound to carry a lot of weight. Also, the Agency did not issue any statement distinguishing its official position from Mr. Jennekens', as it did last September when Mr. Zifferero stated that Iraq's nuclear program was "at zero." Mr. Jennekens had been speaking in his official capacity, and the Agency did nothing to dispel the clean bill of health he gave to Iraq.

As to the central question of whether Iraq violated IAEA safeguards on its HEU fuel without being detected surely it is Mr Kyd not I who is "capricious" in characterizing your remarks at the Atlantic Council press conference in Washington Mr Kyd claims that when you said Iraq "did not touch" the HEU fuel what you "clearly meant was that none of it was ever diverted to non-peaceful use " This is a conveniently revisionist interpretation that is not supported by the transcript of your remarks, as follows

> And the Iraqis never touched the nuclear highly-enriched uranium which was under our safeguards, which in some ways indicate also that the safeguard had an effect Had they touched anything -- (inaudible) -- immediately discovered and these would have been reported, and they would have evoked a governmental opinion and governmental action They didn t want to do that So they never touched the material which was under safeguard

Thus as with your earlier remarks in Japan the clear meaning of your comment was that Iraq had not touched the HEU fuel that safeguards on that material had in no way been violated and that the safeguards had effectively deterred Iraq from attempting such a violation

In fact, the contrary was true Iraq removed the HEU to locations unknown and this was an indisputable safeguards violation Paragraph 63a of INFCIRC/153 clearly requires movement of safeguarded materials to be reported "as soon as possible " Rather than acknowledge this violation Mr Kyd seems to bend over backward to make excuses for Iraq by suggesting that an emergency in response to coalition air raids impeded prompt notification of the IAEA Yet Iraq did not report the relocation of the HEU fuel until more than three months later well after the cease-fire took effect and under duress The NPT safeguards agreement requires that such reports be made "<u>in any event</u> within 30 days of the end of the month" when the safeguarded material is moved [emphasis supplied] Nor are NPT parties permitted to place conditions upon their disclosure to IAEA of the location of special nuclear material as Iraq did in its April 27 1991 declaration

Moreover you are surely aware that no Iraqi diversion of its HEU fuel could have been "immediately discovered" by IAEA This material was only being inspected twice a year despite the fact that it amounted to more than two significant quantities Agency safeguards agreements currently allow many significant quantities of weapons-usable special nuclear material to be treated for inspection purposes as less than one significant quantity provided that the material is split up in smaller amounts among several different material balance areas This is true even if these material balance areas are all located at the same site, as was the case at Tuwaitha

The key point is that Iraq could have quickly gathered and diverted all its HEU fuel for use in weapons without the Agency discovering this diversion for at least several months The fact that actual use in weapons did not occur in no way alters the fact that safeguards were so weak that Iraq could have diverted the material and incorporated it into one or two first-generation fission weapons without detection by the Agency Since the conversion time for HEU is on the order of days or weeks. this makes clear a major gap in IAEA safeguards, and it also makes a strong case for the Agency to acknowledge the obvious limitations of safeguards on direct-use material rather than to continue to obfuscate them

Regarding the two Soviet-type HEU fuel assemblies, Mr Kyd sounds as if he is describing some mystery when he says that they were "found without top and bottom fittings" They were "found" this way because the Iraqis cut off the top and bottom fittings, as they later admitted The UN Special Commission inspectors realizing that this could have been the first step toward diverting the HEU for weapons were not satisfied with Iraq's innocent explanation of why this was done

Yet, Mr Kyd seems satisfied by the fact that "the HEU contained in the two assemblies in question was still there and had not been diverted to non-peaceful uses" Given that the IAEA was not informed of the removal of the fittings, on what basis is the Agency confident that it would have "immediately" discovered the diversion of the HEU subsequent to such removal?

The Iraqi case makes clear why the Agency should not continue to perpetuate the myth of "effective" safeguards on weapons-usable nuclear material The fact that Iraq chose not to use its hidden HEU in weapons should not be twisted into proof that safeguards "worked"

Continued use of HEU in civil nuclear programs on the assumption it can be effectively safeguarded---to borrow the warning by former IAEA Deputy Director General William Dircks about surplus plutonium---"poses a major political and security problem worldwide" Better that you acknowledge that weapons-usable nuclear materials are fundamentally unsafeguardable, given how swiftly they can be converted for use in nuclear bombs Such a warning by you would lift the cloak of legitimacy that now obscures these exceedingly dangerous materials it could hasten their elimination from civil nuclear programs for which they are uneconomical and unnecessary, in any event

Therefore I respectfully repeat my request that you correct your misstatements and set the record straight The public should not be misled on this urgent matter I would appreciate having your reply in time to submit it as part of our exchange of correspondence for the record of the House Foreign Affairs Committee hearing on June 29

Sincerely

Paul Leventhal

INTERNATIONAL ATOMIC ENERGY AGENCY
AGENCE INTERNATIONALE DE L'ENERGIE ATOMIQUE
МЕЖДУНАРОДНОЕ АГЕНТСТВО ПО АТОМНОЙ ЭНЕРГИИ
ORGANISMO INTERNACIONAL DE ENERGIA ATOMICA

24 June 1993

Dear Mr Leventhal,

In the absence of the Director General, Dr. Hans Blix, who will be away from Vienna until July 1, I am again replying to a letter of yours, dated June 23, on the same subjects you chose to raise in your letter of June 4, 1993

Having given your views due consideration, I regret to inform you that there is nothing more of substance I can add to my earlier reply and I must therefore consider this particular exchange of correspondence closed

Yours sincerely,

David R. Kyd
Director
Public Information Division

Mr. Paul Leventhal
President
Nuclear Control Institute
1000 Connecticut Avenue N W
Suite 704
Washington D C 20036

The New York Times
MONDAY, AUGUST 20, 1990

NUCLEAR CONTROL INSTITUTE

The Nonproliferation Hoax

By Paul L. Leventhal

WASHINGTON

The Treaty on the Nonproliferation of Nuclear Weapons is now being reviewed in Geneva by many of the 142 nations that have fied it. Like three previous review ferences held since the treaty ne into force in 1970, this one is ly to extol the virtues of nonprolif tion — the next best thing to moth ood — and ignore flaws that make treaty dangerously out of date In present form in a rapidly changing ld the treaty, for all its good in tions invites catastrophe

The Nuclear Nonproliferation aty is regarded as an interna nal firebreak against the further ead of nuclear weapons But its visions for containing prolifera are like the hospitals that Flor e Nightingale so abhorred They ve served to spread the disease

raq, for example, is a treaty party good standing despite Saddam ssein's decade-long pursuit of nu ar weapons His exercise in bla t proliferation does not run afoul the treaty because only the receipt assembly of a complete nuclear vice not the acquisition of the in edients needed to build one, would olate it

Iraq's continued nonnuclear eapon status is attributable princi lly not to its treaty membership t to Israel's bombing in 1981 of an nfinished research reactor near ghdad That reactor was capable producing plutonium in quantities rge enough to make at least two omic bombs a year It had been cer fied "peaceful" by inspectors from e International Atomic Energy gency, the U.N group that polices e treaty. Israel remains outside the eaty and is hardly a pillar of non roliferation, but its pre-emptive rike capacity and undeclared nu ear arsenal reflect a lack of faith in e treaty's guarantees

Japan is a treaty member in good anding It plans to recover from the astes of its reactors more plu onium than the United States and the oviet Union now have in all their nu lear arms combined This plan does ot run afoul of the treaty because the utonium is to be used as fuel for ower reactors, not bombs

No matter that Japan will have far more plutonium than it needs, because it has postponed into the next century the new reactors for which the fuel was intended. No matter that current reactors do not need this highly toxic, bomb-grade plutonium at all but can continue to function on plentiful low-grade uranium that cannot be made into weapons. No matter that I.A.E.A. inspectors are unable to know in a given year, because of measurement uncertainties, whether 600 pounds of plutonium (enough for 50 bombs) has been simply lost in the pipes of a large processing plant or has been diverted. No matter that these uncertainties and other vulnerabilities make plutonium susceptible to theft by terrorists as well as diversion by nations intent on making nuclear weapons. It's all O.K. Commerce in tons of surplus plutonium — though it is a latent form of proliferation — is not a treaty violation

West Germany is a treaty member in good standing. Its nuclear exports to such non-treaty countries as India and Pakistan, which do not require them to accept the same all-encompassing I.A.E.A inspections that are required of member countries, do not run afoul of the treaty. There are loopholes that even permit West Germany to export some items essential to producing nuclear weapons materials, like heavy water and processing equipment, without being in technical violation of the treaty.

Even Iraq complies with the treaty.

The U.S. and the Soviet Union are *treaty parties in good standing despite* their 50,000 nuclear weapons because they "pursue negotiations in good faith," as the treaty requires. Certainly, recent negotiations and the political realignment in Europe serve to make possible the first substantial cuts in nuclear arms by the superpowers But their quantitative nuclear arms race is fast being eclipsed by a qualitative one Continued testing of weapons, production of materials for weapons and modernization of warheads and missiles keep the superpower nuclear rivalry alive without violating the treaty

Two sets of improvements to the treaty are needed. First, the tripwire for a treaty violation should be possession of weapons-grade materials, not possession of a weapon.

Second, the treaty must obligate the superpowers to curtail, qualitatively as well as quantitatively, the nuclear rivalry that still serves as the ready excuse for other nations to keep their nuclear options open. The superpowers could well halt all testing and weapons-materials productionas they reduce their nuclear arsenals

Failure to consider these improvements now may make it impossible to upgrade and update the treaty by 1995, when the parties must meet *again to extend it. If the needed* changes are not yet in place by then the treaty should be extended for successive short periods only

There should be a longer extension only after the treaty has been made relevent to the real-world dangers of proliferation and terrorism, and to a nuclear arms race that grows more lethal even as the superpower arsenals are reduced.

Unfortunately, U.S policy, shared by the U.S.S.R. and most industrial nations, is to paper over the Nonproliferation treaty's problems That avoids raising concerns about the nuclear industry and does not challenge the nuclear-weapons status quo. But the time has come to view the treaty without rose-colored glasses □

Paul L. Leventhal is president of the Nuclear Control Institute

VIEWPOINTS

Expose All Secret Nuclear Stashes

Rigid inspections and export controls can stop a future Iraq.

By Paul Leventhal
and Steven Dolley

IN 1979, THE partially melted core of the Three Mile Island reactor showed the world that a major nuclear-power accident was no imaginary threat. Now the discovery of a huge Iraqi nuclear weapons program, built right under the noses of international inspectors, has presented the global nonproliferation system with its own kind of Three Mile Island. But just as the Chernobyl meltdown followed Three Mile Island, the spread of nuclear weapons will proceed apace unless real reforms are put in place.

Until the gulf war, Iraq had always been treated as a model citizen by the International Atomic Energy Agency. Now, however, the agency and its boosters in the nuclear industry and bureaucracy worldwide have had to eat crow over a succession of humiliations at the hands of the Iraqis. First, Iraq denied having any weapons-usable material or bomb-building plants, despite the UN cease-fire resolution requiring it to turn over all such materials to the Atomic Energy Agency and to allow the agency to destroy all such plants missed by allied bombing.

Iraq eventually agreed to reveal [illegible] uranium and other nuclear materials, but denied having other weapons-grade materials or weapons plants. Then, after a defector from the Iraqi nuclear program told what he knew to U.S. experts, Iraq tried to conceal [illegible] showed [illegible] of a secret industry for producing its own bomb-grade uranium.

Then, in what must have been the cruelest blow for the international [illegible] Iraq admitted that it had been producing plutonium [illegible] of the Nuclear Nonproliferation Treaty, of which Iraq is a signatory. Although the three grams of plutonium shown to the Atomic Energy Agency [illegible] than the few kilograms needed for a weapon, [illegible] demonstrated Iraq's capability to recover plutonium from spent fuel and raised concerns that Iraq might have hidden away a plutonium production program.

In the interest of world peace, then, we must learn some lessons from this "Three Mile Island" of nuclear proliferation.

First, there may be far more to Iraq's nuclear program. Iraq cannot be expected to volunteer [illegible]

[illegible]

ments and results must be lifted. The Atomic Energy Agency should be empowered to conduct snap inspections — now they must give notice — and be authorized to look wherever they suspect violations. (Now, if a building is declared free of nuclear material, it is off limits, and inspectors may not even report suspicious activities observed between declared sites.) Inspections also should be more frequent. In Iraq, inspectors were checking twice a year on fuel that could be converted into weapons in one to three weeks.

Of course, a stronger inspection system will not help without stricter controls over nuclear exports. U.S. law permits many nuclear components and other items useful to bomb-making to be exported to states that do not adhere to the nonproliferation treaty or accept inspections.

The Nuclear Proliferation Prevention Act, recently introduced by Rep. Edward Markey (D-Mass.) and Sen. Timothy Wirth (D-Col.), would close this and other major export control loopholes. It also directs the president to impose trade sanctions on nations transferring nuclear items under less stringent controls, and to negotiate stronger Atomic Energy Agency safeguards.

Also, there must be a substantial upgrading of U.S. intelligence gathering [illegible] Cold War [illegible] who would [illegible] and threaten world peace.

[illegible]

Paul Leventhal directed the U.S. Senate investigation of the Three Mile Island nuclear accident. He is now president of the Nuclear Control Institute in Washington, D.C. Steven Dolley is the institute's research director.

NUCLEAR CONTROL
INSTITUTE

INTERNATIONAL Herald Tribune
Published With The New York Times and The Washington Post

TUESDAY, SEPTEMBER 24, 1991

The Nuclear Watchdogs Have Failed

By Paul L. Leventhal

CAMBRIDGE, England — The International Atomic Energy Agency has just completed its annual conference in Vienna. After the agency's failure to detect a multibillion-dollar nuclear weapons project in Iraq, the Dutch proposed, on behalf of European Community members, an emergency overhaul of a failed safeguards system. The agency's powerful board of governors has put off action until February and shows every sign of acting like the nuclear faithful failing to see that the emperor has no clothes.

The 23-member board, dominated by industrial states concerned about eroding public acceptance of nuclear energy, is ill-equipped to recognize the nakedness of IAEA safeguards in the presence of a determined proliferator.

To do so risks acknowledging that there is no effective barrier between peaceful and military applications of nuclear energy. This admission could threaten extension of the Nuclear Nonproliferation Treaty when its 25-year charter runs out in 1995 — as well as the lucrative commerce in atom-bomb materials, and the technologies for producing them for civilian uses, now made possible by the treaty.

Perhaps that explains why agency inspectors were making only twice-a-year calls in Iraq on the bomb-grade fuel that could be converted into weapons in two to three weeks. Worse still was the failure of inspectors to find or even suspect secret nuclear weapons plants, or to detect secret production and recovery of plutonium in safeguarded facilities.

To his credit, the IAEA's director-general, Hans Blix, has reported extensively to the board on safeguards weaknesses exposed by Iraq. The Dutch proposal picks up on several of Mr. Blix's points about the need for surprise inspections, more frequent and more intrusive regular inspections, and broader coverage of IAEA safeguards to include natural uranium that cannot be used directly in bombs but is used to produce bomb-grade uranium and plutonium.

But may of the safeguards weaknesses addressed by Mr. Blix and the Dutch are of the governing board's own making. For example, the board has refused to authorize snap inspections of safeguarded facilities to check for unauthorized activities, or to authorize entry by demand into unsafeguarded facilities to determine whether nuclear materials are in production or storage, or to authorize safeguards on natural uranium.

The IAEA's model safeguards agreement with Nonproliferation Treaty members authorizes these inspections, but the board of governors has not permitted them because of objections from members that they would be too extensive and intrusive. The combination of a board that applies a lowest-common-denominator principle to applying safeguards and a nuclear technocracy that applies safeguards to explosive materials that are inherently unsafeguardable is a prescription for catastrophe. Five fundamental reforms are needed.

- The IAEA membership should vote to amend the agency's statute to relieve the board of governors of its safeguards authority and limit the board to pursuing the agency's nuclear promotional activities.
- The director-general should be authorized by vote of the members to report to and serve under the direction of the UN Security Council on all safeguards matters, via a permanent form of the UN Special Commission set up to oversee removal of weapons materials and plants from Iraq.
- Proliferation-related intelligence should be channeled by the U.S. and other governments to the Security Council via the new, permanent Special Commission, which would authorize IAEA challenge inspections or other UN-sponsored actions in any country in which safeguards violations or weapons activities were suspected.
- Since there is no way of knowing whether the IAEA has been effective in verifying that countries other than Iraq are not diverting nuclear materials or building bombs, all of the agency's inspection reports should be reviewed by an independent, blue-ribbon panel named by the Security Council, and the results should be publicly reported.
- The Security Council should authorize the IAEA director-general to propose international arrangements for supply of low-enriched uranium unsuitable for bombs and for custody over reactor-spent fuel and any recovered plutonium. This method of minimizing weapons-capable uranium and plutonium in civil programs is an important "atoms-for-peace" approach long abandoned by the IAEA board of governors, but one that could still work.

Changes in the IAEA statute, which require a two-thirds vote of countries attending the annual conference and acceptance by two-thirds of all IAEA member states, are needed to deal effectively with a governing board that seeks to keep safeguards as weak as possible.

Experts argue the fine points of safeguards, but the public simply wants safeguards to detect nuclear bomb-making. The public does not misunderstand safeguards, as some defenders of the IAEA suggest; the agency misunderstands what the public rightfully expects of safeguards as the price of continuing with atoms for peace and the Nonproliferation Treaty.

The writer, president of the Nuclear Control Institute in Washington, is a visiting fellow at Cambridge University's Global Security Programme. He contributed this comment to the International Herald Tribune.

NEW YORK TIMES, May 22, 1993

The Coming Age of Plutonium

By Paul L. Leventhal

WASHINGTON

For nearly 25 years, the world has depended on the Nuclear Non-Proliferation Treaty to stop the spread of weapons. But Iraq and North Korea have exposed its dirty secret: it legitimates, even facilitates, production of weapons materials — plutonium and bomb-grade uranium.

The world can close this loophole as the United Nations begins considering the future of the treaty, which ends its 25-year term in 1995. Extension of the treaty must be conditioned on a ban on production of bomb-grade nuclear materials. That won't happen if the international nuclear establishment, which is trying to persuade President Clinton to resume nuclear testing, gets its way on the treaty. It wants the treaty, with all its imperfections, extended indefinitely and unconditionally. Mr. Clinton must insist on correcting its four major flaws.

• The treaty is supposed to prevent the spread of the bomb but promotes sharing of "peaceful" nuclear technology that produces plutonium. Every reactor produces plutonium, which cannot be made into bombs until it is recovered from wastes. Instead of banning recovery and promoting waste disposal, the pact approves the use of plutonium in bomb-grade form. A nation only has to promise peaceful use and admit inspectors.

Yet the enforcement arm, the International Atomic Energy Agency in Vienna, admits it could miss diversions of plutonium as large as 600 pounds a year, enough for 60 nuclear weapons. These inspectors certified Saddam Hussein's nuclear program peaceful and declared Iraqi conduct under the treaty "exemplary." They were helpless when North Korea said it was quitting the agreement and keeping enough plutonium to make as many as six bombs.

Japan, pleading "energy security," is about to import tons of bomb-grade plutonium from Europe and produce many more tons at home. South Korea, less than reassured, wants a peaceful plutonium program of its own. North Korea, using Japan's appetite for plutonium as an excuse, continues to produce plutonium with technology acquired as a treaty signatory. The region, festering with ancient enmities, could be awash in plutonium.

> Ban production of bomb-grade materials.

• The treaty rewards nations that refuse to sign. It permits them to receive "peaceful" nuclear materials and technology from member nations without opening all their nuclear facilities to inspection. Brazil, India, Israel and Pakistan have an incentive not to sign the treaty because they qualify for nuclear assistance without it.

• Thirty years ago, the superpowers agreed to negotiate a comprehensive ban on testing. Despite the cold war's end, the negotiations and explosions continue. The treaty does not require a ban and actually permits "peaceful nuclear explosions" by non-nuclear powers. Since some weapons can be built without testing, an essential complement to a ban is a production ban on bomb-grade materials.

• Until recently, international inspectors looked only where countries like Iraq, North Korea and Iran allowed them to look. Embarrassed by bomb programs that proceeded under their noses, the inspectors are ready to look harder. But they lack enforcement power because authority rests with a weak international agency in Vienna. The United Nations Security Council is brought in only after evidence of bomb-making is found.

The nuclear powers must agree to dispose of plutonium from their dismantled warheads safely and permanently, by recombining it with radioactive waste and burying it deep in the earth. Non-nuclear powers must agree to dispose of plutonium from civilian reactors the same way, and not add to a global glut of plutonium.

Failure to act will insure that commerce in plutonium will blossom into world trade exceeding 300 tons by the year 2000. That's one and a half times the plutonium in all the nuclear weapons on Earth. Unless the United States builds a global consensus to strengthen the treaty, the nuclear confrontation of the cold war will be replaced by nuclear terror of a plutonium age. □

Paul L. Leventhal is president of the Nuclear Control Institute.

THE INTERNATIONAL ATOMIC ENERGY AGENCY (IAEA): IMPROVING SAFEGUARDS

HEARINGS

BEFORE THE

SUBCOMMITTEES ON

INTERNATIONAL SECURITY AND SCIENTIFIC AFFAIRS

AND ON

INTERNATIONAL ECONOMIC POLICY AND TRADE

OF THE

COMMITTEE ON FOREIGN AFFAIRS

HOUSE OF REPRESENTATIVES

NINETY-SEVENTH CONGRESS

SECOND SESSION

MARCH 3 AND 18, 1982

Printed for the use of the Committee on Foreign Affairs

U.S. GOVERNMENT PRINTING OFFICE
WASHINGTON 1982

safeguardable

Thank you

[Mr Leventhal's prepared statement follows]

PREPARED STATEMENT OF PAUL LEVENTHAL PRESIDENT THE NUCLEAR CLUB INC

Mr Chairman I appreciate your invitation to testify at this joint hearing of the Subcommittee on International Security and Scientific Affairs and the Subcommittee on International Economic Policy and Trade

The subject of the hearing — to determine what steps are needed and being taken to ensure that our safeguards goals can be met by the International Atomic Energy Agency (IAEA)—is crucial to two complementary sets of interests

First the U S national security interest in assuring that American civilian nuclear exports are not diverted or stolen to produce nuclear weapons that can be used against us or to trigger a war that would engulf us,

Second the global interest in assuring that nuclear violence does not erupt anywhere from conversion of commercial nuclear technology and materials to weapons purposes

Unfortunately neither interest is being served by the IAEA safeguards system In fact, the IAEA safeguards system so-called is a dangerous misnomer It is not safe It does not guard anything, It is not a uniform system

The IAEA is a unique experiment in international politics It has made unprecedented strides in penetrating the sovereignty of nations to impose an international regime of inspections and audits on nuclear energy programs—one of the most sensitive areas of national prerogative But because of the sensitivity and difficulty of its task, the IAEA has been subjected to a multitude of constraints that conspire to render its safeguards system dangerously ineffective and grossly misleading

The weaknesses of IAEA safeguards have been methodically covered up presumably to protect the agency from undue political pressure and embarrassment In fact the secrecy surrounding IAEA safeguards serve the other principal function of the IAEA—namely to promote nuclear power and research programs throughout the world To quote authors Steve Weissman and Herbert Krosney in the recently published The Islamic Bomb IAEA officials often sound as if they are more concerned to make the world safe for nuclear power than safe from nuclear weapons

In fact the IAEA safeguards system is fighting a losing battle against the spread of nuclear weapons To the extent it promises more than it can possibly deliver to the extent it has been used by nuclear advocates to provide a legitimate cover for what otherwise would be seen clearly as illicit trafficking in the means and materials needed to produce nuclear weapons IAEA safeguards constitute 'fraud The extent of the fraud is only now becoming generally understood as are the likely catastrophic consequences of the spread of nuclear weapons material and technology made possible by this gross deception of the public

For years we have been assured by a worldwide nuclear industry and bureaucracy that IAEA safeguards can and do provide an effective barrier between atoms for peace and atoms for war Now we are coming to see that the only real barrier between peaceful and military use of the atom is the intent of the user To quote NRC Commissioner Victor Gilinsky If we don t do something about the spread of nuclear weapons material and technology we better tighten our seat belts because it is going to be a rough ride

I am pleased to testify today on behalf of The Nuclear Club Inc about what can be done and more significantly about what cannot be done to upgrade IAEA safeguards

The Nuclear Club Inc is a non profit educational organization working exclusively on the horizontal proliferation' problem—that is the spread of nuclear weapons through commercial nuclear power and research programs Our membership is a diverse group of citizens seeking to prevent civilian nuclear programs from following technological paths that will lead inevitably to development of nuclear weapons The Nuclear Club seeks to coordinate the activities of other organizations that have an interest in the proliferation problem but cannot devote full time to it

Previously in staff positions in the U S Senate I was responsible for investigations and hearings and for drafting legislation leading to abolishment of the Atomic Energy Commission in 1974 and to enactment of the Nuclear Non Proliferation Act of 1978. I also was Co-Director of the Senate Special Investigation of the Three Mile Island Nuclear Accident in 1979 and 1980. Much of my Senate staff work and current efforts through The Nuclear Club have been devoted to promoting public understanding of the incipient dangers of civilian nuclear programs in the absence of effective safeguards against illicit weapons development

Out of these long overdue hearings hopefully will emerge first a real world assessment of U S options given the political and technical limitations of safeguards and second the realization that prohibition of commerce in nuclear explosive materials not improved safeguards is the key to curbing the proliferation of nuclear weapons

At this point in my testimony I will respond to the three questions you asked me to address in connection with the possible need for more restrictive U S export policies I will then elaborate on some of the points made in these responses

1 What kinds of nuclear facilities and materials is the IAEA unable to safeguard adequately?

The short answer is all kinds While the IAEA is better able to safeguard certain types of materials and facilities than others—for example safeguarding spent fuel in light water reactors is a potentially manageable task while safeguarding plutonium once separated from the spent fuel is not—IAEA safeguards are currently inadequate across the board given

An IAEA inspection force that is understaffed overburdened and beset by Third World and superpower politics

A lack of support by IAEA member nations for safeguards in relation to the agency's promotional role which translates into a lack of financial and technical resources to fully implement and upgrade safeguards

The political discretion of IAEA member nations to bar individual inspectors and to limit the access of those inspectors who are admitted

The technical difficulties in making precise measurements of safeguarded nuclear materials and the absence of direct monitoring of the power levels of reactors to determine how much plutonium is actually produced in their cores

The secrecy that surrounds IAEA safeguards arrangements in each country and the outcome of IAEA inspections and audits made pursuant to these arrangements

The lack of uniformity of inspection and auditing procedures from country to country and from facility to facility within countries

The general unreliability of containment and surveillance devices for detection of unauthorized movements of nuclear materials between visits by IAEA inspectors

The absence of any police authority by inspectors to seek out clandestine activities or undeclared nuclear materials for the production of nuclear weapons

The ease with which nations can renounce safeguards and other obligations under the Nuclear Non Proliferation Treaty after acquiring all the materials and know how needed to manufacture nuclear weapons

The lack of prompt and effective international sanctions against an offending nation in the event the IAEA detects and announces a diversion of nuclear materials

Given all of these weaknesses it is unreasonable to expect that the IAEA can fulfill its basic safeguards objective That objective is to detect on a timely basis and thereby deter diversions of civilian nuclear materials to weapons purposes or to provide sufficient advance warning that a diversion has occurred to permit the international community to respond before clandestine nuclear weapons can be assembled and used

And yet Mr Chairman despite documentation of these weaknesses in a recent succession of technical and press reports civilian nuclear enterprise continues in a headlong rush along technological paths that will overwhelm the already beleaguered safeguards system and flood the world with tons of plutonium and highly enriched uranium eventually enough for hundreds of thousands of Nagasaki - and Hiroshima type bombs

I am referring of course to the programs of this Administration and of the governments of several industrialized and Third World nations to proceed with the reprocessing of spent fuel the recycling of plutonium as fuel and development of the breeder - a reactor that will produce more plutonium than it consumes as fuel. I am also referring to the development and widespread deployment of centrifuge and laser technologies for enriching uranium technologies that will provide the capability to produce weapons grade as well as reactor-grade fuels

Further in a particularly disturbing development the Reagan Administration is actively considering breaking down a real barrier between atoms for peace and atoms for war by utilizing spent fuel from commercial nuclear power plants as a source of plutonium for production of nuclear weapons This would be a horrible example to set for the world—one that almost certainly would be followed by other nations if the United States leads the way

So that the hearing record can include a full accounting of the weakness of IAEA safeguards and the system's inability to cope with the advanced technologies I have just described I would like to submit for the record a number of recently released or published technical reports as well as a number of excellent articles that have appeared recently in The New York Times The Wall Street Journal The Christian Science Monitor The Baltimore Sun The Washington Post and The Bulletin of the Atomic Scientists [1]

2 To what extent is the United States involved in the export of these nuclear materials and how would more restrictive export policies be carried out?

The United States has exported thousands of kilograms of highly enriched uranium for research reactors and hundreds of kilograms of plutonium for breeder programs throughout the world Exports of highly enriched uranium should be terminated because research reactors can be adapted to accommodate lower-enriched uranium unsuitable for weapons Plutonium exports also should be stopped as a first step toward discouraging further development of breeder reactors

Although the exports of weapons usable uranium and plutonium are obviously sensitive and dangerous the export of low enriched uranium unsuitable for weapons is equally sensitive and dangerous if the end-use of this material is to be reprocessing—that is the separation of plutonium from the spent fuel of light water reactors This unfortunately has been a neglected area of nuclear export policy So-called MB-10 applications from foreign governments for permission to transfer U S origin spent fuel to reprocessing plants have been routinely approved by the Department of Energy with Congressional acquiescence over the past several years It is time for Congress to take a hard look at reprocessing in the light of the inability of the IAEA to effectively safeguard separated plutonium

The Nuclear Regulatory Commission now has the authority to withhold exports of low-enriched uranium if the recipient country intends to reprocess spent fuel and if the NRC believes that safeguards cannot be effectively applied to the separated plutonium However it appears unlikely that the NRC will take such bold action against the obvious preferences of the President and Executive Branch agencies without a clear directive by Congress to do so

It is incumbent upon this Committee and the Congress in general therefore to establish such a policy in law This would be strong medicine admittedly but it may be the only remedy available to prevent a plutonium epidemic Without such strong action by Congress there is virtually no hope that the nuclear industry and bureaucracy in this country and abroad will voluntarily limit civilian nuclear development to the current generation of reactors and will forego reprocessing plutonium recycling and deployment of breeder reactors

Yet only in the exercise of such technological restraint is there any hope that the IAEA safeguards system can "catch up" with nuclear development that already has taken place Only by assigning the IAEA the task of safeguarding what is safeguardable is there any hope to prevent the spread of nuclear weapons

3 Can more restrictive export policies be effective in meeting safeguard goals if the U S acts alone rather than in concert with other supplier nations?

Obviously restrictive export policies by the United States alone without cooperation by other suppliers, cannot be effective in the long run However there is much the United States can do on its own to lead the way toward an effective non proliferation regime worldwide

Much has been made of the argument that U S leverage to attain non proliferation objectives is a "wasting asset"—that we no longer have the influence we once had because we are no longer the sole or dominant supplier of nuclear equipment and materials The only course open to us so this argument goes is to help "manage the proliferation problem"—that is to "manage a proliferated world" rather than to seek to prevent the world from proliferating

This is self defeating strategy Of course proliferation will be inevitable if we assume it to be The problem is that a proliferated world is irreversible and inherently unmanageable Once plutonium is separated from spent fuel there is no putting it back Once plutonium begins to accumulate in the tens and hundreds and eventually thousands of tons in the commercial sector—in the absence of effective safeguards—it is only a matter of time before it will be put to violent use by nations or by terrorists

Proliferation management is the truly wasting asset Over time in the face of regional instabilities and global crises, in the historical process of friends becoming enemies and enemies becoming friends in the face of the growing sophistication and boldness of international terrorists—it appears inevitable that regional wars will become nuclear wars that urban terrorism will become nuclear terrorism

If we are to avoid such a nuclear Dark Age the United States must act decisively now Our leverage to prevent widespread nuclear proliferation has eroded only if we assume erroneously that our leverage is confined to the arena of nuclear commerce

Clearly we have other cards to play in the considerable interest of preventing the spread of nuclear weapons that can be used against us

Even in the confined area of nuclear commerce we remain a potent force The latest data from the Energy Department shows for example that we still provide enriched fuel for 31 percent of the free world's nuclear power reactors This is down from 68 percent in 1978 but in OPEC-oil terms we still are the equivalent of a Saudi Arabia! DOE projections indicate that our share of the enrichment market for the next two years will remain in the 15-30 percent range

Thus if we are prepared to do so we can leverage our position as a principal supplier of enriched fuel to attain non proliferation objectives We can withhold low enriched uranium if the end product is to be plutonium We also can offer a positive incentive for customer countries to forego the production and use of plutonium namely to offer an assured and economic supply of low-enriched uranium in exchange for a commitment to forego plutonium and to dispose of spent fuel in unaltered form The Hart bill S 1488 would establish such a system and should be supported

However U S efforts to prevent the spread of nuclear weapons capabilities should not be limited to nuclear commerce Surely our only chance is not to serve as a "reliable nuclear supplier" as the industry and its advocates would argue There is a whole range of economic political and military leverage both negative and positive at our disposal

It is not a question of whether we have leverage Of course we do—not to the extent we had in the immediate post war era but still in very large measure We remain the most powerful economic moral and military force in the free world It is really a question of to what degree we are prepared to exercise leverage on the proliferation problem in relation to all the other problems on our current foreign policy agenda

The real dilemma is that proliferation is generally deemed a distant long term problem and is inevitably relegated to a lower order of priority than the "front burner" issues of the day that require prompt exercise of U S leverage and influence Competing foreign policy priorities more than any other factor undermined the non proliferation initiatives of the Carter Administration

The Carter non proliferation policies have been declared a failure by the Reagan Administration which is now seeking a prompt reversal of these policies by promoting reprocessing and breeder programs at home and acquiescing in their continued development abroad Ironically the Reagan Administration is assigning the major responsibility for curbing nuclear weapons proliferation to the International Atomic Energy Agency expressing confidence that the IAEA system can be upgraded to meet the test If the Administration pursues this course and the Congress concurs in it the worldwide civilian nuclear program perhaps the world itself will be set on self-destruct

Precious little time remains to avoid a world of nuclear anarchy and nuclear violence What can still be done?

1 End secrecy The weaknesses of the IAEA safeguards system must be openly acknowledged so that public pressure can be brought to bear to remedy them to the extent politically and technically feasible The secrecy surrounding safeguards must be lifted

Only in publicly airing the weaknesses and the limits of international safeguards is there any hope of strengthening the agency to the point that it can perform a limited inspection role effectively Only in laying bare the technical and political limits of IAEA safeguards is there any hope to steer commercial nuclear enterprise away from technological paths that are unsafeguardable and therefore too inherently dangerous to be pursued for peaceful purposes

There are technological and political means available to upgrade safeguards on reactor spent fuel But there is no hope for developing effective safeguards on vast quantities of plutonium and high grade uranium or on the reprocessing and enrichment facilities that produce these weapons usable materials

In this context the Administration should explain the following confidential assessment of the safeguards system by the Department of Defense

DOD wishes to express its reservations about the effectiveness of IAEA safeguards the weakness of the IAEA as an international institution its susceptibility

[1] [illegible]

to Third World and East Bloc politics its lack of an intelligence capability, and the limits of its scope and jurisdiction in order to guard against undue reliance on the IAEA by those responsible for national security within the United States government

The President's non proliferation statement last July made no reference to this warning by the Department of Defense although it did contain commitments to work for "an improved international safeguards regime" and to "seek to prevent the spread of nuclear explosives to additional countries" These commitments were offset, however by the President's commitment not to inhibit plutonium reprocessing and breeder development abroad in advanced nations where it does not constitute a proliferation risk and later in his domestic nuclear policy statement to promote reprocessing and breeder development in the United States

It is difficult to understand how commercial reprocessing and breeder activities anywhere do not constitute a proliferation risk in the absence of effective safeguards And if safeguards cannot be effectively applied now or in the future on separated plutonium how can these advanced technologies be justified—especially when sufficient low grade uranium not usable in nuclear weapons is available to meet the fuel needs of all the current generation of power reactors that are now operating or that can be built well into the next century?

2 Upgrade Safeguards on What Is Safeguardable IAEA safeguards should be upgraded in facilities and on materials that are safeguardable The IAEA should be split into separate and independent regulatory and promotional agencies—as was done with The Atomic Energy Commission

Particular emphasis should be placed on improved containment and surveillance In particular the United States should press for the IAEA's acceptance and deployment of the advanced technology Operation RECOVER and Operation TRANSEAVER systems These systems now being tested on a pilot basis would permit satellite transmission directly to the IAEA on a real time basis of camera surveillance of nuclear facilities and shipments as well as the monitoring of electronic (fiber optic) seals This system would represent a quantum leap beyond the present system of unescorted nuclear shipments and the labor intensive highly inefficient process of overburdened inspectors traveling from facility to facility around the world checking cameras that often do not work and antiquated seals that can be defeated

In addition a standardized IAEA materials accounting system should replace the myriad national accounting systems that IAEA inspectors somehow must oversee and verify

The number of IAEA inspectors should be increased and the technical competence of the inspection force improved It is scandalous that in an industry in which individual plants cost upwards of a billion dollars the entire IAEA safeguards program is financed at $25 million a year utilizing only about 140 inspectors to monitor over 700 facilities in 50 countries In fact figuring in a 20 percent turnover rate and sick leave the actual number of available Inspectors is about 100—at least ten times too small to fulfill the agency's own technical objectives

3 Tighten U S Export Controls The United States should assertively pursue a policy of withholding nuclear assistance and applying economic sanctions to nations that insist on pursuing reprocessing enrichment and breeder development The heart of a successful nuclear non proliferation policy is the control of nuclear explosives—separated plutonium and high-grade uranium The best way to control them is to provide leadership to bar their use in commercial nuclear programs

Chairman Zablocki Thank you, Mr Leventhal

Mr Sokolski

STATEMENT OF HENRY DAVID SOKOLSKI, VISITING SCHOLAR, THE HERITAGE FOUNDATION

Mr Sokolski First I would like to thank you, Mr Chairman, for making it possible for me to appear here and giving me the opportunity to present my views.

I feel, looking at my watch that I am object lesson in the wasting asset of time So I am going to try to keep my comments very brief

I was asked to appear here to make some comments about what we can do without the IAEA to slow nuclear weapons spread

NUCLEAR WEAPONS SPREAD A NATIONAL SECURITY ISSUE

I think that we can do a good deal if we are willing to look at the problem of nuclear weapons spread as a national security issue Unfortunately there is a tendency to emphasize solutions with regard to nuclear weapons spread that assume that the problem doesn't exist

In specific I think that the left tends to talk about arms control and international regimes that might be established some day and the right tends to talk about cartels and atomic deals that will be in place and producing leverage a decade away

The problem of nuclear weapons spread though is something that is with us now Fortunately there are things that we can do here and now without necessarily securing the cooperation of a lot of other people abroad that could make a difference

RAPID DEPLOYMENT FORCE

I also want to emphasize that the national security threat posed by the spread of nuclear weapons is quite real Right now we are spending several scores of billions of dollars to put together a Rapid Deployment Force This force is necessary to help secure and stabilize the Persian Gulf for ourselves and our allies

The prospect of being able to do that when the force itself won't even be complete until the 1990's will not be improved by several more nations in that region getting nuclear weapons Not only will the spread of nuclear weapons in this region increase our difficulty in securing bases, which is absolutely essential if this force is to make any sense but if we do get bases it is going to be more expensive to protect them Indeed, the targets that we are trying to protect the oilfields, are going to be much more vulnerable and we are more likely to get hurt along with a lot of other people

That is just blood and treasure I think the bigger problem is that with nuclear weapons in that region you are simply going to have a very unstable situation And, Lord knows, it is already unstable That makes for good opportunities for the Soviets, much better opportunities for the Soviets to do the things that they do well already

I think then that we ought to start looking at the problem in these terms If we do there are several steps we can take which will not increase the budget very much or require interagency studies In fact, there are suggestions in my paper, approximately 12 or so, which are, as someone who read it this morning said absolutely mundane

These mundane suggestions are the place to begin precisely because they can be done and because for all their mundaneness they are the things that will make the most difference

STEPS TO CURB NUCLEAR WEAPONS SPREAD

I am not going to go through those suggestions They are underlined in the text

What I will do though, is hone in on what I think the most important of those suggestions—to increase the bureaucratic likelihood that action will be taken when trouble is found

Nuclear Safeguards and Non-Proliferation in a Changing World Order

LAWRENCE SCHEINMAN*
Cornell University, Ithaca NY

1. Non-proliferation and Safeguards

INTERNATIONAL SAFEGUARDS are an essential element of the nuclear non-proliferation regime. In discussing safeguards, the words *element* and *regime* are central: although some critical assessments of international safeguards tend to equate their effectiveness with *preventing* proliferation, safeguards were never designed to prevent proliferation, so to judge them according to this criterion is to raise the wrong question and to foster the wrong expectations.

Safeguards are only one part of a regime of norms, rules, institutions and procedures developed to support efforts to control the spread of nuclear weapons.[1] The regime is anchored in the Nuclear Non-Proliferation Treaty of 1968 (NPT) and, in addition to the Treaty, includes national nuclear non-proliferation policies, supplier-state export controls, regional nuclear weapon-free zones, security assurances, and verification arrangements – principally the safeguards applied by the International Atomic Energy Agency (IAEA). The NPT codifies the norm of non-proliferation and establishes the legal basis upon which non-nuclear-weapon states can contract undertakings not to produce or receive nuclear weapons or nuclear explosive devices, and to submit their peaceful nuclear programs to international verification.

Safeguards are a technical means of verifying that states comply with their legal undertakings.[2] The legal undertakings define the scope of the safeguards to be applied. In the case of the NPT, the purpose of safeguards is to provide, through verification of operating records and reports and on-site inspection, assurance that states are fulfilling their commitments to use nuclear energy for exclusively peaceful purposes. In so doing they provide confidence about the character of nuclear activity in the safeguarded state, reinforce non-proliferation, and facilitate international nuclear cooperation for peaceful purposes. Although non-nuclear-weapon states are obliged under the NPT 'not to receive the transfer ...of nuclear weapons or other nuclear explosive devices...; not to manufacture or otherwise seek or receive any assistance in the manufacture of nuclear weapons or other nuclear explosive devices',[3] safeguards extend only to verifying that nuclear energy (specifically nuclear material) is not diverted from peaceful uses to nuclear weapons or other nuclear explosive devices.[4] Creating confidence involves the capability to detect (and, by risk of detection, deter) violations of this undertaking regarding the use of nuclear energy.

As safeguards are carried out by an international organization that lacks independent political authority, their capability to provide assurance and to build confidence is largely determined by the authorities, resources, and political support that the instituting sovereign member-states provide. The leadership and determination of the international secretariat, which is responsible for day-to-day implementation of safeguards, also is relevant to their success in providing the sought-after confidence.

Preventing proliferation is a matter of political will to which the regime as a whole contributes. But prevention begins at home. The first and most important line of defense against proliferation is the political decision that nuclear weapons do not serve the political or security interest of the state and that they are not in the national interest. Many factors enter into this calculation, both domestic and international.[5] Decisions are influenced by perceptions of local and regional security and stability, the dependability of alliances or security commitments, and by the general international environment – whether it is marked by tension and uncertainty, which may increase interest in nuclear weapons, or by detente and stability, which may diminish that interest. If nuclear-weapon states continue to emphasize the importance of nuclear assets to national security, this is bound to affect thinking in other states – just as progress toward nuclear disarmament as reflected in the INF and START agreements can encourage reinforcement of the commitment to non-proliferation, as well as to an extension of the NPT in 1995, and to a strengthening of the regime. Safeguards contribute to shaping the environment against which assessments of national interest are made. If perceived as effective, they build confidence in security and reduce incentives to acquire nuclear weapons, or to preserve the option of doing so; if perceived as ineffective, they can work in reverse.

2. Safeguards and Security

While safeguards have always been a critical factor in national assessments of the value of the non-proliferation regime, they have become even more so in the post-Cold War period. As long as the Cold War persisted and the superpowers pursued a global competition, it was always presumed that the United States and the Soviet Union would control the threat of proliferation among their allies or clients. To have done otherwise would have been to defeat the purpose for which the superpowers supported the concept of non-proliferation in the first place. The security guarantees they provided through their alliance systems made it unnecessary for those states to acquire nuclear weapons. Safeguards were important, but they were not alone.

Where alliances or credible security guarantees did not exist – as in the case of India, Pakistan, Israel, South Africa – the situation was more problematic. Since none of these states contracted non-proliferation obligations, legal restraints on proliferation were non-existent; but for largely political reasons, including the probable costs and risks of a regional nuclear arms race and of flying in the face of strong normative preferences against the spread of nuclear weapons held by states of importance to would-be proliferators, overt proliferation was nevertheless avoided. Safeguards in these states were limited to material, facilities, or equipment acquired from outside suppliers; in these situations of only partial verification, safeguards provided little if any confidence regarding the character of national nuclear activity. However, from a political perspective, since confidence ends where safeguards end, outside states did not harbor false illusions about the nuclear programs in these countries.

With the end of the Cold War, the situation is different. The changed circumstances have brought about new opportunities and new challenges – opportunities to capitalize on the end of bipolarity and ideological conflict, to establish a new basis for world order and to introduce a measure of collective security; challenges to ensure that a nuclear multipolarity does not emerge. The United States and Russia are no longer engaged in a global competition; their active involvement in regional and local controversies in the Third World has sharply diminished, and so, in many cases, has their influence. Local and regional conflicts have displaced the older 'relationship of major tension' on the international agenda; and some countries in unstable regions, even though they are NPT parties, may see nuclear weapons as a means of promoting policies and interests which in some cases are expansionist, and which in the new situation become more feasible. This change creates new challenges for the non-proliferation regime and, as the discovery in the wake of the Gulf War of a major clandestine nuclear weapons development program in Iraq has made clear, imposes the challenge of new expectations on international verification and specifically on IAEA safeguards. It is this latter set of issues that draws our attention here.

3. Safeguards Before Iraq

Successive NPT Review Conferences have considered and validated the contribution of IAEA safeguards to non-proliferation. The consensus final document of the 1985 conference offers a succinct statement to this effect in saying that 'IAEA safeguards provide assurance that States are complying with their undertakings... promote confidence among States and...help to strengthen their collective security.'[6] These conclusions were echoed in the 1990 NPT Review

Conference draft final document Of equal significance was the decision of Argentina and Brazil, two non-parties to the NPT, to accept IAEA full-scope safeguards to verify their recent bilateral non-proliferation arrangement,[7] confirming the perceived security value and legitimacy of the system

In short, safeguards have performed largely as expected, and the IAEA has had a believable probability of detecting diversion of significant quantities of declared nuclear material What happened in Iraq was not a breakdown of safeguards on declared material, but a circumventing of the system as designed, and of the regime as a whole Export controls failed to stem the flow of equipment relevant to nuclear weapons development, and national intelligence failed to identify clandestine activities

Importantly, from the very outset, the comprehensive safeguards system devised in 1970 to implement IAEA verification responsibility under the NPT had in view the nuclear fuel cycles of the advanced industrial states, which at the time were the only states capable of mounting any kind of nuclear program These states were concerned to minimize the risk that the distinction between themselves and the nuclear-weapon states inherent in the NPT would extend to the realm of peaceful nuclear activity and competition At the same time their joining the NPT was the main concern of the United States and the Soviet Union, who were spearheading the negotiation of the Treaty. This led to the establishment of a verification regime that kept intrusion to the minimum consistent with credible verification, which focused on the flow of nuclear material rather than on nuclear facilities per se, and which resulted in certain constraints on how the Agency exercised the rather liberal rights originally granted it in its statute[8]

The system is based on material accountancy, supplemented by containment and surveillance, to verify that all nuclear material under safeguards can be accounted for The frequency of inspection is determined by the amount of nuclear material in a facility and not by the amount of nuclear material in the state as a whole Non-discrimination between states is one of the underlying principles of implementation, the Agency does not make political judgments about the credibility of a state's non-proliferation commitment

One consequence of this system is that the amount and the intensity of safeguards increase with the size of the material inventory being verified States with large nuclear programs consequently account for a very large proportion of IAEA inspection effort Small programs on the other hand, with only modest inventories of nuclear material, are subject to only limited inspection activity. The irony is that the states that have in fact become objects of proliferation concern in the past few years fall into this category These new realities define one of the challenges for future verification

While the IAEA assumes that states entering into comprehensive safeguards agreements will declare and submit to safeguards all nuclear material that should be submitted, it does not discount the possibility of non-compliance, or that clandestine nuclear facilities capable of producing fissile materials that could be used in a nuclear explosive device might exist in a safeguarded state, and it takes these possibilities into account in establishing its safeguards implementation plan.[9] On the other hand, IAEA safeguards are not an intelligence or policing mechanism. Agency inspectors cannot roam the countryside of states in search of undeclared nuclear material or facilities, and the prevailing expectation has been that if there were information indicating the existence of undeclared activity the state having that information would bring it to the attention of the IAEA or the UN Security Council, as it saw fit. As indicated above, the system has generated substantial confidence, and there is no reason to think that material under safeguards has been diverted from peaceful use. But it is equally clear that, as devised, the system assumed that all nuclear material subject to safeguards actually was declared, and it was not designed to detect fully clandestine nuclear activity; the capability to do so would have been seen by key interested parties as controverting the objective of minimizing intrusiveness. It is fortuitous that the countries that could have diverted nuclear material had no interest or incentive to do so, and hence the need to intrude further on national sovereignty never arose. This circumstance can no longer be assumed.

4. The Impact of Iraq on Safeguards: The Emergence of New Expectations

The effect on safeguards of the discovery of the extensive clandestine nuclear-weapons development program in Iraq was two-fold: First, it underscored that even under conditions of international treaty obligations and full-scope safeguards, a state that was determined to cheat on its undertakings could successfully do so by pursuing a strategy of developing a totally clandestine program that did not rely on material under safeguards.[10] In doing so, it illuminated some of the limitations of conventional safeguards and the non-proliferation regime — the emphasis on nuclear material rather than both facilities and material, which made it possible to acquire or construct facilities without informing the IAEA of their existence before introducing nuclear material into them; determining the frequency of on-site inspections by the amount of nuclear material in a single facility rather than the amount of material in the country as a whole; limitations on knowledge about the scope of national nuclear activities resulting from the fact that NPT verification focuses only on diversion of nuclear material, and does not subject other NPT obligations to international verification, thus providing only partial transparency; weaknesses in national export control policies and laws, especially for dual-use items. Countries can get rather close to nuclear-weapons-capability without being detected in the process, and in certain respects without violating the black letter law of the Treaty. In a sense, Iraq was an opportune event, for it directed attention to the limitations and weaknesses of the regime and of safeguards at the very outset of the post-Cold War world, and provided the justification for evaluating what would be required to sustain confidence in the regime under new political circumstances.

The second effect of the Iraqi affair was to alter political expectations regarding the breadth of safeguards coverage. Hitherto, the expectation was that the IAEA would verify that all *declared* nuclear material could be accounted for. Now, the expectation extends to providing assurance that no *undeclared* material or clandestine facilities or activities exist in states that have ratified the NPT and have entered into comprehensive safeguards agreements with the IAEA. Redefining expectations means reassessing the authorities, resources and political support which the international community that now holds these expectations is prepared to provide to the institutions charged with implementation.

5. Satisfying New Expectations

Since strengthening safeguards is only part of the problem of strengthening non-proliferation, the issue is *how* to satisfy this new expectation — whether it can be achieved within the framework of existing institutions and authority, whether additional authority needs to be prescribed, or whether a totally new approach involving new institutions is required. It is imperative to keep in mind the interdependence between expectations, authority, and resources. To meet expectations, appropriate authority must be granted and adequate human, technical, and financial resources made available. In addition, political support for the responsible implementing institutions is essential — especially the will to enforce compliance with legal commitments and to take sanctioning action against violations when these are brought to the attention of political authority. Of course, the implementing institution must have leadership and direction from its senior management as well as a professional and dedicated staff.

6. New Institutions or Strengthening the IAEA?

In response to the new situation, some have advocated establishing a new verification authority based on the United Nations Special Commission (UNSCOM) that was created pursuant to UN Security Council RES/687 to carry out the provisions of that resolution for inspection, removal, destruction, or rendering harmless of all chemical and biological weapons and all ballistic missiles and supporting materials and facilities in Iraq. (The tasks related to Iraq's nuclear activities were entrusted to the IAEA with the assistance and cooperation of the Special Commission.) Partisans of this approach include (a) those who are instinctively distrustful of international organizations and prefer to maintain control through bilateral arrangements or, if that is not feasible, something closely controlled by, and directly responsible to, a limited membership body such as the UN Security Council which is predominated by the major states; and (b) those who have never had much confidence in the IAEA, because of its promotional responsibilities which are seen as countervailing effective regulation, or the emphasis given to cooperation in conducting inspections, or the large and heterogeneous governing Board through which crucial decisions would have to pass.

There is not much that can be said to those who distrust anything that they do not directly control, other than that this is too narrow and unrealistic an approach to international order. As for those who have reservations about the IAEA, some of their concerns are legitimate – but in the main correctable – and others are inherent in any organization. It is naive to assume that by creating a new institution one will escape attributes of bureaucracy that affect all organizations. As far as emphasis on cooperation is concerned, it is clear that even the 'adversarial' bilateral agreements such as INF and START require considerable cooperation to achieve their objectives, and that while they may have more adversarial roots, they are not necessarily any less cooperative. IAEA cooperation has always been predicated on the principle that, in the final analysis, nothing less than independent verification will suffice to allow it to reach a conclusion regarding accountability and non-diversion. The capacity of a heterogenous Board of Governors consisting of advanced and developing states, nuclear-weapon and non-weapon states, and both parties and non-parties to the NPT to take hard decisions swiftly, was demonstrated in July and September 1991, when the Board twice condemned Iraq for violating its safeguards undertakings and reported these violations to the Security Council. It is also well to remember that governing bodies of international organizations act on the instructions of governments, and that the actions of representatives to the IAEA or to the United Nations are defined by the same government. There is no inherent reason why political determination vis-a-vis non-proliferation should differ, whether it entails an action by the Board of Governors or the Security Council acting in response to a report of non-compliance from the IAEA Board.[11]

The main effort to meet new circumstances and new expectations has focused on re-examining existing safeguards authority and clarifying or building on it as appropriate. Considerable attention has been given to the Agency's right of special inspection which derives from the statutory right to access 'at all times to all places and data...'[12] and is inscribed in the safeguards document, INFCIRC/153, that governs IAEA full-scope safeguards agreements. This is to be distinguished from the inspection rights given the IAEA under the authority of Security Council RES/687, which in a number of respects extended beyond the rules, procedures, and techniques normally applied by the Agency.

7. Special Inspections

Special inspections are normally precipitated by reports submitted by the inspected state concerning a loss of material or change of containment, or by the Agency because the information made available by the state is not sufficient to enable the Agency to fulfill its safeguards responsibilities.[13] Pursuant to a recommendation of the 1990 NPT Review Conference that the IAEA take full advantage of special inspection rights to address questions about the completeness of the safeguards coverage of a state's nuclear material, the Agency examined their scope and applications and concluded that its right to conduct special inspections was *not* limited only to other locations within a declared facility, but also included locations and facilities other than those notified to the Agency by the state. It also concluded that the request could be based on plausible information from sources other than safeguards inspections, including national intelligence information.[14] The Board of Governors subsequently reaffirmed this right, and acknowledged the Director General's indication of how he intended to implement special inspection authority. Given the context in which the scope of special inspections has been discussed, it is clear that what had at one time been seen principally as a means of resolving uncertainties and ambiguities has now also become an instrument to investigate suspected non-compliance and clandestine activity.

Clarifying the authority for special inspections is one thing; having the information upon which to predicate a call for such an inspection is another. The Director General has emphasized that information regarding where to look in a state has been an even more decisive factor in successfully carrying out inspections in Iraq under RES/687 than the extensive rights of access granted the Agency under that resolution. Following this line of reasoning, then, if the IAEA not only makes optimal use of the many sources of information available to it through its routine safeguards, technical assistance, and safety activities, but is also assured timely access to information from member states resulting from their intelligence activities, this can significantly enhance the scope of safeguards credibility.

However important it is to have information, it also is important to have assured access to locations that might have undeclared material or facilities. Access depends on the state. Presumably, a state that has something to hide will not readily admit international inspectors into its territory even if it is obligated to do so.[15] Refusal of access can lead to a finding of non-compliance which, under its statute, the IAEA Board of Governors is obliged to report to the UN Security Council.

8. SECURING COMPLIANCE

The convergence of responsibility for enforcing compliance with international undertakings in the Security Council underscores a third element, along with information and access, in the equation of effective safeguards. In Iraq, enforcement has been taking place pursuant to Security Council resolutions based on a finding of a threat to international peace and security resulting from Iraqi aggression against Kuwait. Enforcing treaties is not, however, a routine Security Council responsibility, and unless the Council were to resolve that violations of non-proliferation undertakings or safeguards commitments *ipso facto* constituted a threat to international peace and security, reports of violation and non-compliance would have to be evaluated on a case-by-case basis. Even so, the very fact of sustained action to divest Iraq of all capabilities to produce weapons of mass destruction, puts would-be violators on notice that comparable action could be agreed again, even in the absence of a compelling need to answer an aggression in violation of the Charter.

In January 1992, the President of the Security Council, following a meeting of Heads of State and Government of Council members, stated that the proliferation of all weapons of mass destruction constitutes a threat to international peace and security. On nuclear proliferation, the members of the Council noted the importance of the decision of many states to adhere to the NPT and 'the integral role in the implementation of that Treaty of fully effective IAEA safeguards'. It was also stated that members of the Council 'will take appropriate measures in the case of any violations of safeguards notified to them by the IAEA.'[16] The importance of this step cannot be disputed; nor should it be exaggerated, given that it was made in the midst of a continuing crisis in Iraq, and a then present sense of unity of purpose on the Council. What would be still more helpful, and of even greater deterrent value, would be a formal Security Council resolution declaring that violations of non-proliferation and of international safeguards *prima facie* will be regarded as threats to peace and security and addressed under the Chapter VII authority of the Council.

9. NUCLEAR TRANSPARENCY

The second main area of attention has been in enhancing nuclear transparency. The more that is known about a country's nuclear profile, the more comprehensive the analysis and the verification can be, and the more confidence the verifying agency can have in its conclusions. The decision of the Board of Governors to endorse a proposal calling upon all parties to comprehensive safeguards agreements to inform the Agency of initial design information at the time of the decision to construct or to authorize construction or modification of any nuclear facility, and for adapting, where appropriate, the related subsidiary arrangements thus establishing a basis of obligation, paved the way to developing an early warning system.[17] Access to such information not only expands the information base upon which the IAEA can formulate verification strategies for the state; it also provides the IAEA with the opportunity to visit the construction site periodically, even though nuclear material may not yet be present, thus getting around the stipulation in the NPT safeguards system that the flow of nuclear material is what is subject to safeguards.

Another means of increasing transparency is through a comprehensive system of reporting exports, imports and production of nuclear material, equipment particularly relevant to nuclear activity, and sensitive non-nuclear materials (e.g. pure graphite, heavy water). Efforts to achieve consensus on this are still under discussion at the IAEA. Significant reporting requirements already exist, but even comprehensive safeguards agreements do not provide for complete reporting. A system of obligatory reporting of all of these elements will require establishing new bases of legal obligation, as would other measures that, if agreed to, could enhance transparency and build early warning into safeguards – such as requiring all full-scope safeguards states to provide complete information on their nuclear research and development activities in addition to all programs involving peaceful use of nuclear energy; or allowing for re-verification of design information even in the absence of a change in the operating conditions of the facility in question (the normal condition calling for a re-examination of design information).

The point of all of this is that today, confidence in verification is being measured not only by the ability of a system to confirm that what a state which has accepted comprehensive safeguards declares to exist can be accounted for, but that everything that should be declared is known and under safeguards, and that activities or violations that put at risk the security of others will be detected before they become an actual threat. Thus far, the means to this end has been to identify the limitations of the existing safeguards system, to examine its authority base, to ensure that existing authority will be used to its fullest, and where necessary to seek to reinforce and expand that authority. All of this is occurring, or should be occurring, with the understanding that safeguards – even robust, intrusive, 'adversarial' safeguards – are not panaceas and cannot prevent a determined state from seeking to cheat and to acquire nuclear weapons. But an effective system can raise the costs of cheating, and in doing so, contribute to deterring the effort.

10. Limits of the Possible

As just suggested, even with an optimally invigorated safeguards system there is no 100% guarantee. If anything demonstrates this truth it is the difficulty encountered by the United Nations in Iraq in implementing, under exceptionally favorable circumstances, a draconian verification program and in achieving assurance that all that should be known about Iraq's nuclear development program and assets has been discovered.

Even if safeguards are strengthened and reinforced along the lines discussed above, there can be other problems, such as verifying the initial inventory of a state that has had an unsafeguarded nuclear program in existence for some time before accepting comprehensive safeguards. South Africa and North Korea are current cases in point; while unlikely, it is not completely out of the question that at some time in the future India, Pakistan, and even Israel might accept full-scope safeguards as part of a political settlement that removes their incentive for at least maintaining a nuclear option. How is one to know that the submitted inventory is correct? To raise a question one must have information; if there is no information on which to act, perhaps because activities were undertaken at a time when intelligence gathering was not focused on the state or in the right place, then one does not know where to ask to go. South Africa operated an enrichment facility for a number of years before joining the NPT and accepting full-scope safeguards. North Korea operated a 5 MW unsafeguarded reactor for a period of six years prior to completing its safeguards agreement with the IAEA. Records and reports may provide a picture of apparent completeness, but there will always be a measure of doubt. At some point, it must be decided to accept the risk of incompleteness and, as political relationships improve and the sense of security increases and normalization sets in, the possibility that the initial inventory was incomplete becomes increasingly irrelevant. If the world ever were to adopt agreement on zero nuclear weapons, this risk would have to be factored in: one would never be certain that all the weapons were accounted for; one only could hope that political relationships were moving in a direction that would make irrelevant any weapons that might never have been reported.

11. Regional Approaches to Safeguards and Non-Proliferation

Finally, there is the question of how relevant regional verification arrangements are to the efficacy of international safeguards. In some regions like the Korean peninsula, the Middle East, or South Asia, additive regional measures may be not only desirable, but in fact necessary. In South America, where Argentina and Brazil have long been engaged in a political competition involving a threatening development of nuclear capabilities that could have been converted into a local nuclear arms race, a move to democratization, as well as changes in national political leadership and in the broader international environment, have led to mutual pledges of non-proliferation, progress toward ratification and implementation of the Latin American Nuclear Weapon Free Zone, and the establishment of a regional verification regime that relies substantially on the safeguards system of the IAEA. The regional system is both a stepping stone to assimilation into the broader international verification system and a necessary element to support and to consolidate the foreclosing of nuclear weapons as a way of achieving security or promoting political status.

In the Korean peninsula, where tensions have been high for the past four decades, the governments of North and South Korea in December 1991, concluded an agreement on a non-nuclear Korea. This involved commitments not to receive, possess, produce, test or deploy nuclear weapons; to ban both enrichment and reprocessing; and to establish a mutual inspection regime to verify implementation of the agreement. In April 1992, North Korea also ratified a long-overdue safeguards agreement with the IAEA. While the IAEA agreement is now being implemented, at the time of this writing there has been less progress with respect to the bilateral agreement than had been anticipated. Questions continue regarding the status and future of the partially completed reprocessing facility in North Korea which already served to produce a gram quantity of plutonium, and the bilateral verification system is yet to be activated. A robust regional inspection arrangement in Korea would help to increase openness and transparency in what has been a very closed society; it would also serve to complement and reinforce IAEA safeguards. With a two-tiered inspection arrangement, each system could not only add to the credibility of the findings of the other, but difficulties encountered in implementing one system would put the other on alert regarding its completeness and its integrity.

The Middle East today, as in the past, poses a particularly dangerous proliferation situation It is widely assumed that Israel has produced nuclear weapons, and the discoveries in Iraq revealed a long-standing and extensive nuclear weapons development program Other countries in the region including Libya and Iran, both NPT parties, and Algeria, a non-party, are frequently mentioned as sources of proliferation concern The challenge here is not only how to avert further proliferation in the region, but how to facilitate nuclear reversal by states which have taken steps toward weapon development The verification measures incorporated in UN Security Council Resolution 687 are often cited as precedent for a region-wide arrangement, and language suggestive of such an approach is to be found in the resolution. However, 687 is more a punitive instrument than a precursor for verification among states that have voluntary negotiated a non-proliferation or nuclear weapon-free zone agreement. On the other hand, here as in the Korean peninsula, it seems evident that some kind of regional verification system providing for very liberal, swift, and assured access by nationals of states party to such agreements will be essential to securing any such type agreement. Here also a two-tiered system of verification could be mutually reinforcing and provide the level of assurance and credibility necessary for confidence-building to take place

Whatever their value, regional verification arrangements should not be considered as substitutes for international verification, which should remain a *sine qua non* Rather, they should be seen as *parallel* structures, endowed with an authority which goes beyond what could reasonably be expected to be granted to an international organization, but which is necessary in situations where mistrust is the essence of relationships and mutuality and reciprocity the only basis for agreement Regional arrangements can include measures beyond what can plausibly be agreed for an international authority which must necessarily approach its responsibilities in a nondiscriminatory fashion and which is unlikely to be granted the depth of authority that might be granted to a regional institution Among the measures that might be included in a regional arrangement are challenge inspections in which no justification may be required and which may be carried out at any location designated by the challenger, and/or quota inspections involving a designated number of inspections at either previously specified sites, or at any site selected by the inspecting party Regional investigative arrangements conducted by nationals of directly concerned states will enjoy a higher political credibility in the latter than even the most rigorous international verification system However, international verification remains the only means by which to satisfy out-of-region states, many of whom may have fundamental interests in regional security and stability

NOTES AND REFERENCES

* Lawrence Scheinman is Professor of Government (International Law & Relations) at Cornell University and Associate Director of the Peace Studies Program He has served in senior posts in the United States Department of State (Principal Deputy to the Deputy Undersecretary of State for Security Assistance, Science and Technology) and Energy Research and Development Administration (Head of Office of International Policy Planning) as well as in the International Atomic Energy Agency (Special Advisor to the Director General) He is a member of the Council on Foreign Relations, the Washington Council on Nonproliferation, the National Council of the Federation of American Scientists, the Core Group of the Programme on Promoting Nuclear Nonproliferation, and the Advisory Committee on Nonproliferation of the Atlantic Council of the United States His most recent book on the subject of non-proliferation is *The International Atomic Energy Agency and World Nuclear Order*

1 For a general discussion of the concept of regime see Stephen Krasner ed, *International Regimes* (Ithaca, NY. Cornell University Press, 1983), Oran Young, 'International Regimes Problems of Concept Formation', *World Politics*, 32, April 1980, pp 331–356 For a discussion of regime as applied in the case of non-proliferation see Lewis A Dunn, *Controlling the Bomb*, (New Haven, CT Yale University Press, 1981), Lawrence Scheinman, *The Nonproliferation Role of the International Atomic Energy Agency* (Washington, DC Resources for the Future, 1985)

2 For a comprehensive introduction to the nature and scope of international safeguards see David Fischer and Paul Szasz, *Safeguarding the Atom A Critical Appraisal* (Stockholm and London SIPRI and Taylor and Francis 1985)

3 Treaty on the Non-Proliferation of Nuclear Weapons, A II

4 *Ibid*, Article III

5 For analysis of the decision-making in several critical non-nuclear weapon states see Mitchell Reiss, *Without the Bomb The Politics of Nuclear Non-Proliferation* (New York Columbia University Press, 1988)

6 Final Declaration of the Third Review Conference of the NPT as reproduced in Jozef Goldblat, *Twenty Years of the Non-Proliferation Treaty Implementation and Prospects* (Oslo PRIO, 1990), Appendix XII

7 See John R. Redick, 'Argentina and Brazil's New Arrangement for Mutual Inspections and IAEA Safeguards', (Washington DC Nuclear Control Institute, February 1992) for a discussion of the Foz de Iguaca agreement and the Argentine-Brazil Agency for Accounting and Control of Nuclear Material

8 See Jon Jennekens, 'IAEA Safeguards – Emerging Issues', Fourth International Conference on Facility Operations – Safeguards Interface', (Albuquerque, NM, 29 September–4 October 1991)

9 This is managed in the case of safeguarded material by use of interim inspections conducted at sufficiently frequent intervals to be able to detect a diversion of such material The timeliness goal for detecting the diversion of spent nuclear fuel which if reprocessed would yield separated plutonium is currently three months

10 It is significant that Iraq chose a totally clandestine approach rather than relying on diversion of safeguarded nuclear material This suggests that Iraqi nuclear personnel were of the view that IAEA safeguards would detect a diversion

11 It cannot go unsaid that the Iraq situation was exceptional in the sense that its action against Kuwait had been universally condemned and it was under severe Security Council sanctions when the Board met to consider findings regarding the Iraqi program and that under more ambivalent circumstances Board action might not have been so clear But neither might Security Council action be as determined and unanimous under less egregious conditions It may also be noted that while the Board of Governors

has endorsed a number of measures to strengthen safeguards, a number of states have done so grudgingly and with concern that they may be opening a Pandora's box

12 Statute of the International Atomic Energy Agency, Article XII A 6

13 International Atomic Energy Agency, *The Structure and Content of Agreements Between the Agency and States Required in Connection with the Treaty on the Non-Proliferation of Nuclear Weapons*, INFCIRC/153 (Corrected), para 73

14 GOV/INF/613, June 1991

15 In some cases, access may be denied for reasons other than non-compliance with safeguards undertakings, such as safety-related considerations but this does not release the state of its obligation to satisfy the verification authority that all material and facilities that should be reported and placed under safeguards in fact have been

16 United Nations Security Council, S/23500, 31 January 1992

17 See IAEA Press Release PR 92/12, 26 February 1992

Lessons From Post-War Iraq for the International Full-Scope Safeguards Regime

Lawrence Scheinman

The discovery after the Gulf War of an extensive Iraqi nuclear weapon development program severely shook public confidence in the nuclear non-proliferation regime in general, and the safeguards program administered by the International Atomic Energy Agency (IAEA) under the nuclear Non-Proliferation Treaty (NPT), in particular.

This questioning of IAEA effectiveness contrasts sharply with the judgment rendered by the NPT parties as recently as 1990. Repeating almost verbatim the conclusion reached in the 1985 NPT Review Conference, the final draft document of the Fourth Review Conference reaffirmed that the NPT "is vital to preventing the spread of nuclear weapons and in providing significant security benefits." It strongly endorsed the effectiveness of the IAEA, saying the agency's safeguards "provide assurance that States are complying with their undertakings and assist States in demonstrating this compliance," and that these safeguards "promote further confidence among states and, being a fundamental element of the Treaty, help to strengthen their collective security."[1]

Original Safeguards Political Factors

If there is now a diminished confidence in some quarters in the effectiveness of the IAEA, it stems from a basic change in the expectations brought on by the Iraqi experience about what degree of non-proliferation assurance safeguards *should* provide. When the system was devised in 1970 to implement IAEA verification responsibility under the NPT, it was focused on the nuclear fuel cycles of the advanced industrial states, which at the time were the only states capable of mount-

Lawrence Scheinman is professor of government and associate director of the Peace Studies

> ***"[Iraq] provided the justification for evaluating the safeguards regime under new political circumstances, so that appropriate corrective measures could be taken when necessary. It is now up to the individual states within the international system to take advantage of this opportunity."***

ing any kind of nuclear weapon program. The United States and the Soviet Union, which were spearheading the negotiations, were chiefly concerned about ensuring the participation of these states in the NPT.

Even conceding the political and security benefits of non-proliferation, the advanced non-nuclear-weapon states were intent on guarding against the risk that the distinction between weapon and non-weapon states inherent in the NPT would extend to peaceful nuclear activity and competition. In particular, they wanted to ensure that in agreeing to forswear nuclear weapons or explosives they would not hamper their ability to make full use of nuclear energy and technology for peaceful purposes and to compete in what was seen nuclear energy. For these states, the sa- guards system devised to ensure their co pliance would have to be crafted carefu. to cause as little interference as possib and protect as far as possible their comm cial interests and proprietary informatio

Limited Intrusiveness a Goal

These considerations led to th development of a verification system th kept intrusion to the minimum consiste with credible verification, and to th development of certain constraints on ho the IAEA exercised the rather liberal righ granted to it in its statute. In contrast wi the IAEA's pre-NPT system, NPT sa guards focus on nuclear materials rath than on nuclear materials and facilities c the theory that with total coverage material there is no need to safeguar facilities *per se*. The NPT system em phasized establishing material balan areas and designating key measureme points where safeguards could be appli and the flow and inventory of nucle material could be determined. It stresse the importance of using instrumentati wherever possible so as to minimize th extent of human inspection.

Routine inspection activities were be supplemented by exceptional measure (namely "special inspections") only cases where the IAEA was unable to inde pendently verify that all nuclear materi under safeguards could be accounted fo or where it was informed of the existence undeclared nuclear material. A few spec inspections were carried out under th former provision but none on the basis special information because the IAE never received information regarding po sible undeclared nuclear material upo which it could act.

Legally, states entering into full-scop safeguards agreements with the IAEA...

obligated to declare all nuclear material being used in peaceful nuclear activities In practice while the IAEA assumed that states would comply with this obligation it did not discount the possibility of non compliance or that clandestine nuclear facilities capable of producing fissile materials that could be used in a nuclear explosive device might exist in safeguarded states and it took these possibilities into account in establishing its safeguards implementation plan

It is worth noting that because of the concerns of these states the system, from the outset, was not focussed on ferreting out and detecting fully clandestine nuclear activities that did not rely in any way on safeguarded nuclear material It was assumed that states would declare all their material When the NPT was being created and consensus was being solicited the level of intrusiveness necessary to find fully clandestine nuclear activities would have been seen by the key interested non-nuclear weapon states as controverting their objective of minimizing intrusiveness It was thus generally assumed that the IAEA would detect the diversion of any declared nuclear material but that any undeclared or clandestine activity would be detected by other means primarily intelligence sources and presumably brought to the agency's attention

Iraq as a Case Study

Until Iraq safeguards although not trouble free performed largely as expected and the IAEA had a reasonable probability of detecting diversion of significant quantities of declared nuclear material On balance the system was consistent with the expectations of the states that designed it with the dispersion of capabilities necessary to acquire nuclear weapons and with the bipolar political environment dominated by two superpowers whose alliance structures and nuclear umbrellas deterred most states from seeking to acquire nuclear weapons What happened in Iraq was not the breakdown of safeguards on declared nuclear material but a circumventing of the system and the regime as a whole Export controls failed to stem the flow of equipment and components relevant to nuclear weapon development Safeguards which were not geared to cope with a totally clandestine nuclear program failed to identify the existence of undeclared nuclear activities Moreover national intelligence apparently failed to identify the extent of clandestine activities

Iraq s Impact on the Regime

The impact of Iraq on the safeguards regime was twofold first it underscored that even under conditions of verified international treaty obligations and full-scope safeguards, a state that was determined to cheat on its undertakings could successfully do so developing a totally clandestine program that did not rely on material or facilities under safeguards This reality highlighted some of the limitations of a system that placed primary emphasis on nuclear material accounting when for example there was the possibility for a country to acquire or construct nuclear facilities without informing the IAEA until it was ready to receive nuclear material

Another limitation illuminated by the Iraqi experience was the practice of coupling the frequency of inspection to the amount of nuclear material in a particular plant or material balance area rather than in the country as a whole a practice which could and did result in less frequent inspections than might have been warranted by political concerns about the safeguarded state As an international organization it was not feasible for the IAEA to overtly discriminate in the application of safeguards between states under a common system.

Moreover there were limits on how much knowledge the IAEA had about the scope of national nuclear activities because NPT verification focused only on the diversion of nuclear material and not on the full range of obligations implied by a commitment to non-proliferation

In a sense the Gulf War was an opportune event because it directed attention to the limitations and weaknesses of safeguards and of the NPT regime at the very outset of the post Cold War period Moreover it provided the justification for evaluating the safeguards regime under new political circumstances so that appropriate corrective measures could be taken when necessary It is now up to the individual states within the international system to take advantage of this opportunity.

The second effect of the Iraqi affair was to alter political expectations regarding the breadth of safeguards coverage As already noted until now the expectation was that the IAEA would verify that all *declared* nuclear material could be accounted for Now the expectation extends to providing assurance that no *undeclared* material or *clandestine* facilities or activities exist in states that have ratified the NPT or equivalent non proliferation agreements with the IAEA Redefining expectations means reassessing the authority resources and political support that the international community which now holds these expectations is prepared to provide to the institutions charged with implementation of this broader safeguards regime [2]

Focus on Special Inspections

Thus far the main effort to meet new circumstances and new expectations has focused on re-examining existing safeguards authority and clarifying or building upon it as appropriate Considerable attention has been given to the IAEA s right of special inspection which derives from the statute allowing access "at all times to all places and data and is incorporated in safeguards document INFCIRC/153 that governs IAEA full-scope safeguards agreements

This special inspection right is different from the inspection rights given the IAEA under the authority of UN Security Council Resolution 687 the Gulf War cease-fire resolution In a number of important respects resolution 687 extends beyond the rules procedures and techniques usually applied by the agency and cannot realistically be viewed as the new standard practice for safeguards activities in normal circumstances [3]

The IAEA Board of Governors has confirmed that the right of special inspection extends not only to additional locations at declared sites but also to undeclared locations and facilities if there is plausible evidence that undeclared nuclear material may be present at these sites

While the IAEA and the UN Special Commission (UNSCOM) the UN body tasked with eliminating Iraq s weapons of mass destruction have been publicly criticized as having not done the job in Iraq or for having done it poorly an examination of the facts leads to the conclusion that the IAEA adapted well to the newly imposed mandate from the Security Council UNSCOM s executive chairman said in a statement before the Security Council "IAEA inspections have been very successful . . . the nuclear area is the most emotional and political of the Iraqi weapons programs One should not believe all that he reads in the media on this issue

The decision to invoke a special inspection rests with the IAEA director general although in all probability he would first consult with members of the Board of Governors If an inspection team is denied access it would be reported to the board which, based on the evidence, would call upon the state to comply with the request. If conditions require it, the request for special inspection can be declared urgent and the state in question must then respond very quickly. Failure to provide access would result in a finding of non-compliance, which the board would report to the Security Council (as it did on two occasions with respect to Iraq in 1991).

This idea of confirming the right of special inspections at undeclared locations at the initiative of the safeguarding authority establishes an authoritative basis for a more robust safeguards system in which states presumably can have more confidence. Whether such a system actually emerges in the near future depends on several *considerations that can be divided* into two components: external and internal.

The Need for Information

From an *external* perspective, as the IAEA director general has noted, success depends in the first instance on the availability of information upon which to predicate a request for a special inspection. Primarily, but not exclusively, this means the availability of national intelligence information, which, as noted below, must also include safety analysis, research and development cooperation, technical assistance and so on, if the IAEA is to have a comprehensive information base.

With regard to the issue of the sharing of intelligence information, the jury is still out on the extent to which relevant information would be shared, and whether, as some contend, another institutional filter such as UNSCOM is needed to receive and evaluate such information.

Even now, however, some mythology can be dispelled. In the case of Iraq, although intelligence information was provided to UNSCOM for the purpose of site selection, virtually the same information was shared with the IAEA, which was responsible for conducting the actual inspections. In the case of the IAEA visit (not inspection) to Iran in February 1992, agency site selection for that visit was based in part on information provided from national intelligence sources. While it is true that intelligence authorities are inherently uncomfortable about sharing information with international institutions, there is no basis for the argument now made by some that an institutionalized UNSCOM would be provided with relevant information while the IAEA would not. There may be nuances between the two, but it is too facile a proposition to argue that the IAEA would *a priori* be excluded.

The possibility should not be ruled out that as a result of the integration and analysis of information drawn from routine safeguards activities, coupled with information derived from technical cooperation programs, nuclear safety activities, published material and the like, the agency could acquire a plausible base of information to justify a request for further inspection in a state. In this regard, measures now in place to establish country officers with the responsibility to assimilate and evaluate information concerning the nuclear programs of inspected states, to brief inspectors before they go into the field and to participate in their debriefing upon return from an inspection, are excellent steps toward the goal of achieving increased knowledge and sensitivity about the character of national nuclear activities. How well these measures are implemented remains to be seen. One concern is that while there is now much greater attention to country analysis, this responsibility comes in addition to existing IAEA activities, but without the additional resources to do a proper analytical job.

Several other external requirements are necessary for robust and credible safeguards. These include assuring the IAEA the right of unimpeded access to designated locations to carry out any special inspection, and, related to this, the support of political authorities (primarily the Security Council) to ensure that this right is respected.

'Organizational Culture' Problems

The *internal* component to successful implementation of a regime involving a higher reliance on special inspections in the future involves the mind-set, attitudes and behavior—what is being called the "organizational culture"—of the agency and of those responsible for implementing international safeguards. While the IAEA has earned the confidence of its membership in implementing safeguards, as reflected in the previously mentioned NPT review co ferences, there also has existed a cert sense that the IAEA is perhaps more co servative or more cautious than it should or need be. Over the past two decades agency has experienced restraints on rights of access, on the intensity a frequency of inspection efforts, and even the extent to which it could exercise discretionary judgment in planning, sch uling and conducting inspections. Patter of conservatism and self-constraint beca internalized to the extent that the ager occasionally gave more ground than nec sary in negotiating subsidiary arran ments that regulate the operational side safeguards agreements.

Moreover, the emphasis on mater accountancy has led to an almost obsess focus on sharpening and improving the tainment of quantitative goals, as precision and objectivity alone provid credibility. This came all too often to exclusion of any awareness of the setting which nuclear activity was taking pla This has led some observers to right criticize the IAEA for having satisfied its regarding Iraq's nuclear compliance by a counting for declared nuclear mater while ignoring the obvious large-scale tivity going on around the safeguard facilities.

Overcoming Past Limits

To overcome these limitations requir two things: leadership at the level of t Board of Governors and leadership in th secretariat. The board is a reflection of th political will and interests of memb states. If the political will is present at t national level to ensure that the IAEA fully effective in carrying out its respo sibilities, there is *no reason* such a sentime should not be represented in the governi board. If this assumption is correct, t IAEA should be able to implement a mo far-reaching and intrusive safeguar regime, not only with respect to spec inspections, but for routine inspection a tivity as well. However it should not forgotten that it took extraordinary

> ***". . . winning the non-proliferation battle is a multifaceted proposition involving a range of national, regional and international policies, processes and institutions of the states involved."***

circumstances to move the board to endorse the Secretariat's proposals accepted so far (special inspections early reporting of design information universal reporting of nuclear material and equipment particularly relevant to nuclear activity) More to the point the endorsement was granted with some anxiety because sovereignty remains a vigorous and contradictory force against empowering international institutions with far reaching authority On the other hand if governments would be willing to institute strong non-proliferation measures at the Security Council level they should be equally willing to support vigorous measures by a technical international organization whose conclusions regarding treaty compliance may ultimately be the source for forceful action that is then needed at the political level To act otherwise would be not only illogical but counterproductive For this reason concerned states such as the United States should be taking active leadership roles in bringing increased political and other support—including intelligence support—to the IAEA and to the Security Council (see p 3)

Strong Leadership at the Top

Leadership within the Secretariat is no less important Here the director general has set a tone by making clear his intention to invoke agency authority where appropriate He is also seeking to inculcate new values by encouraging the staff to be more sensitive to the new political conditions in which the IAEA will operate in the future and to be more aware of the relationship between its technical responsibilities and the overriding political purpose of safeguards. But it is difficult to say whether the necessary coherence of mission morale and team building that is fundamental to an effective new orientation toward safeguards has taken firm root Leadership by example at all levels of management rather than leadership by directive is what is ultimately required to inspire and sustain a sense of purpose and to achieve the necessary integration and coherence The IAEA has operated heretofore primarily on the principle of leadership by directive

All of this suggests what lessons the IAEA has—or should have—drawn (but not necessarily internalized) from the Iraq experience On one level there is the need to integrate method and purpose more systematically to be more probing more alert more sensitive to the political environment and to the risk of change and unpredictability The IAEA Secretariat must understand that achieving quantitative goals of accounting for declared nuclear materials and equipement is only one step toward attaining international credibility it is also necessary to be aware of the total context in which safeguards are applied

On another level member states must also draw lessons from the experience with Iraq if international safeguards are to be truly effective The idea that access to information and political support for implementation of authority are prerequisites for effectively meeting political expectations must be incorporated into the consensus among member states in their support for the Secretariat. It cannot be underscored too heavily that the IAEA is not just a secretariat but an international organization consisting of sovereign states that define the Secretariat's authority furnish its resources, and provide the political support that enables an international institution to function credibly and effectively International organizations are the creatures of their constituent member states

A determined Secretariat can influence the understanding and the behavior of its members and the process of interaction the institution can provide a learning experience that changes how states perceive and interpret their national interests But there are real limits to what even the most enlightened and persuasive Secretariat leadership can achieve and judgments about international institutions and their perceived weaknesses must keep this reality in perspective

These limitations and weaknesses notwithstanding, it must be stressed that the IAEA over its lifetime has done and can continue to do critical service in support of non proliferation The consensus on this conclusion consistently restated by the NPT membership at virtually all quinquennial treaty review conferences is one to build upon The existence of flaws is not a reason for abandoning the agency in favor of the uncertainties that any new institution would inevitably bring, or even necessarily to create additional institutions to support it although that possibility should not be ruled out Furthermore those who favor alternative institutions that would threaten draconian action against delinquent states from the outset should recall that the UN action against Iraq was based on aggression not NPT violations and that ultimately legitimacy not force is the soundest basis for a long term stable order IAEA safeguards provides a foundation for achieving non proliferation legitimacy and should therefore be preserved and strengthened in the interests of establishing universal non proliferation and moving us closer to an eventual nuclear weapon free world.

Lessons for the Future

In making any assessment about the IAEA its safeguards and its role in the post-Cold War era three factors must be considered First the international environment is still very much in transition The outcome of the major shifts occurring in the world order will be an important factor in determining the role and relevance of safeguards in building and maintaining states confidence that their neighbors are not acquiring nuclear weapons

Second virtually no acceptable system of verification will by itself ever be enough to ensure—in any but the smallest states—that there is no clandestine activity whatsoever Such a system could however provide some assurance that there is no clandestine activity, and it could confirm or refute suspicion that such activities exist when a specific charge or challenge is raised

Third winning the non proliferation battle is a multifaceted proposition involving a range of national regional and international policies processes and institutions of the states involved While safeguards have a critical role to play in this effort they are not the first or even the second line of defense against proliferation First come political decisions by governments not to acquire nuclear weapons (a decision that reflects the security and political assessments of the state) and solemn international undertakings codifying those decisions The durability of these undertakings requires a collective effort in support of the totality of measures that constitute the non proliferation regime all working in a harmonious and mutually reinforcing way Expectations regarding safeguards and the IAEA must be considered in this light ACI

NOTES

1 See NPT/CONF IV DC 1 Add 3 A

2 For a comprehensive analysis of the problem of post Iraq safeguards see Lawrence Scheinman *Assessing the Nuclear Non Proliferation Safeguards System* Atlantic Council of the US Occasional Paper Series October 1992 and Lawrence Scheinman, Nuclear Safeguards and Non Proliferation in a Changing World Order *Security Dialogue* V 23 No 4 1992

3 For a useful study of UN Security Council Resolution 687 see Eric Chauvistre The Implications of IAEA Inspections Under Security Council Resolution 687 UNIDIR Research Paper 11 1992

August 10, 1993

STAFF STUDY MISSION

INTERNATIONAL ATOMIC ENERGY AGENCY

VIENNA, AUSTRIA

JULY 6-9, 1993

PURPOSE

The primary purpose of the staff study mission by David Barton and Walker Roberts of the Committee on Foreign Affairs was to receive comprehensive briefings on all activities, operations, and decisionmaking of the International Atomic Energy Agency (IAEA) in Vienna, Austria There was also a strong interest in current IAEA activities and inspections in Iraq, Iran, North Korea, and South Africa

Chairman Hamilton and Ranking Minority Member Gilman had requested that staff make recommendations to them regarding ways to strengthen the role of the IAEA as a part of efforts to maintain and strengthen international nuclear nonproliferation controls, enforce and supplement, if necessary, existing treaties, and establish new stricter norms of international behavior

GENERAL PREMISE

As the world has had to adjust to a new post-Cold War setting so the IAEA has had to adjust to new challenges and demands of the post-Gulf War nuclear environment.

It is clear that the IAEA is changing dramatically as a result of past and on-going activities in Iraq and North Korea. The Board of Governors, faced with politically difficult decisions and the need to conclude issues by consensus, is finding the necessary political will to address new challenges and demands successfully. It is essential, however, that political leadership and resources are forthcoming from the United States and other Member states in order to reinforce the pace and breadth of continued change.

Since the IAEA has been the subject of criticism regarding the Iraqi development of a nuclear weapons program, it is important to underline that the failure in Iraq was a failure of the total worldwide nonproliferation regime, including the lack of stringent export controls and timely intelligence gathering and analysis, and not a failure of the IAEA-safeguarded part of the Iraqi nuclear program. In fact, the IAEA maintains that none of the elements of the IAEA-safeguarded Iraqi program aided Iraq's undeclared nuclear program.

The basic philosophy of the IAEA regarding technical cooperation with countries around the world which do not have nuclear technology remains valid and an important motivator for political cooperation. Current funding levels for technical assistance should be maintained. Nuclear technology can accomplish things in the developing world such as the elimination of flies and worms harmful to domestic animals which would otherwise not be possible nor available to these countries.

OBSERVATIONS

1. Board of Governors and Decisionmaking

The IAEA was established in Vienna, Austria in 1957. President Eisenhower's Atoms for Peace program is normally cited as one of the instrumental factors in stimulating the establishment of the IAEA.

The IAEA consists of 114 Member States. The Member States meet together once a year in a General Conference to approve the budget for the coming calendar year and to provide overall direction for the agency. In addition there is a Board of Governors composed of 35 Members who meet five times a year to approve specific actions and oversee and report on the operations of the agency The Board of Governors appoints the Director General after obtaining the approval of the General Conference. It is the Director General who manages the daily functioning of the Agency.

New challenges in nuclear nonproliferation and nuclear safety have faced the IAEA in increasing frequency in the last two or three years and this has activated the IAEA's decisionmaking process The result has been an expansion of IAEA activities, the exercise of pre-existing authorities which were never before used such as special inspections, and future planning for a more action-oriented agency which can address such things as the hard task of uncovering undeclared nuclear weapons programs, nuclear safety at previously unsafeguarded nuclear facilities, support for implementation of a comprehensive test ban, and supervision of a fissile material cut-off and long-term storage.

The Board of Governors and the General Conference have made the following decisions and mandated the following actions which illustrate the new dynamism and evolving activism of the agency:

o ordered special inspections in North Korea,

o reaffirmed the agency's legitimate right to carry out special inspections in any facilities in order to verify that there is no nuclear weapons program operating,

o approved a universal reporting system for the international trade in nuclear material and equipment, o mandated a thorough exploration of ways in which the agency can conduct long-term monitoring such as environmental sampling to detect any undeclared nuclear weapons programs;

o accepted the advisability of having a centralized data and intelligence-gathering network to maximize the potential for uncovering suspect activities;

o approved an ambitious program of inspection and destruction activities in Iraq even though those activities stretch way beyond the normal safeguards activities of the agency;

o accepted that the IAEA must plan for a long-term monitoring role in Iraq;

o responded to the South African request to involve IAEA in verifying information regarding nuclear materials and South Africa's revelation of a nuclear weapons program;

o mandated that the IAEA's Safeguards Advisory Group (SAGSI) look into improvements in effectiveness and efficiency for the safeguards system as it exists today;

o ordered the establishment of a Nuclear Safety Convention which would facilitate the international review of nuclear safety and assist the IAEA in responding to numerous requests to assist in safety provisions for many countries, Member and non-Member countries.

A clear yardstick to measure the progress of the IAEA in becoming a more dynamic and action-oriented agency will be the 1995 Nonproliferation Treaty Review Conference. By that time the IAEA must show that demonstratable progress is being made or one can expect numerous concerns regarding extension of the NPT to be raised by both developed and less developed nations.

2. More Aggressive Policy to Detect Undeclared Nuclear Weapons Programs

In the post-Gulf War environment there has been a basic change in approach by the IAEA and its Board of Governors to meet the challenge of undeclared nuclear weapons programs which may exist in countries which are adherents to the Nuclear Nonproliferation Treaty (NPT) and which have safeguards arrangements with the IAEA This change in approach is a result of the experience in Iraq where the system as designed did not work The change is underway to a more aggressive policy by the IAEA to attempt to detect undeclared nuclear weapons programs thereby heightening the risks of detection and increasing the advantages of comprehensive adherence to the NPT

The shared experience of the UN and the IAEA in Iraq has motivated both international agencies to pursue realistic, aggressive policies regarding intrusive inspections and long-term monitoring The U S. Director of Central Intelligence, Mr. R. James Woolsey, pointed out in testimony before the Subcommittee on International Security, International Organizations, and Human Rights of the House Foreign Affairs Committee on July 28, 1993 that: "Iraq's harassment of inspectors has not deterred the UN from continuing to destroy a vast chemical munitions and agent stockpile, to dig out details about past activity, and to search for hidden missile, biological, and nuclear capabilities...Neither we nor the UN have lost sight of the basic fact that critical elements of Iraq's programs remain hidden. Therefore, intrusive inspections remain an important element of any monitoring regime."

This new approach reflects the view that over two-thirds of safeguard activities are taking place in countries of less proliferation concern. While the motto should remain "we do not trust anyone nor suspect anyone", safeguards activities must be made more effective and efficient and clearly targeted to countries of concern Clearly this issue cuts to the heart of the debate over apportionment of resources as well· activity must be kept high on declared facilities but increased resources must be dedicated to undeclared programs as well.

The IAEA notes that this change in approach involves numerous aspects. First, greater information is needed by the IAEA through national technical means, the media, special publications and scientific journals and export/import data To access this information requires interactive relationships with Members states, non-Member states and organizations such as the Security Council and London Suppliers Group. The IAEA believes that if the Member states and international organizations are willing to provide this information on a timely basis, the intrusiveness of safeguard inspections can be dramatically increased

A second central element of this new approach would be additional training seminars for IAEA safeguard inspectors IAEA inspections would reflect this new approach by moving away from a mechanical, routine, "blinders" type of approach to a rigorous and intrusive inspection regime utilizing comprehensive inspection rights provided to the IAEA. The U S would be particularly helpful in this regard given its experience in training On-Site Inspection Agency (OSIA) inspectors to implement U S.-former Soviet Union arms accords.

The IAEA acknowledges that it is only in the beginning phase of developing this new, more aggressive approach to detecting undeclared nuclear weapons programs. This new approach will include use of special inspections and perhaps the institution of other types of inspections to monitor suspicious activities, deter clandestine programs, and investigate suspected undeclared programs. The IAEA also would like to increase its ability to do enhanced analysis of waste products and soil.

In addition to special inspections the new approach being developed by IAEA would also include long-term monitoring such as environmental monitoring and coordinated worldwide data and intelligence collection.

3. Long-term monitoring

There must be long-term monitoring in Iraq if the international community is to deter the Iraqis from recreating their nuclear weapons development and production program. The IAEA is currently developing extensive plans to address this need including environmental monitoring of air, ground, and water samples; video/ground, aerial, and satellite surveillance; human monitoring by routine and special inspections; data collection on all nuclear and dual-use technology and equipment being exported to Iraq; and oversight of the Iraqi scientific community.

4. Export controls

While both IAEA officials and outside experts stress the importance of export controls and the need for all countries and private companies to recognize their own responsibility to restrict exports which could potentially be used in nuclear weapons programs, both also underline the difficulties and limitations of export controls. As difficulties and limitations, they cite the desire of all countries to promote their own manufactured goods and technology in the face of intense international competition; the dilemma of dual-use items being crucial to a country's manufacturing base at the same time that those same items may be the key components for a nuclear weapons program; the relative ease with which private companies may skirt export controls by exporting to front-companies, transferring items to foreign subsidiaries, or disguising controlled items with false licenses or smuggling.

Therefore, it is clear that export controls should be viewed as important particularly when adopted at a significant international level on a multilateral basis, but only as one element of "arms control" when it comes to controlling the potential development of nuclear weapons by countries which are determined to do so

5. International Intelligence-Sharing

International intelligence-sharing and data collection are essential if the IAEA is to progress successfully from its traditional role of safeguarding declared nuclear facilities and providing technical assistance to a new role of uncovering clandestine nuclear weapons programs, monitoring suspicious activities in the nuclear field, and enforcing relevant treaties. The IAEA depends on its Member states for information regarding each Member states' nuclear activities and now it must expand its capabilities to create a data base of information which includes input from a number of Member states about one country's nuclear program or about nuclear trade and activity in general. Obviously, the more countries that participate in the intelligence-sharing and data collection the better the product in terms of a reasonably accurate picture of every country's nuclear programs and worldwide nuclear activity. In addition, the IAEA should work with Member states to promote greater interaction and access with appropriate international organizations such as the London Suppliers Group.

6. Fissile material storage and monitoring

Unusual developments in the Ukraine and in South Africa have created situations regarding nuclear weapons where the IAEA might be asked to step in and assist with the storage, accounting, and monitoring of the fissile material in those nuclear weapons. The IAEA does not have the expertise nor the mandate to actually handle, transport, or dismantle the nuclear weapons themselves That work has to be done by experts from the nuclear-weapon states such as the United States.

The two cases of Ukraine and South Africa offer an opportunity to the IAEA to develop some expertise, background, and experience in managing this fissile material. This might be very useful in the future in other countries where there are nuclear weapons to be dismantled or if there is an international agreement to limit or stop fissile material production and then that agreement will need to be monitored and "safeguarded"

7. Clean-up, safety, and safeguards at facilities previously unsafeguarded

There is an urgent, new concern regarding the clean-up, safety, and safeguards at nuclear facilities in Eastern Europe and in the former Soviet Union which were previously unsafeguarded but which may now be placed under safeguards. The IAEA is addressing this concern and it has set in motion a series of explorations and assessments to determine exactly what can and should be done with these facilities and what role the IAEA can properly play.

8. <u>Iraqi nuclear weapons program</u>

IAEA statements are clear concerning what has been accomplished in Iraq under UN resolutions 687, 707, and 715 and what remains to be done in order to provide some assurance to the world community that Iraq will not succeed in producing nuclear weapons.

In testimony submitted to the House Foreign Affairs Committee on June 29, 1993 the IAEA stated that it "has been successful in identifying, destroying, removing or otherwise rendering harmless the key components of a hitherto secret and broadly-based Iraqi program aimed at the acquisition of nuclear weapons capabilities." The IAEA describes its assessment of just how complete a picture of the Iraqi nuclear weapons program it judges that it has been able to piece together by asserting that "As to the completeness of the picture obtained, it is the considered opinion of the IAEA, based on the results of nineteen inspection missions, the analyses of thousands of samples, the evaluation of several hundred documents confiscated in Iraq, the assessment of procurement and other information obtained from Member States of the IAEA, that the essential components of the clandestine program have been identified." The IAEA credits the success in rapidly unmasking the secret Iraqi program to the provision of experts and intelligence by Member states combined with rapid and intrusive field inspections.

In the same testimony the IAEA describes its mandate from the United Nations and what it has accomplished in the following manner: "The tasks entrusted by the Security Council to the IAEA are essentially threefold. search, destroy and prevent any reconstitution [of the Iraqi nuclear weapons program] The IAEA has searched, has found and has destroyed. The basis has been established for preventing a reconstitution of the Iraqi nuclear program Effective control of future Iraqi activities can be put in place if adequate measures are maintained at the political level and sufficient resources continue to be provided."

The IAEA testimony to the House Foreign Affairs Committee also details two areas which will hinder any future efforts by the IAEA to successfully monitor Iraqi nuclear activities. UN resolutions 707 and 715 specify that Iraq should provide the names of all suppliers and intermediaries who worked with Iraq on its nuclear weapons program and that Iraq must approve IAEA plans for long-term monitoring of compliance by Iraq to UN resolution 687. It is the IAEA's position that the UN must maintain its sanctions on Iraq until there is full compliance by Iraq with all of its obligations under all UN resolutions and particularly these two provisions if IAEA long-term monitoring is to be effective in detecting or deterring any effort by Iraq to reconstitute its nuclear weapons program.

As a result of UN Security Council Resolution 687 an Action Team was established at the IAEA to assume responsibility for fully enforcing that resolution The Action Team's report on their activities to fully carry out the resolution's mandate to destroy, remove, or render harmless all nuclear weapons and prohibited precursor materials is included as an appendix to this report.

9. People and books

Much of the press and other media attention to IAEA activities in Iraq have focused on buildings, reactors, machine tools and other dual-use equipment. Much of this "nuclear hardware" has either been destroyed, sealed, tagged, or inventoried. Obviously, there has also been attention to Iraq's quantities of weapons-usable nuclear material such as its highly enriched uranium in the form of reactor fuel elements. However, several experts at the IAEA pointed out that there has been little focus on a very crucial element to the Iraqi nuclear weapons program which has not been destroyed its scientists and engineers and the availability of scientific information.

These two elements, people and books, form a crucial part of any Iraqi ambition to reconstitute their nuclear weapons program The objective of mentioning this is to provoke thought in the international community of ways to address this problem of scientists and scientific information in order to come up with creative and effective solutions to diverting these people and this knowledge into peaceful, civilian endeavors.

10 Technical cooperation

Technical cooperation between nuclear and non-nuclear states to share the fruits of nuclear energy and power lies at the heart of the founding of the IAEA In addition to IAEA's responsibility to ensure that nuclear energy assistance is not used for military purposes, the IAEA's Statute describes another basic assignment for the IAEA "to accelerate and enlarge the contribution of atomic energy to peace, health, and prosperity throughout the world."

The IAEA has undertaken a number of projects in developing countries which apply nuclear technology to resolve development problems in the fields of medicine, agriculture, health, and food. For example, the IAEA has succeeded in applying nuclear technology to the eradication of a number of pests and insects such as the medfly, screwworm, and tsetse fly in a number of different locations. This year the IAEA is embarking on a new approach of model projects which will include a very interesting project in Sri Lanka supporting a human tissue bank This human tissue bank in Sri Lanka has, since the 1960's, supplied over 30,000 corneas to over 61 countries. With the assistance of the IAEA and new nuclear technology in sterilization techniques, this tissue bank may be able to expand its operations

It is interesting to note that the technical cooperation activities of the IAEA only absorb about $42-$45 million of the IAEA budget but that amount funds approximately 1,000 technical projects per year many of which have a very rapid and high impact on the development process in developing countries.

11. Iraqi Action Team and Future

In order for the IAEA to successfully continue the work of the Action Team in Iraq and to be able to apply it elsewhere it is essential that the concept and practice of long-term monitoring be firmly established as standard operating procedure for the IAEA, that the strongest possible political will be maintained to pressure for the establishment and sustaining of long-term monitoring, and that substantial resources be devoted to this effort and remain committed for some time to come. The long-term monitoring in Iraq will allow the IAEA to refine many monitoring techniques such as human and satellite intelligence, special techniques such as remote sensors and environmental sampling, and surveillance by video or aerial surveillance

The best way of getting a true picture of exactly what the Action Team is accomplishing in Iraq is to include here the last full report of the Action Team (see below).

12. IAEA and CTB

The IAEA is aware of the proposal made at the UN Conference on Disarmament in Geneva to have the IAEA implement and oversee a comprehensive nuclear test ban. The proposal would have the IAEA coordinate different national centers of detection in order to establish a worldwide system for monitoring the test ban The IAEA representatives seemed open to this proposal and predicted that the Board of Governors would probably also be open to the proposal. These positive responses to this proposal can be seen in the same light as the other new challenges and demands being addressed by IAEA The IAEA appears to be adapting and responding in a thoughtful and positive manner to these multiple proliferation challenges, demands, and needs that are being thrust upon it.

13. Safeguards vs. Technical Assistance

It is essential that the IAEA do more to involve developing countries in safeguard activities. Rightly or wrongly, the perception remains within the IAEA that the U.S. and other developed nations are interested only in safeguard side of IAEA activities. This perception is reinforced by the fact that the U.S. and developed nations fund 98 percent of the safeguards budget. In this regard, IAEA officials indicated that it would not be helpful for Member states to earmark additional funds for safeguards activities without addressing the technical assistance funding as well.

In order for LDC's and technical assistance recipients to be more involved in safeguards activities, it is important that these nations view nonproliferation as a major issue. One approach to this end is to integrate representatives from these nations in the programs which support safeguards activities, at more senior levels of management and on the technical teams which carry out the inspections; in short involve them in the management of the safeguards regime.

LIST OF OFFICIALS AND EXPERTS INTERVIEWED AT IAEA
JULY 6-8, 1993

Hans G Blix, Director General IAEA

Qian Jihui, Deputy Director General Department of Technical Co-operation IAEA

Sueo Machi, Deputy Director General Department of Research and Isotopes, IAEA

Bruno Pellaud, Deputy Director General Department of Safeguards IAEA

David Waller, Deputy Director General Department of Administration, IAEA

John Tileman Special Assistant Office of the Director General, IAEA

Mohamed ElBaradei Director, Division of External Relations IAEA

Maurizio Zifferero Leader UNSC 687 Action Team, IAEA

Robert Kelley, Deputy Leader UNSC 687 Action Team, IAEA

Demetrius Perricos, Director, Division of Operations, and Deputy Leader UNSC 687 Action Team IAEA

Richard Hooper Section Head Division of Concepts and Planning Department of Safeguards, IAEA

William Lichliter Section Head Program and Resources Department of Safeguards, IAEA

Muttusamy Sanmuganathan Secretary of the Policy-Making Organs, Secretariat IAEA

Michael Von Gray and Michael J Lawrence, U S Mission

O

71-404) - 93 (216)

Printed in the USA
CPSIA information can be obtained
at www.ICGtesting.com
CBHW071156030624
9480CB00017B/112

9 781021 500991